THE CONCORD REVIEW

Emerson Prize Issue, Number One   Summer 2012

Editor and Publisher

Will Fitzhugh

E-MAIL: fitzhugh@tcr.org

WEBSITE: **www.tcr.org**

Managing Editor: Caroline Lee

First Special Emerson Prize Issue of *The Concord Review*
– Print Edition.

Partial funding was provided by:
Subscribers, the Consortium for Varsity Academics®, and
the Carnegie Corporation of New York

EDITORIAL OFFICES: *The Concord Review*, 730 Boston Post Road, Suite 24, Sudbury, Massachusetts 01776 USA [1-800-331-5007]

The Concord Review (ISSN #0895-0539), founded in 1987, is published quarterly by The Concord Review, Inc., a non-profit, tax-exempt, 501(c)(3) Massachusetts corporation. Subscription rates: $60 + s&h ($10 US / $50 international) for four printed copies ($70/$110), or $40 for one year of ebooks (PDF). Orders for 26 or more subscriptions (class sets) will receive a 40% discount.

Subscription orders must be paid in advance, and change-of-address information must be sent in writing.

TCR SUBSCRIPTIONS: Subscribe at www.tcr.org, or by check mailed to 730 Boston Post Road, Suite 24, Sudbury, MA 01776 USA; email: fitzhugh@tcr.org

Ralph Waldo Emerson Prize 2003

THE GREAT DELUSION:
CHAIM RUMKOWSKI'S ATTEMPT
TO SAVE THE JEWS OF LODZ

Rachel E. Hines

This paper is dedicated to the members of my family who lived, perished and survived in the Lodz ghetto.

"Arbeit Macht Frei"—"work sets you free." This Nazi slogan pervaded concentration camp and ghetto propaganda during the Holocaust, most infamously greeting those who faced the entrance gates of the Auschwitz death camp. The motto was also embraced in the Lodz ghetto during the four difficult years of its existence, through the policies of its Chairman, Chaim Rumkowski. The city of Lodz which, prior to WWII, was home to the second largest Jewish population in Poland, was the first ghetto to be enclosed and the last Polish ghetto to be liquidated. Chaim Rumkowski was deluded by the Nazis into believing that "arbeit macht frei"—that productivity and compliance with Gestapo orders would earn the Lodz Jews survival—a misconception that made the ghetto's ultimate demise after its unique longevity all the more tragic.

A sizable Jewish community began to spring up in Lodz in 1820 as Lodz's growing industry drew increasing numbers of

The author is an MD candidate at the University of Maryland. She wrote this paper at Richard Montgomery High School in Rockville, Maryland, for Mr. Gilbert Early's history course in the 2000/2001 academic year.

Jews to the city. By the outbreak of the second World War, the Jews had grown to comprise about one-third of the city's population and owned an even greater proportion of factories in Lodz, mostly textile-producing.[1] But the interwar years brought economic devastation to the Jewish community. The loss of its vital Russian market with the creation of an independent Poland was compounded by the anti-Jewish fiscal policies of Polish Finance Minister W. Grabski and the international Depression of 1929. In the mid-1930s, as Hitler rose to power in Germany, the Nazi party disseminated anti-Semitic propaganda to the German minority in Lodz. By 1934, such sentiments had spread, allowing an anti-Semitic party to gain the majority in municipal elections with a platform of purging the town of Jews.[2]

The Nazi occupation of Lodz, which the Germans called Litzmannstadt, began on September 8, 1939. SS Brigadier General Friedrich Uebelhoer issued a top-secret report on December 10, 1939, concerning "the establishment of the ghetto in Lodz."[3] The report made clear that the formation of a ghetto would be only a temporary measure, since the complete evacuation of the city's large Jewish population was not possible immediately. The report included plans for a Jewish autonomous administration consisting of several departments as well as an outline for the exchange of foodstuffs for manufactured products.[4] This, according to Uebelhoer, was a suitable solution to "the Jewish question in the city of Lodz...for the time being."[5] The report concluded with an emphasis on the transitory nature of the ghetto as an intermediate step towards the final solution:

> The creation of the ghetto is, of course, only a temporary measure. I reserve to myself the decision concerning the times and the means by which the ghetto and with it the city of Lodz will be cleansed of Jews. The final aim must in any case bring about the total cauterization of this plague spot.[6]

The report made clear the ultimate goals of the Nazis in creating the Lodz ghetto; although Uebelhoer's provision regarding the exchange of foodstuffs for "materials, such as textiles, etc." suggested that the Nazis were willing to provide for the Jews for as long as they had something to offer in return, under no circumstances would the Jews of Lodz be granted long-term survival. In January 1940, Jews were segregated into the Old City and Baluty quarters of Lodz, which were officially established as the parameters of the Lodz ghetto by a police order on February 8, 1940.[7] When the ghetto was sealed on April 30, 1940, its population numbered 164,000, which excluded the 70,000 Jews who had previously left the city. Upon Lodz's occupation, the Nazis immediately disbanded the city's Jewish Community Council, of which Mordechai Chaim Rumkowski was vice-chairman. They replaced it with a formal Judenrat, a Council of Elders,[8] to which the Nazis appointed Rumkowski as *Judenaeltester*, the "Elder of the Jews."[9] Rumkowski was granted wide powers over the ghetto's inhabitants but was in turn accountable to orders received via Hans Biebow, the German head of the Lodz ghetto administration.[10]

From the beginning of his leadership, Rumkowski focused on the means by which Lodz could survive the war. His plan was threefold: to create a community that would operate as a fully-functioning society; to make the ghetto economically indispensable to the Nazis through high productivity; and to make intermittent concessions to Biebow's orders to avoid terror and mass deportations. All three goals were dependent on a highly-organized system of internal work, which would become an integral aspect of Lodz ghetto life. However, though Rumkowski's strategies may have prolonged the ghetto's existence, his plan proved inadequate for ensuring its long-term survival.

Rumkowski aimed to make Lodz a permanent ghetto that embodied a community of Jewish culture and nationalism[11] and maintained various departments that would control the needs of the population. The "Rumkowski Manifesto" which was spread throughout the ghetto via posters and newspapers, declared the necessity of "work, bread, care, and welfare for the children, the aged, the sick; law and order."[12] The departments and other organizations which sprung up in Lodz to fulfill these necessities were far more extensive than the "Jewish autonomous administration" mandated by Uebelhoer.[13] In addition to the departments of nutrition, finance, housing, and others which were responsible for the most basic workings of the ghetto, Rumkowski established systems of education and recreation, a postal service, as well as a network of hospitals, and most importantly, of factories. Rumkowski described his goal of organizing all facets of the ghetto community: "I have made it my aim to regulate life in the ghetto at all costs. This aim can be achieved, first of all, by employment for all. Therefore, my main slogan has been 'to give work to the greatest number of people.'"[14] Under Rumkowski, unemployment was practically non-existent among those over the age of ten,[15] excluding the sick and very elderly, because work was used to regulate food rations; if one who was deemed able-bodied was not engaged in any kind of work, he simply did not eat. By instituting work as the means for obtaining all physiological needs, Rumkowski not only assured a greater regularity of life with little resistance, but also achieved his greater goal of maintaining ghetto productivity.

When the question first arose of how the ghetto was to be maintained and its population fed, Rumkowski responded that "he had in the ghetto a gold currency of the highest caliber—the labor of Jewish hands."[16] This "currency" would be the ghetto's basis for exchange with the Nazis for foodstuffs and raw materials with which to produce textiles and German armaments,[17] and in doing so, would make the ghetto valuable to the German war economy. Thus, according to Dobroszycki, editor of *The Chronicle of the Lodz Ghetto*;

> The deciding factor in all aspects of ghetto life was whether or not a given person was employed. Even in 1943, a relatively peaceful year when mass deportations in and out of the ghetto had ceased, there were periods when people without working papers were grabbed on the streets and in their homes day and night and deported to a death camp.[18]

Rumkowski undoubtedly succeeded in making the ghetto a remarkably profitable enterprise for the Germans—toward the end of 1943 it contained more than 90 enterprises employing over 75,000 workers. In addition to the tons of munitions, equipment, uniforms, boots, and other goods the Germans extracted from the Jewish laborers, Berlin recorded a net profit of 46,211,485 Reichmarks from the ghetto as of its liquidation.[19]

The ghetto's productivity did not go unnoticed by certain prominent members of the Nazi party, most especially Hans Biebow, head of the German ghetto administration, as well as Albert Speer of the German Armament Ministry,[20] who weighed the affairs of the ghetto, as he recognized the benefits of the nature of its production. Although Speer may have been able to exert some influence on the ghetto's fate, "exploitation was in the foreground," he explained thirty-five years later.[21] In his introduction to The Chronicle of the Lodz Ghetto, Lucjan Dobroszycki says:

> Apart from Biebow, none of the Nazis realized so clearly how much the ghetto could benefit the Reich economically. Biebow was well acquainted with every workshop in the ghetto...and had a precise sense of what every factory was producing and at what low cost.... The initiative to liquidate the ghetto certainly did not originate with him, although he rarely displayed even the slightest sign that the fate of its inhabitants was of any concern to him. His sole interest was the ghetto's productivity and the profit to be derived from it... He never forgot that he was a German, and he ruled the ghetto with a firm hand."[22]

Perhaps Rumkowski's conviction that it was beyond the realm of logic for the Nazis to eliminate such a center of productivity stemmed from his contact with Biebow, whose interest in ghetto production was not representative of general German sentiment, which was far more concerned with the execution of the final solution. Unfortunately for Rumkowski and Lodz, Biebow was not responsible for the city's fate, being subordinate to Goering, the Plenipotentiary of the Four-Year Plan,[23] and Himmler, the SS-Reichsfuhrer and Chief of the German Police (Gestapo).[24] Himmler himself may have played a role in propagating Rumkowski's emphasis on work as a key to survival; Szmul Rozensztajn's daily notes recorded a conversation between Rumkowski and Himmler upon the latter's visit to the ghetto in June 1941:

When Herr Himmler arrived at Balut Market with his entourage, he had the following exchange with Chairman Rumkowski:

"How are you doing here?" asked Herr Himmler.

"We work, and we are building a city of labor here...My motto is Work, Peace, and Order."

"Then go on working for the benefit of your brethren in the ghetto. It will do you good." Herr Himmler finished the conversation.[25]

Himmler's support for the work of the ghetto epitomizes the great deception of Nazi policy. It was ultimately Rumkowski's efforts to demonstrate the worth of the ghetto's existence to the Nazis that turned Lodz into a center for war industry that worked faithfully to arm its enemy.

    The third major element of Rumkowski's policy—his compliance with orders from the German Ghetto Administration—defined his controversial position in the ghetto and exemplified his deluded beliefs. He believed that concessions to the Nazis would alleviate terror and avoid mass deportations; in this respect, Rumkowski succeeded for a time but only at great costs to the ghetto. Before a system of labor was formed in Lodz, the Nazi occupiers of the city would conduct forced roundups for manual laborers, yanking people off the streets and out of their homes. Adelson describes how "when the problem [of forced labor] had reached catastrophic proportions, the Chairman stepped in. A decision was made to voluntarily place a contingent of workers at the authorities' disposal..."[26] From this point forward, Rumkowski sought young, able-bodied men to fulfill the Germans' demands for labor outside the ghetto, which consisted of tasks such as building roads or straightening riverbanks, rather than await the use of force to achieve these ends. Rumkowski obeyed all such Nazi requests, as he would say, so that they would "not be executed by others," who would employ terror and give less regard to particular choices of workers.[27]

    Rumkowski applied the same philosophy to the deportation quotas that he received from the Nazis; if it remained under his own jurisdiction to select who would be "resettled," then he could assure that the most productive members of society would remain in the ghetto. Rumkowski was unaware that, beginning in the latter half of 1941, the Nazi's final solution entered a new phase of direct genocide, during which the principal means of exterminating the Jews shifted from starvation to deportation to death camps[28]—Chelmno, in the case of Lodz. In the beginning stages of the new phase, Rumkowski himself was probably not aware of the true nature of the transports, so he reiterated Biebow's promise to him with no apparent skepticism: "The fate of the ghetto deportees would not be so tragic as generally anticipated in the ghetto. They won't be behind barbed wire, they will be doing agricultural work."[29] Convinced of this, Rumkowski followed the orders from the German authorities, supplying the requested numbers of people for the deportations. Rumkowski's decisions concerning who would be included in the resettlements reveal his determination to retain in Lodz those persons who contributed to the ghetto's productivity and vice-versa. The first transport out of Lodz in December 1941, necessitated by an influx of new residents, was comprised of 10,000 people who included, "in addition to criminals...those who received rations but ignored their work assignments."[30] On March 2, 1942, Rumkowski delivered a speech referred to as "Work Protects Us From Annihilation" to an invited audience of administrators, factory managers, and his advisors regarding further requests for deportations:

> Thousands more [people] were requested [for resettlement]—this time, in accordance with the agreement that only people who can work can remain in the ghetto. The order must be carried out, or it will be carried out by others. After painful deliberation and inner struggle, I've decided to deport the people on relief: They too are at fault, if not fully, then partially, in that they stayed outside the ghetto workforce.[31]

The ghetto chronicle from Spring 1942 confirmed Rumkowski's decree, citing that the first thousand deportation cards were sent to families in which no one worked, while people who were employed were not receiving deportation cards.[32]

In late May 1942, about 6,000 Jews from neighboring Pabianice and Brzeziny were sent to Lodz—not including any children under ten or the aged.[33] This observation instilled a mood of deep unrest among the Jews of Lodz, who began to distrust the principle upon which they had lived to this point. Bernard Ostrowski, one of the ghetto chroniclers, expressed this doubt in an entry from May 21 and 22, 1942:

Until now, people had thought that work would maintain the ghetto and the majority of its people without any breakup of families. Now it is clear that even this was an illusion. There were plenty of orders [for new work] in Pabianice and Brzeziny, but that did not protect the Jews against wholesale deportation.[34]

Ostrowski's insight foreshadows not only the deportation of children and elderly from Lodz later that year, but the eventual liquidation of the ghetto entirely, as by this point, the Nazis' drive to win the war was second to the priority of the final solution.

By September of 1942, the Nazis made it clear that all non-workers must be unconditionally removed from the Lodz ghetto. Rumkowski, of course, complied with their order for the deportation of more than 20,000 Jews, believing it to be a sacrifice necessary for upholding the productive interests of the greater population. In his infamous "Give Me Your Children" speech, delivered on September 4, 1942, Rumkowski regrettably accepted that there could be no other suitable course of action if the whole of the ghetto was to be saved:

"I must perform this difficult and bloody operation—I must cut off limbs to save the body itself!—I must take children because, if not, others may be taken as well, God forbid....

"There are, in the ghetto, many patients who can expect to live only a few days more, maybe a few weeks. I don't know if the idea is diabolical or not, but I must say it: 'Give me the sick. In their place, we can save the healthy...'"[35]

Rumkowski cooperated with the Germans even on such extreme measures since he still clung to the belief that as long as productivity was sustained in the ghetto via a population capable of working, "the body itself" would be saved. However, Rumkowski was not aware of the much broader scheme that controlled the fate of the ghetto—Hitler's final solution.[36]

The tragedy of Rumkowski's situation lay in the fact that the Germans would have deported Jews with or without his assistance. Dobroszycki points out that with each new demand from the authorities "he continued to delude himself that this was the last, that he would succeed in saving at least a part of the populace." In fact, by taking it upon himself to fill quotas, Rumkowski shifted the culpability of the Nazis to himself, so that any bitterness regarding ghetto life and attempts at resistance arose principally against him and his administration.

Resistance of any kind could not succeed under Rumkowski's administration because of his control over all sources of force and power in the ghetto—namely, the police, food supply, and choice of deportees. As workers' strikes arose over the course of the ghetto's existence, Rumkowski simply closed those factories in which they originated and withheld food from those involved.[37] Socialists and other groups suspected of opposing Rumkowski's policies were infiltrated by the security police[38] and would assuredly be included in any upcoming deportations. Conversely, those closest to Rumkowski received privileged food rations; as food supplies decreased, corruption within the ghetto bureaucracy, especially among the police, increased.[39] Any attempts on Rumkowski's part to remedy the corruption within the ghetto leadership would most likely have been rendered ineffective by his complete dependency on just such dishonest people for support.[40] Leon Hurwitz, a resident of the Lodz ghetto, suggested that Rumkowski too, and perhaps most of all, was corrupted by the power he possessed as Judenaeltester, thinking of himself as "the Jewish King Lear."[41] Hurwitz gives a description of Rumkowski's obsession with power in 1940:

"Everybody in the clique Rumkowski has gathered around him sings paeans to his genius and his mission. Once, speaking to an associate about his mission, he declared, 'What do you know about power? Power is sweet, power is everything, is life.' And with a fanatical gleam in his half-crazed eyes, he finished, 'But woe to him who makes the slightest attempt to wrest power from me.'"[42]

Rumkowski had always envisioned himself as a father-like savior of his people,[43] but as his control over ghetto affairs and population increased, an almost dictator-like cult of personality sprung up around him. In physician Jakub Szulman's diary, he contends that "even before the ghetto was sealed, [Rumkowski] had an inner certainty that his name would be remembered."[44] Paintings of him, and poetry in his honor were published, albums were created to record his works, and a postage stamp with his face on it was prepared for circulation but banned by the Nazis.

Rumkowski's power, however, was only an illusion. Although he was firmly convinced that he was always in the right in his program of "work and peace,"[45] in reality, it was the Germans who made all decisions concerning ghetto affairs. If, on a rare occasion, Rumkowski refused to comply with an order, he was threatened with death, or Biebow would personally inflict physical punishment on him.[46] The scant news he received from outside the ghetto and especially his two trips to the Warsaw ghetto,[47] only further deluded him into thinking that his program was successful. A comparison of early mortality rates in the Warsaw and Lodz ghettos indicates that people were dying of hunger in nearly identical proportions in both places.[48] The difference, according to Dobroszycki, was that "while in Warsaw the dead lay on the streets for a long time before they were buried, in Lodz burial took place almost immediately."[49] In 1943, the liquidation of the Warsaw, Radom, Vilna, Cracow, and Lublin ghettos[50] made Lodz the last existing ghetto in Poland and seemed to affirm unequivocally the ghetto's success.

It is not certain at what point, if ever, Rumkowski was made aware of the fates of the resettled persons from Lodz. During the summer of 1942, a Jew relocated to the Lodz ghetto brought with him a letter written by Rabbi Jakub Szulman of Grabow,[51] a town northwest of Lodz, which contained the following information:[52]

> ...An eyewitness who by chance was able to escape from hell has been to see me...I learned everything from him. The place where everyone is being put to death is called Chelmno...People are killed in one of two ways: either they are shot or gassed... This is what happened to the towns of Dabie, Izbica Kujawska, Klodo Wava and others...And for the past few days, they have been bringing thousands of Jews from Lodz there, and doing the same to them.[53]

Sources do not agree on whether Rumkowski ever actually saw this letter; however, most concede that he was well aware of the fates of the ghetto deportees. However, it is not clear when Rumkowski recognized that such a fate inevitably awaited all residents of the ghetto, even the most productive. In August of 1944, when Biebow issued the order to dissolve the Lodz ghetto completely, it was accompanied by the promise that all would survive; Rumkowski repeated this promise to the population whom he strongly encouraged to report for resettlement.[54] The entire population was in fact taken to the Auschwitz death camp, where the vast majority, including Rumkowski, were gassed.

Although Rumkowski did not achieve his goal of earning the ghetto survival through its productivity, his agenda undoubtedly bought the Lodz Jews extra time. Lodz became the last Polish ghetto in existence in 1943, maintaining a population of nearly 100,000 when the others had been completely liquidated. On September 18, 1944, the War Refugee Board in Washington cabled the American Ambassador in Moscow, W. Averell Harriman, regarding the large number of Jews still living in Lodz to that point:

> It is reported that many Jews, perhaps 60,000 persons, survive in Lodz, Poland. The Soviet authorities are undoubtedly aware of the danger that the Germans may attempt to exterminate these people before evacuating the city...[55]

At the time this message was sent, the Russians were only one-hundred-some miles from Lodz but the ghetto was not liberated until January 19, 1945, when the population had been reduced to a mere 877 people.[56] Perhaps the legitimacy of Rumkowski's policies would have been proven had the Russians arrived just months sooner. Even so, according to Adelson, survivors commonly assert that more Jews are alive today from the Lodz Ghetto than from any other concentration of Jews under Nazi rule.

Rumkowski's deluded impression of the ghetto's ability to earn its survival through work was a product of an extensive scheme of Nazi deception designed to utilize every ounce of the Jews' productive capabilities before exterminating them. The goals of the Germans' evil final solution—to destroy the Jews even at the cost of losing a productive and profitable element of a war economy—were so illogical as to be quite unfathomable to Rumkowski and his peers. The plight of Rumkowski and the Jews of Lodz was representative of the plight of other Jewish communities under Nazi rule in using rational tactics to try to appease the irrational masters of their fates during the Second World War.

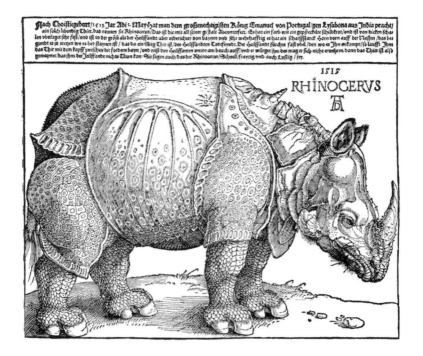

[1] "Lodz," Encyclopaedia Judaica Volume 11 (Jerusalem: Keter Publishing House, Ltd., 1971) p. 426

[2] Ibid., p. 432

[3] Friedrich Uebelhoer, "Report by Uebelhoer on the Establishment of the Ghetto in Lodz," 10 December 1939, rpt. in Documents on the Holocaust Yitzchak Arad, Israel Gutman, Abraham Margaliot, eds. (Lincoln: University of Nebraska Press, 1999) p. 192

[4] "The principle must be that foodstuffs and fuel can be paid for only by means of an exchange of materials, such as textiles, etc. In this way we should succeed in getting from the Jews all their hoarded and hidden items of value." Uebelhoer, in Documents, Arad, et al., eds., p. 194

[5] Ibid., p. 194

[6] Ibid., p. 194

[7] "Lodz," Encyclopaedia Judaica, p. 433. The entire area was less than two square miles, consisting of houses fit for demolition, and generally lacking a system of sewage disposal.

[8] Judenrate were first instituted in occupied Poland in September 1939, and subsequently in other countries conquered by Germany, to be responsible for the implementation of German policy regarding the Jews. The Judenrate were composed of prominent men from their respective communities in order to ensure that orders were carried out to the fullest possible extent and to discredit Jewish leadership in the eyes of the Jewish population. Beginning in 1940, the Judenrate were given the responsibility for providing the Germans with forced labor for the camps being set up, where no contact with the community was possible. In most instances, the Judenrate chose to comply with such demands, but those who didn't faced death. When Nazi policy shifted and the question of obedience turned to sending Jews to extermination camps, far fewer agreed to cooperate, no longer seeing their role as a contribution to the community's struggle to survive. Figures from Isaiah Trunk's 1972 study on the Judenrate indicates that close to 80 percent of Judenrate members in Eastern Europe died before or during deportations to extermination camps from their communities. "Judenrat," Encyclopedia of the Holocaust Vol. 2, Israel Gutman, et al., eds. (New York: MacMillan Publishing Company, 1990) pp. 762-766

[9] It is not certain as to why the Nazis selected Rumkowski for this position; prior to the war, he had been only a peripheral politician, focusing his efforts primarily on the

welfare of orphans in Lodz. Alan Adelson, author of <u>Lodz Ghetto</u>, cites several reasons for the choice, including Rumkowski's energy, ability to speak German, or even his striking white hair. The possibility that Rumkowski's early proposals to appease the Nazis by delivering daily quotas of Jews rather than see them seized off the streets in acts of Nazi terror, may have signaled that he could, and possibly wanted to, be counted on to continue to deliver Jews on command. Alan Adelson and Robert Lapides, <u>Lodz Ghetto</u> (New York: Viking Penguin, 1989) p. xvi

[10] Biebow enjoyed wide powers in administering the Lodz ghetto, from which he was able to extract great profits by exploiting the manpower in its factories and confiscating Jews' property. Biebow did not want the ghetto administration to pass to other hands, so in order to maintain high profits from the ghetto factories, he worked to ensure the ghetto's continued existence until the summer of 1944. Biebow excelled in deception tactics, convincing the Jews that transports from Lodz to Chelmno and Auschwitz would merely take them to work camps connected to German factories. "Biebow, Hans," <u>Encyclopedia of the Holocaust</u> Vol. 1, pp. 214-215

[11] "The Story of Chaim Rumkowski and the Jews of Lodz," videocassette. Produced by Peter Cohen and Bo Kuritzen. Lucjan Dobroszycki, historical consultant. Produced in association with Yad Vashem Remembrance Authority, Israel and the YIVO Institute for Jewish Research, New York. Poj Filmproduction AB, Switzerland.

[12] Ibid.

[13] Uebelhoer, in <u>Documents</u>, Arad, et al., eds., p. 194

[14] Chaim Rumkowski, "Address by Rumkowski to the Officials of the Judenrat in Lodz," 1 February 1941, rpt. in <u>Documents on the Holocaust</u> D. Dabrowska and L. Dobroszycki, eds., p.237

[15] Bernard Ostrowski, "The Drive to Employ Children Over the Age of Ten," 2 July 1942, rpt. in Lucian Dobroszycki, ed., <u>The Chronicle of the Lodz Ghetto 1941-1944</u> (New Haven, Connecticut: Yale University Press, 1984) p. 218

[16] Adelson and Lapides, p. 45

[17] "The Story" videocassette

[18] Dobroszycki, p. lx

[19] Adelson and Lapides, p. xix

[20] Albert Speer was named minister of armaments and war production in September 1943. As such, he was able to raise

armaments production significantly, using millions of forced laborers. He received assignments from Hitler personally and developed a close friendship through working with him. "Speer, Albert," Encyclopedia of the Holocaust Vol. 4, pp. 1395-1396

[21] Dobroszycki, p. lx

[22] Ibid., p. xiii

[23] The Four-Year Plan was the Nazi economic plan to make the German army operational and the German economy fit for war within four years. "Four-Year Plan," Encyclopedia of the Holocaust Vol. 2

[24] Ibid.

[25] Szmul Rozensztajn, "Daily Notes," 6 June 1941, rpt. in Adelson and Lapides, p. 152

[26] Adelson and Lapides, p. 23

[27] Dobroszycki, Chronicle, p. li

[28] Ibid., p. li

[29] Ibid., p. li

[30] Chaim Rumkowski, "Only Undesirable Elements Will Leave," 20 December 1941, rpt. in Adelson and Lapides, p. 191

[31] Chaim Rumkowski, "Work Protects Us From Annihilation," 20 March 1942, rpt. in Adelson and Lapides, p. 231

[32] Unspecified chronicler, "Resettlement," 1-3 May 1942, rpt. in Dobroszycki, p. 159

[33] Bernard Ostrowski, "The Mood of the Ghetto," 20 and 21 May 1942, rpt. in Dobroszycki, p. 182

[34] Ibid., p. 182

[35] Chaim Rumkowski, "Give Me Your Children," rpt. in Dobroszycki, p. 328

[36] In January of 1942, the Wannsee Conference was called as a general clarification of Nazi policy and direction, specifically with the purpose of creating "a draft plan concerning the organizational, practical, and economic aspects of the final solution of the European Jewish question." The plan called for the extermination of 2,284,000 Jews from the Government-General (Poland) to be carried out "as quickly as possible." It was proposed that those Jews employed in essential war industries not be evacuated, but Secretary of State Buhler emphasized the urgency of executing the final solution and that "consideration of labor supply would not hinder the course of [the current evacuation] Aktion." "Protocol of the Wannsee Conference," 20 January 1942, rpt. in Documents on the Holocaust V. Dabrowska and L. Dobroszycki, eds. p. 250

[37] "The Story" videocassette

[38] A system of Jewish ghetto police was set up with the establishment of the ghetto to maintain general order within the ghetto. A special unit within the force took orders from the Gestapo while the police generally took part in roundups and in protecting Rumkowski and his position. "Lodz," Encyclopaedia Judaica, Vol. 3

[39] Ibid.

[40] Ibid.

[41] Leon Hurwitz, "Leon Hurwitz, Life in the Lodz Ghetto," rpt. in Adelson, Lodz Ghetto p. 94

[42] Ibid., p. 94

[43] "The Story" videocassette

[44] Jakub Szulman, "Jakub Szulman's Notebook 21.3.41," 21 March 1941. rpt. in Adelson and Lapides, p. 87

[45] Dobroszycki, p. 1

[46] "The Story" videocassette

[47] Dobroszycki, p. 1. As Chairman, Rumkowski was permitted limited contact with neighboring ghettos. Dobroszycki does not name, however, the specific purposes of his two visits to Warsaw.

[48] Ibid., p. 1

[49] The burial system in Lodz was much more efficient than that in Warsaw because Rumkowski organized teams of workers to collect bodies, transport them to grave sites, and dig graves at a pace that nearly kept up with the death rate in the ghetto. Adelson and Lapides.

[50] "The Story" videocassette

[51] This letter writer is not to be confused with the physician of the same name whose diary was previously cited.

[52] Martin Gilbert, The Holocaust: A History of the Jews of Europe During the Second World War (New York: Holt, Rinehart, and Winston, 1985) p. 279

[53] Jakub Szulman, "Letter to Relations in Lodz Regarding the Chelmno Death Camp," 19 January 1942, rpt. in Adelson and Lapides, pp. 490-491

[54] "The Story" videocassette

[55] "Cable to Ambassador Harriman, Moscow, U.S.S.R.," 18 September 1944, Washington, D.C., National Archives, Record Group 59, Box 47, 095-101502/7-1844, rpt. in Fifty Years Ago: Darkness Before Dawn, 1994 Days of Remembrance (Washington, D.C.: United States Holocaust Memorial Museum, 1994) p. 129

[56] Dobroszycki, pp. lxv-lxvi

Bibliography

Works Cited

Primary

"Cable to Ambassador Harriman, Moscow, USSR"
18 September 1944, Washington, DC: National Archives,
Record Group 59, Box 47, 095-101502/7-1844, rpt. in <u>Fifty
Years Ago: Darkness Before Dawn, 1994 Days of Remembrance</u>
United States Holocaust Memorial Museum; Washington, DC.,
1994, p. 129
    Provides an insight into the outside world's conception
of the situation in Lodz a short time before the ghetto's
liquidation. It is interesting to note the War Refugee Board's
accuracy in their estimation of the number of surviving Jews in
Lodz and its sense of the impending threat of liquidation.

    Hurwitz, Leon, "Leon Hurwitz, Life in the Lodz Ghetto,"
rpt. in Alan Adelson and Robert Lapides, <u>Lodz Ghetto</u> New
York: Viking Penguin, 1989, p. 94
    Provides a unique portrayal of Rumkowski as a man
obsessed with his own power but is blatantly biased against the
Chairman, whom Hurwitz views as "fanatical and half-crazed."

    Ostrowski, Bernard, "The Drive to Employ Children Over
the Age of Ten," 2 July 1942, rpt. in Lucjan Dobroszycki, ed.,
<u>The Chronicle of the Lodz Ghetto 1941-1944</u> New Haven,
Connecticut: Yale University Press, 1984, p. 218
    Indicates the extent to which Rumkowski strove to include
as many people as possible under the "shelter" of work in the
ghetto, including relatively young children.

    Ostrowski, Bernard, "The Mood of the Ghetto," 20 and
21 May 1942, rpt. in Lucjan Dobroszycki, ed., <u>The Chronicle
of the Lodz Ghetto 1941-1944</u> New Haven, Connecticut: Yale
University Press, 1984, p. 182
    Excellent summary of the ghetto residents' disillusionment
with the Nazis and distrust regarding the promise that work
would allow families and individuals to survive.

Rumkowski, Chaim, "Address by Rumkowski to the Officials of the Judenrat in Lodz," 1 February 1941, rpt. in <u>Documents on the Holocaust</u> D. Dabrowska and L. Dobroszycki, eds., p. 237—Exemplifies Rumkowski's attitude stressing the importance of work in the ghetto.

Rumkowski Chaim, "Give Me Your Children," 4 September 1942, rpt. in Alan Adelson and Robert Lapides, <u>Lodz Ghetto</u> New York: Viking Penguin, 1989, p. 328
Powerful example of Rumkowski's desperation in his attempts to save at least some of the ghetto by cooperating with the Germans.

Rumkowski, Chaim, "Only Undesirable Elements Will Leave," 20 December 1941, rpt. in Alan Adelson and Robert Lapides, <u>Lodz Ghetto</u> New York: Viking Penguin, 1989, p. 191
Indicates Rumkowski's distaste for those who did not contribute to the ghetto through work.

Rumkowski, Chaim, "Work Protects Us From Annihilation," 20 March 1942, rpt. in Alan Adelson and Robert Lapides, <u>Lodz Ghetto</u> New York: Viking Penguin, 1989, p. 232
Indication of Rumkowski's utilitarian position regarding which persons were "worth" retaining in the ghetto, and who was not.

Szulman, Jakub, "Jakub Szulman's Notebook 21.3.41," 21 March 1941, rpt. in Alan Adelson and Robert Lapides, <u>Lodz Ghetto</u> New York: Viking Penguin, 1989, p. 87
An interesting perspective on Rumkowski's impression of his role in history as a hero-like figure. The account seems generally critical of Rumkowski's policies, depicting them as unreasonable or egocentric.

Uebelhoer, Freidrich, "Report by Uebelhoer on the Establishment of the Ghetto in Lodz," 10 December 1939, rpt. in <u>Documents on the Holocaust</u> ed. Yitzchak Arad, Israel Gutman, Abraham Margaliot, Lincoln: University of Nebraska Press, 1999, p. 194
Excellent and reliable documentation of initial German intentions in creating the Lodz ghetto from a General of the SS.

Unspecified chronicler, "Resettlement," 1-3 May 1942, rpt. in Lucian Dobroszycki, ed., <u>The Chronicle of the Lodz Ghetto 1941-1944</u> New Haven, Connecticut: Yale University Press, 1984, p. 159
Relatively objective report on the proceedings of the first resettlements of 1942.

Secondary

Adelson, Alan, and Robert Lapides, <u>Lodz Ghetto</u> Viking Penguin; New York, 1989
A compilation of primary sources from various authors within and outside the Lodz ghetto. The diaries and journals included may be biased but add unique perspectives not offered in the documentary chronicle.

Dobroszycki, Lucjan, ed., <u>The Chronicle of the Lodz Ghetto 1941-1944</u> New Haven, Connecticut: Yale University Press, 1984
The chronicle is an overall objective record of the chroniclers' observations of life in, and affairs of, the Lodz ghetto. However, as Dobroszycki points out, it is not known to what extent the content of this official chronicle was censored by Rumkowski or others. Overall, it takes a laudatory view of Rumkowski while his opponents are portrayed as being unreasonable or somehow in the wrong.

Gilbert, Martin, <u>The Holocaust: A History of the Jews of Europe During the Second World War</u> New York: Holt, Rinehart, and Winston, 1985
An account of the Jews throughout Europe, including several references to Lodz, during the Holocaust. Included several references to primary sources found in either the ghetto chronicle or journals and diaries included in <u>Lodz Ghetto</u>.

<u>Fifty Years Ago: Darkness Before Dawn, 1994 Days of Remembrance</u> United States Holocaust Memorial Museum; Washington, DC., 1994
A compilation of primary sources regarding various aspects of the Holocaust.

"Lodz," <u>Encyclopaedia Judaica</u> Volume 11, Jerusalem: Keter Publishing House, Ltd., 1971

"The Story of Chaim Rumkowski and the Jews of Lodz,"
videocassette. Produced by Peter Cohen and Bo Kuritzen.
Lucjan Dobroszycki historical consultant. Produced in
association with Yad Vashem Remembrance Authority, Israel
and the YIVO Institute for Jewish Research, New York. Poj
Filmproduction AB, Switzerland. A documentary film that
summarizes the events that occurred during the course
of the Lodz ghetto's existence, from its establishment to
its liquidation. Takes an objective standpoint in regard to
Rumkowski's leadership.

Works Consulted

Secondary

"Biebow, Hans," Encyclopedia of the Holocaust Vol. 1, Israel
Gutman, et al., eds., New York: MacMillan Publishing Company,
1990

Fifty Years Ago: Revolt Amidst the Darkness, 1993 Days
of Remembrance Washington, DC: United States Holocaust
Memorial Museum, 1994

"Four-Year Plan," Encyclopedia of the Holocaust Vol. 2,
Israel Gutman, et al., eds., New York: MacMillan Publishing
Company, 1990

"Judenrat," Encyclopaedia of the Holocaust Vol. 2, Israel
Gutman, et al., eds., New York: MacMillan Publishing Company,
1990

"Rumkowski, Chaim," Encyclopedia of the Holocaust Vol.
3, Israel Gutman, et al., eds., New York: MacMillan Publishing
Company, 1990

"Speer, Albert," Encyclopedia of the Holocaust Vol. 4, Israel
Gutman, et al., eds. New York: MacMillan Publishing Company,
1990

Ralph Waldo Emerson Prize 2003

Rhodes Scholarship 2006

ANNE HUTCHINSON: A LIFE IN PRIVATE

Jessica Leight

Anne Hutchinson, a member of the pantheon of American heroes for more than three hundred and fifty years, has always been the stuff of legend. According to Nathaniel Hawthorne in The Scarlet Letter, she is a holy martyr who caused rose bushes to spring up at her feet; she is a phenomenon, an American Joan of Arc who heroically stood her ground alone against Puritan tyranny. Although such descriptions are not completely inaccurate, they overlook a basic fact about Anne Hutchinson. She was not alone. Her enemies deliberately construed her as isolated and abandoned in an effort to contain the threat she posed, but that was most emphatically not the case. Though she is perhaps the most famous leader of what we now know as the Antinomian movement, there was another—her fiery brother-in-law Reverend John Wheelwright, an admirably effective incendiary who also gave the movement a religious authority and validity that Hutchinson, as a woman, could not provide.

There is, however, a crucial difference between Anne Hutchinson and John Wheelwright that made and still makes the former more radical, more hated, and ultimately, more important, a difference revealed in the punishments each received for their

---

The author is a Ph.D. candidate at MIT. She graduated summa cum laude from Yale and was a Rhodes Scholar. She graduated early from Cambridge Rindge and Latin School in Cambridge, Massachusetts, where she wrote this paper as a Junior for an independent study supervised by Mr. Michael Desimone in 2001.

seditious and blasphemous rebellion. Both were banished from the Massachusetts Bay Colony, and those who overtly supported them faced penalties. However, only Hutchinson was excommunicated, and Wheelwright's banishment was eventually revoked, though he never returned to Massachusetts. And never was John Wheelwright, who became a respected minister in New Hampshire following his banishment, subject to the same revulsion, vitriol and contempt that was heaped on the head of his female counterpart.

Quite simply, the difference between them lay in the threat each posed. Wheelwright's rebellion was primarily in the political and the politicoreligious spheres—ministerial appointments, gubernatorial elections, and public sermons. Throughout his life, he remained within this recognizable framework of sanctioned political engagement. Hutchinson, while she participated as fully in such engagements as was possible for a woman at that time, went even further: she radically politicized the private sphere. Rather than attempt to gain an appointment or win an election, she denied the necessity of either; she spoke at home, she spoke directly to her ministerial opponents in private and personal conversation, and she spoke of direct revelations and communions with God that could only be private experiences. Moreover, she was a midwife, presiding over one of the most private and mysterious experiences of daily life, and one from which men, who more or less constituted the public at this point, were entirely excluded. Everything she did went against the grain of Puritan New England religion and society, which was entirely public—publicly displayed, publicly regulated. By affirming and exalting the primacy of privacy, Anne Hutchinson struck to the heart of a society in which making the private public was a virtual mania. And thus she earned more bitter hatred and retrospective praise than John Wheelwright ever garnered, or deserved.

The two people around whom the Antinomian controversy would one day swirl had similar experiences with the tyranny of state-imposed religion in the old country before taking refuge in the Puritan wilderness—a wilderness that later proved to be inhospitable for them. John Wheelwright is thought to have been born at Saleby, England, a tiny town twenty-four miles from Boston in Lincolnshire, sometime during the year 1592. He attended Cambridge as a classmate of Oliver Cromwell and then became a zealous Puritan minister; as "he was of too frank and independent a spirit to leave his position in doubt,"[1] he was eventually silenced for non-conformity. Following the loss of his parish, he lived privately for three years until the departures of his friends and colleagues for New England convinced him to follow them. He, his wife, originally Mary Hutchinson, and their five children landed at Boston, Massachusetts on May 25, 1636, where they joined Mary's brother William, his wife Anne, and their family.

Anne Hutchinson was raised by a rebellious clergyman not unlike the brother-in-law she eagerly welcomed that May day, and she inherited from him a healthy sense of religious radicalism. Born in 1591, she grew up under the tutelage of her father, Francis Marbury, who never identified himself as a Puritan but waged an endless struggle for ecclesiastical reform, most notably more rigorous training for ministers and the providing of a minister for every parish.[2] He was silenced for these views during Hutchinson's childhood (which was what enabled him to take charge of his precocious daughter's education); within a few years, however, he had settled down sufficiently to obtain a comfortable and prestigious post in a prominent London parish. There, Hutchinson spent her adolescence in one of the great political and intellectual centers of Europe, with an insider's view of the ecclesiastical hierarchy as well as close ties to her mother's ardently Puritan relatives.[3] As a young woman she also gained her first practical training in midwifery, an occupation in which she would become highly skilled.

Following her father's death, Anne Marbury took the conventional step and married William Hutchinson, a wealthy merchant from her home town. The couple lived in Alford and immediately began having children, while Hutchinson, just as she would do later in New England, quickly gained the admiration and respect of the women around her because of her gifts as a midwife. She and her husband were also lucky enough to find a religious mentor in keeping with their Puritan tastes—John Cotton, the extraordinarily popular and defiantly rebellious preacher in Boston, twenty-four miles away.[4] Thus through the first years of her marriage, life for Hutchinson seemed stable and happy. Sometime in the mid-1620s, however, the death of her son William, the couple's eighth child and the first to die, triggered a wrenching personal crisis. She later described it as lasting "a twelvemonth altogether":

> When I was in old England, I was much troubled at the constitution of the churches there, so far as I was ready to have joined to the Separation, whereupon I set apart a day for humiliation by myself, to seek direction from God.[5]

Contributing to Hutchinson's personal distress was the alarming state of political and politicoreligious affairs in England at that time. Continuing official harassment from quasi-Catholic Archbishop William Laud was making it more and more likely that John Cotton would be silenced, leaving the Hutchinsons with no sanctioned alternative to the established church. England was ravaged by drought, flooding and plague, while the new, clearly Catholic, and even more clearly incompetent King Charles provided little or no help. Though Hutchinson would probably have been ready to leave England right then and there, she and her husband were determined to follow the example Cotton set, and in a 1629 tract he rejected Separatism and pledged to remain in England and purify the Church.

In the early 1630s, however, illness forced John Cotton into retirement and took the lives of two of the young Hutchinson daughters, a triple tragedy for the family. Though they found themselves a new ally in the fiery John Wheelwright, the Hutchinsons, infuriated by Laud's papist tendencies and the economic pressures Charles's government was placing on middle-class merchants such as William, decided they could not remain any longer in England. At the same time, Cotton, upon recovering, found himself in serious danger because of his unacceptable religious sympathies; bowing to necessity, he made his way in disguise to south England and departed for Massachusetts from there. The Hutchinsons had planned to go on the same ship, but were forced to postpone their plans because of yet another pregnancy. They departed from London at last on June 4, 1634.

The first hints of the tumultuous life Hutchinson would find in Boston appeared during this voyage, or rather, immediately before it. The departure of the ship the family traveled on was delayed significantly, and during the interval they stayed with fellow traveler William Bartholomew in London. Hutchinson, thinking that she was at last surrounded by sympathetic Puritans, eagerly poured her heart out and told him, as he later repeated, "that she had never had any great thing done about her but it was revealed to her beforehand...And also that she was to come to New England but for Mr. Cotton's sake." Once on the ship, she repeated this alarming assertion of personal communion with God to the orthodox misogynist Reverend Zechariah Symmes, challenging him in front of the entire ship to disprove the truthfulness of her revelations. "What would you say if we should be at New England within three weeks?"[6]

She soon found out what he would say. Following the Griffin's arrival in Boston on September 8, William Hutchinson was immediately admitted into the Boston church, indicating his acceptance as one of God's elect. Anne's declarations on board, however, were considered significantly alarming to bar her immediate accession to that honored title. A special hearing was assembled at which she was expected to recant and apologize for her outrageous statements; presiding were the governor Thomas Dudley, pastor of the Boston church John Wilson, Reverend Symmes and her old friend John Cotton, who had since become teacher of the Boston church. Though Hutchinson seems to have passed the test and Dudley stated he was "satisfied that she held nothing different from us," former governor and Puritan founding father par excellence John Winthrop later argued in his account of the entire Antinomian scandal that she had "cunningly dissembled and colored her opinions," and that those present had simply failed to see through her deception.[7] Having barely accustomed herself to walking on New World land, Hutchinson was already a cause for controversy.

Once she was admitted into the church, however, Hutchinson and her husband seemed to settle into a respectable life as prominent members of the community. Their house stood in the "fashionable quarter of the town,"[8] close to that of John Winthrop—later one of Hutchinson's most prominent adversaries—and to the church. Her husband became a well-known businessman, and she gained tremendous renown as a sympathetic and effective healer capable of helping women to survive the ten to twenty pregnancies and births they might undergo in a lifetime. Even beyond the sphere of her professional duties, her charisma soon made its presence felt, as Adams, an early historian of the controversy, remarked:

> ...above all Anne Hutchinson, though devoid of attractiveness of person, was wonderfully endowed with the indescribable quality known as magnetism—that subtle power by which certain human beings—themselves not knowing how they do it—irresistibly attract others, and infuse them with their own individuality.[9]

Thus when Hutchinson began to hold weekly women's meetings to discuss the sermon of the previous Sunday, she found a ready audience. It is difficult to know exactly what impelled her to begin these meetings. Perhaps experience had taught her the difficulty of weekly church attendance for mothers with small children; perhaps her natural religious fervor and acute intelligence craved an outlet. In the transcript of her political trial, she stated that the reason was a desire to dispel accusations of impiety and pride.

> The ground of my taking it up was, when I first came to this land because I did not go to such meetings as those were, it was presently reported that I did not allow of such meetings but held them unlawful and therefore in that regard they said I was proud and did despise all ordinances, upon that a friend came unto me and told me of it and I to prevent such aspersions took it up, but it was in practice before I came therefore was I not the first.[10]

Though Hutchinson was quite right in pointing out she was not the first to preside over such gatherings, her popularity caused her meetings to take on unheard-of proportions. Forty, sixty, or even eighty women would come several times a week, and they hung upon Hutchinson's every word. Adams attributes her success merely to the sort of temporary fashionableness bestowed by a fickle public and compares her meetings to the events of the "season;"[11] however, this unsympathetic statement reveals no understanding of the tremendous importance Hutchinson, as a skilled and sympathetic midwife, had for the women of Boston. In the move to New England, these women had lost the ties to mothers, sisters and friends that had sustained them through a life of continuous childbearing and childrearing. The loneliness they experienced raising families in hostile and isolated environments drove some nearly to insanity. Then Anne arrived, a woman who could heal them, who would talk to them, who would lead them. And so of course they came to the meetings, scores of them.[12]

At first, the church hierarchy was pleased at this outburst of religious enthusiasm and female piety; it was almost a revival.[13] Hutchinson, after all, was a prominent and devout member of the Boston church, and only the most suspicious churchmen found immediate fault in the meetings. But soon, Hutchinson's soirées became less innocuous. In response to her audience's interest—in fact, their near-adulation—and in keeping with her own brilliance and constant theological introspection, she moved from repeating sermons to commenting on them, and from commenting to formulating her own distinct doctrine. As Winthrop sardonically remarked, "the pretense was to repeat sermons, but when that was done, she would comment...and she would be sure to make it serve her turn."[14] What was actually happening, however, was far more radical and far more significant than Hutchinson making the words of others "serve her turn." She was not using anyone else's words; she was preaching a new brand of Puritanism, and this is what is now known as Antinomianism.

As nearly all students of the Antinomian controversy have discovered to their chagrin, the differences between the Antinomian beliefs and those of their adversaries are frequently so subtle as to be indistinguishable. However, boiled down to its simplest principles, Antinomianism[15] is relatively basic, and it is described succinctly and lucidly by John Winthrop in what is also the first mention of Anne in his diary.

One Mrs. Hutchinson, a member of the church of Boston, a woman of a ready wit and bold spirit, brought over with her two dangerous errors: 1. That the person of the Holy Ghost dwells in a justified person. 2. That no sanctification can help to evidence to us our justification.[16]

Consider the second statement first. According to Catholic doctrine, good works on earth are necessary to personal salvation after death. John Calvin rejected this idea but stated that the performance of good works, i.e. the living of a moral life in accordance with the dictates of the church, is evidence that a person has been chosen for salvation. This, however, is a slippery idea, and could easily lead to piety and morality being construed as the cause of one's salvation, rather than simply the outward signs of it.

Hutchinson fully grasped the ambiguity in the Puritan position on this point, and to eliminate it she took Protestant doctrine a step farther, stating that outward forms of godliness—known in New England parlance as sanctification—bear no relation, either causal or evidential, to personal salvation. In other words, she rejected the notion of man's ability to change his ultimate fate even more thoroughly than Calvin did. One could live by the laws of the Bible and the Church, one could be moral and sober and godly, but that did not necessarily mean that one was chosen as one of God's elect, and similarly, one could sin nonstop and still find ultimate salvation. When asked how then one could know if one was saved, the Antinomians replied that such knowledge could only be obtained through a revelation, an assurance of salvation sent directly by God. A person who received such assurance would be serene enough in his faith that he would never doubt the state of his soul again. To the prudish and authoritarian Puritan elders, this doctrine was viewed as nothing more than an open door to sin; after all, if one did not have to behave oneself to go to heaven, who would bother?

The other "dangerous error" Winthrop alluded to relates essentially to the question of Church authority—or rather, challenges to that authority. The Antinomians believed that a justified person (one who has been chosen for eternal salvation) experiences a personal union with the Holy Ghost. As theological doctrine, this is simply blasphemous, since it amounts, more or less, to stating that every justified person is another Christ. More importantly, what it implies is a degree of personal communication between the Divine and the chosen on earth that supersedes the Bible, the church, the ministers, or any other go-betweens. And that, of course, is rebellion.

Despite the radical nature of these two doctrines, the most important and explosive aspect of Antinomianism actually lies not in either one, but in the way Hutchinson used them to anathematize the Puritan hierarchy, by exploiting the concept of a covenant of works versus a covenant of grace. The covenant of works is the original Christian idea, now held by the Catholic church, which states that God has made a covenant with mankind granting man the ability to earn salvation through the performance of good works on earth. (Good works here should be taken in the broader sense of living a moral life, rather than simply giving to charity.) On the other hand, the covenant of grace as conceived by Luther states that one cannot "earn" salvation. Men are saved only through the free gift of God's grace, which was granted to a certain number of people, known as the elect, at the beginning of time.

The Puritans, however, were unwilling to assert that one's behavior in life bore no relation to one's fate after death, and so they developed the principle that "sanctification" does not earn but evidences membership in the covenant of grace. It is this belief that being good doesn't cause you to go to heaven but proves to everyone else that you're going to heaven that the Antinomians rejected as a new covenant of works. According to Hutchinson and her followers, the "legalist" ministers in Boston who preached that all saved persons would and should lead holy lives were under a covenant of works. In other words, they were indistinguishable from their greatest enemies, the Papists. Those who agreed with her that salvation comes through a personal revelation and is completely unrelated to moral behavior (or lack thereof) were under a covenant of grace. Needless to say, the difference between these two definitions in Puritan New England was vast.

The wheels of the Antinomian controversy, greased by this new brand of blasphemy, began turning in earnest in early October 1635, when two notable persons arrived in Boston. One was John Wilson, the pastor of the Boston church, who was returning from a trip to England to fetch his wife. A pillar of the Puritan establishment, Wilson was "hard, matter-of-fact, unimaginative"[17] and noted for unrelenting adherence to the tenets of orthodoxy, however bigoted they might be. In other words, he was exactly the kind of man Hutchinson detested.

The second newcomer was as yet unknown to the people of Boston and no less to Hutchinson, though his reputation preceded him. This was Henry Vane—young and aristocratic, the son of one of the King's closest advisors, sent to New England so he would not pester the court with his Puritan sympathies. Boston was, quite understandably, smitten with the young Vane; it was widely hoped that his presence would help the colony's standing with King Charles at a time when the King was perpetually threatening to rescind its charter. Nothing was too good for this rising star, and so within two months of his arrival it was agreed that prior to the institution of a lawsuit in Boston the case would be submitted to Vane and two other elders of the Boston church for review. This was heady praise for an arrival so new and inexperienced, and it could not help but rub the more established members of the community the wrong way.[18]

Matters were not improved when the upstart Vane called a meeting on January 18, 1636 with the intention of reconciling Thomas Dudley and John Winthrop, who were widely perceived not only as rivals for the position of governor, which both had previously held, but as ideological opponents. Winthrop had been the first governor of Massachusetts and was still the most powerful man in the colony at this time; he had been briefly ousted by the stiff-necked Dudley who condemned him as too lenient. At the time, neither was actually in power. The panel assembled included leading ministers as well as the current governor John Haynes, and intending to usher in "a more firm and friendly uniting of minds, especially of the said Mr. Dudley and Mr. Winthrop," it declared the need for "strict discipline...tending to the honor and safety of the Gospel." This was a bitter blow to Winthrop, who had effectively been chastised for lax discipline by a group led by a man young enough to be his son. In the coming controversy, he would not forget this.[19]

During these events, our fiery heroine was absent for quite a simple reason: she was pregnant. At forty-four, Hutchinson underwent her fifteenth pregnancy, and she gave birth to her twelfth living child in March. Due to a difficult pregnancy at her relatively advanced age, she seems to have more or less retired from society before the birth, but she was soon back in full vigor, at which point she encountered her pastor John Wilson preaching for the first time. (Though he had been present at her hearing held the previous fall, he had evidently departed soon after for England, and so Hutchinson had never seen him in his ministerial capacity.) Especially in comparison to her beloved Cotton, Wilson's bluntness must have been more than unappealing. Hutchinson soon began to boycott the Boston church, once leading a group of women out of services when Wilson began to preach and resuming her former practice of meetings in her home now, bigger and better than ever.

By the spring of 1636, Hutchinson's renewed efforts had paid off, and she had a new and crucially important convert, Henry Vane. Whether Vane joined to gratify his propensity for making trouble, (he had, after all, been sent from the royal court because his ardent Puritanism was too great an irritation to be borne) or because of religious convictions, is both unknowable and irrelevant, but his election as governor in May of that year, with Winthrop his deputy, was indisputably an Antinomian victory. The very next day, John Wheelwright and his family arrived in Boston. Now things really began to move for Hutchinson. She had Wheelwright and she had the governor; her husband was active in local politics; and "to [her] living room every Monday and Thursday now paraded the highest concentration of wealth in the colony."[20] The Antinomian movement was coming into its own, well-known and well-established, the enthusiasm of its members testified to by the colonial observer Edward Johnson.

> Come along with you, says one of them, I'll bring you to a woman that preaches better gospel than any of your black-coats who have been at the university, a woman of another kind of spirit, who has had many Revelations of things to come, and for my part, says he, I had rather hear such a one that speaks from the mere motion of the spirit, without any study at all, than any of your learned scholars, although they may be fuller of Scripture and admit they may speak by the help of the spirit, yet the other goes beyond them.[21]

Nevertheless, there was one thing lacking—the overt support of a member of the appointed clergy. Cotton was making a determined effort to be neutral, either out of concern for his social position or simple preoccupation, and so naturally Hutchinson and her supporters turned to Wheelwright. Soon after his arrival, it was proposed that he be made an assistant teacher in the Boston church, and as was the custom, a date was set for formal debate of the idea by the congregation. Five days before this occurred, however, a number of ministers from outside Boston met with Cotton, Wheelwright and members of the General Court in an attempt to resolve theological differences. Though there was no direct reference to the proposal to appoint Wheelwright, it was clear that the purpose of the assembly was to ascertain whether or not he was in fact a suitable candidate. The assembled ministers ostensibly came to an agreement that sanctification does evidence justification but could not decide on the possibility of a personal union of the Holy Ghost; this agreement or lack thereof had no bearing on the debate on the Boston church.[22]

In fact, only one thing truly had bearing on that debate, held on Sunday, October 30, 1636: John Winthrop's opposition to Wheelwright's appointment. Despite the huge majority of the congregation in support of Wheelwright, Winthrop's moral and political authority in the community gave him the deciding vote, and so he emerged victorious from this passage of arms. Wheelwright did not become assistant teacher. Instead, he was appointed leader of a new, small, daughter congregation developing at Mount

Woolystone, on the outskirts of Boston where, it was hoped, he would be too far away to make trouble.

The month of December following these events was one primarily of talking, and these conversations would later be examined in excruciating detail in the various trials dealing with the Antinomian controversy. First, Vane announced he was returning to England because his personal affairs demanded his attention, presumably with the intent of reminding his opponents, most notably Winthrop, that his august presence could be removed from them if offended. The Boston church came in on cue and refused to give their permission, and so things remained as they were. Meanwhile, a number of ministers got together with the members of the General Court to bemoan the present state of affairs especially in reference to Vane's participation, and Wilson made a bitter speech—a "veritable jeremiad"[23]—on the present condition of the churches in which he blamed the Antinomians for their downfall. During this time, virtually everyone was engaged in long and barely intelligible correspondence about fine points of theological doctrine with John Cotton, who was being pressed to take a definitive stand. Cotton, on the other hand, was playing compromiser as always; he held a meeting at his house between Hutchinson and a number of ministers, among them the die-hard conservatives Wilson, Hugh Peter and Thomas Weld, in the hope that a face-to-face conference would lessen the tension. Unfortunately things didn't work out quite as planned—Hutchinson simply told the ministers outright they were under a covenant of works. Later, this conference would play a key part in her trial.

Seeing that their attempts to smooth things over had not been particularly successful, the ministers of the colony called for a general fast day of repentance and prayer to attempt to heal and/or atone for the division in the churches, to be held on January 20, 1637. On that day in the Boston church, following Watson's sermon, John Wheelwright was invited to "exercise as a private brother." In other words, he was allowed to make a speech but reminded that the privilege did not elevate him to the status of minister. Perhaps stung by this subtle barb, Wheelwright delivered

the infamous Fast-Day Sermon, a veritable battle-cry for the Antinomians. Though it seems to the modern reader much like the
other sermons of its day, i.e. long, boring, and virtually unintel-
ligible, Wheelwright's address was considered to be tantamount
to an open declaration of war between those under a covenant of
works and those under a covenant of grace—and that was a radical development in a controversy that specialized in ambiguities,
obfuscation and general beating-around-the-bush.

      Though the fast-day sermon would later loom large in the
accounting of the Antinomian controversy it did not produce an
immediate reaction; rather the next significant event revolved
around Wilson's "jeremiad" of December. Perhaps fired up by
Wheelwright's rousing address, the Boston congregation attempted
on January 31 to censor their pastor for those imprudent remarks,
described as "nothing less than an angry arraignment of almost
the whole body of his people, including both Cotton and Vane."[24]
Winthrop described this attack on his close friend and ally, which
ended not in formal censure, but in an "exhortation" to Wilson
by Cotton as follows:

> ...they called him to answer publicly, and there the governor pressed
> it violently against him, and all the congregation except the deputy
> and one or two more, and many of them with much bitterness and
> reproaches...It was strange to see, how the common people were led
> by example to condemn in that, which (it was very probably) divers
> of them did not understand, nor the rule which he was supposed to
> have broken; and that such as had known him [Wilson] so long, and
> what good he had done for that church should fall upon him with
> such bitterness for justifying himself in a good cause.[25]

Perhaps having this humiliation of one of the most respected
conservative clergymen in the colony in mind, the General Court
when it met early in March decided to strike back, and it did so
by using the most convenient tool available, the Fast-Day sermon.
It was, in a way, poetic justice. Wilson had been reprimanded in
church for a sermon in court; now Wheelwright would be reprimanded in court for a sermon in church. Before this could get
underway, however, the Boston congregation stepped in and sent
the court a petition asking that "proceedings in judicial cases

should be conducted publicly, and that matters of conscience might be left for the church to deal with."[26] The court ignored the petition, returned it and continued its proceedings behind closed doors. Those proceedings, though protracted, were quite simple. Wheelwright confirmed he had denounced all those who walked in a covenant of works; the ministers, in an odd but effective self-condemnatory gesture, said that they walked in such a covenant; Wheelwright was declared guilty of sedition and contempt.

This straightforward account masks what was truly going on behind the closed door: a bitter struggle for domination between Winthrop and Vane. After the decision was reached, Vane protested and was ignored, and another petition was presented, which was also ignored. There had been a decisive swing of power towards the conservatives, partially because the late political developments had excluded completely the driving force behind the Antinomians, Anne Hutchinson. Aware, however, that their victory had been slight, Winthrop & Co. postponed sentencing of Wheelwright until after the upcoming annual election, hoping that at that point they would have a more sympathetic court that would pronounce a harsh sentence without any fuss. Their last action was to take steps to ensure that they would indeed win the election that could pack the court with their supporters: they moved it from Boston, the bastion of Antinomian power, where a large turnout of Vane/Wheelwright supporters was inevitable, to Newtown, now Cambridge, where it was hoped residents of the more conservative outlying towns would carry the day.

The long-awaited election was held on May 17, 1637 on the Cambridge common, presided over by Henry Vane. As expected, he opened the meeting by attempting to resubmit the petition on behalf of John Wheelwright that had previously been dismissed by the court. Winthrop, as deputy governor, said it was out of order, and eventually those who desired an immediate election won out over those hoping to postpone it via debate over the petition. Winthrop was restored to his position as governor, with Thomas Dudley as deputy. Again, it was a straightforward result but one arrived at only after a bitter struggle, as Winthrop described. "There was a great danger of a tumult that day for those of that side [Vane supporters] grew into fierce speeches, and some laid hands on others; but seeing themselves too weak, they grew quiet."[27] In fact, according to a perhaps apocryphal source quoted by Thomas Hutchinson in his work, the events of the day roused such passions that the rather elderly and stiff-necked Wilson had to climb up in a tree and call loudly for election in order to be heard over the clamor.

Following the election, both sides engaged in petty re-criminations, with Vane's honor guard refusing to attend Winthrop, and the General Court rejecting Vane and two colleagues as Boston representatives on the ground that not all freemen had been informed of the election. (A new election returned the same representatives who were then accepted.) Raising the stakes a little, the General Court passed an alien exclusion act barring any newcomers from remaining in the colony for more than three weeks without the permission of the magistrates, a move clearly intended to prevent the importation of more blasphemers. Then Hutchinson and her followers refused to support the Pequot War (May 26–July 28, 1637) because Wilson had been chosen as military chaplain. They rejected all requests for money, supplies or soldiers, enraging those in power, who believed they were waging a holy war, and given that the progress and success of the war were unaffected, this sudden spurt of pacifism harmed the Antinomians more than it did anything else.

This tit-for-tat sparring would no doubt have continued had it not been abruptly terminated by a matter of much greater import to both sides. Twice in June 1637, ships arrived in Boston bearing orders from the King that substituted appointed commissioners for the locally elected government and insisted that "there was no lawful authority in force" in the colony.[28] Massachusetts, the first house divided in North America, was dangerously close to being taken over by powers in London who valued stability more than salvation or sanctification. Determined to save the colony he had helped to build, Winthrop called for a religious synod at Newtown, beginning on August 30, to obliterate all differences and prove that Massachusetts was in fact harmonious and well-governed.

At this point, it was clear that the Antinomians were on their way down. The election had been the beginning of the end. Vane, disgruntled by his defeat and evidently unwilling to stick it out when he was no longer being treated as the honorable young sir, had quietly returned to England on August 3. Wheelwright was awaiting sentence. Cotton, always vacillating, appeared to be moving closer to Winthrop. And the synod, after engaging in nine days of singularly meaningless obfuscation, took on a decidedly conservative tone, coming up with eighty-two opinions supposedly held by the dissenters and declaring them all blasphemous. Moreover, it took aim at Hutchinson herself, recently deprived of both her political and her clerical allies, by declaring[29]

> That though women might meet (some few together) to pray and edify one another, yet such a set assembly (as was then in practice at Boston) where sixty or more did meet every week, and one woman (in a prophetical way, by resolving questions of doctrine, and expounding scripture) took upon her the whole exercise, was agreed to be disorderly, and without rule.[30]

With this denunciation as a sort of mission statement, the religious and political conservatives moved the controversy from the theological into the political spheres. Anne Hutchinson was called to appear before the November session of the General Court.

Before this occurred, however, the court elected the previous May was suddenly dissolved by the governor, and a new one was elected that included only twelve of the original deputies. The justification Winthrop offered for this action is completely obscure; in fact, it is quite possible that he offered no justification whatsoever. Recently reprimanded for softness and with the ambitious Dudley shadowing him at every step, Winthrop too had his back against the wall. He could not afford to let either Antinomianism or his unpleasantly persistent reputation for leniency survive, and if a new court was needed to achieve these ends, so be it.

Prior to the first sitting of this court, a more private affair in the life of Anne Hutchinson transpired which would eventually throw a great deal of light on its behavior. On October 17, 1637, the principal midwife of Boston hurried to the home of Mary Dyer (later turned Quaker and hanged as an old woman on Boston common), who had borne three children in the last four years and was in the midst of an excruciating and difficult labor two months before term. Eventually, Hutchinson and another midwife, Jane Hawkins, managed to deliver the stillborn, deformed baby girl while the mother lay close to death. Then, uncertain what to do, Hutchinson went to John Cotton for advice. This is perhaps the most inexplicable part of the whole affair. Cotton certainly could not have given her medical guidance; perhaps she wondered whether the baby should be baptized or given similar rites before being buried, but she had not previously shown herself to be particularly mindful of such conventions. She had not been closely associated with Cotton for years, and it seems that her brother-in-law (who was still in Boston awaiting sentence) would have been the more logical choice for a dispenser of clerical advice.

But for whatever reason, to Cotton she went, and he told her, as he later repeated to Winthrop, "that, if it had been his own case, he should have desired to have had it concealed. He had known other monstrous births, which had been concealed, and that he thought God might intend only the instruction of the parents."[31] Hutchinson and Hawkins then buried the baby together to protect the weak and ill mother from the shock of seeing it when she regained consciousness. Cotton's action suggests that he still retained at least some personal ties to Hutchinson, since he could easily have construed the failure of a birth she supervised as evidence of her corruption, as others would later do; it also testifies to his personal experience of barrenness and stillbirth. His first wife had not born a living child in their eighteen years of marriage, and so he was doubtless more sympathetic to Mary Dyer's case than most others would have been. (It is also interesting to note that Hutchinson almost certainly was the midwife at the birth of Cotton's own daughter to his second wife in September 1635, and so in a way he owed her for the fulfillment of a hope he had cherished through nearly two decades of marital infertility.) [32]

Though Cotton's refusal to publicize Dyer's tragedy or use it as evidence to incriminate Hutchinson afforded her and her followers some hope, it soon became clear that the court was not prepared to be so tolerant. The first thing it did when it convened on November 2 in Newtown was to reject the deputies Boston had sent by dredging up the petition, or rather petitions, that had been submitted on behalf of John Wheelwright to the previous court earlier that year. William Aspinwall, who had signed and helped to draft the offending document, was not only rejected as deputy but also disfranchised and banished for "seditious libel." John Coggeshall, who had not signed, was dismissed and disfranchised simply for verbally stating "he would pray that our eyes might be opened to see what we did...for he did believe the Master Wheelwright did hold forth the truth."[33] William Coddington retained his position, partly because he had not signed the petition and partly because he was the wealthiest man in the colony. To replace its dismissed deputies, Boston elected William Colburn and John Oliver. The latter had signed the petition and was also rejected. Colburn and Coddington were left, and no attempt was made to elect a third deputy.[34]

Following these ominous proceedings, the court began the work at hand—the punishment of the Antinomians. First, Wheelwright was sentenced to banishment. He asserted that he would appeal to the King for commutation of his sentence, but the court replied that under the Massachusetts charter there could be no such appeal; he then agreed to leave the colony within fourteen days and eventually went north to New Hampshire. Next, Edward Hutchinson, Anne's brother-in-law, and William Baulston were accused of disloyalty because they had refused to attend as sergeants on Winthrop as they had on Vane. Hutchinson made an irate reply to this charge and spent the night in jail. Following his apology the next day, he was disenfranchised and fined along with Baulston.

Having disposed of these secondary troublemakers, the court at last turned to Anne Hutchinson herself. In a strange way, she had thus far been protected by her sex; she had not signed the petition, and she could not be disenfranchised. But her opponents had not forgotten that all those previously mentioned were "but young branches, sprung out of an old root, the Court had now to do with the head of all this faction...a woman had been the breeder and nourisher of all these distempers, one Mistress Hutchinson...a woman of a haughty and fierce carriage, of a nimble wit and active spirit, and a very voluble tongue, more bold than a man."[35] The time had come for this woman to be subdued once and for all.

The ensuing trial was transcribed both by Winthrop and by an anonymous observer who appears to have been more sympathetic to Hutchinson, as he turned over his notes to her for her perusal between the first and second days of the trial. Winthrop also began the trial, as governor and principal moral authority in the community, in the following words.

> Mrs. Hutchinson, you are called here as one of those that have troubled the peace of the commonwealth and the churches here; you are known to be a woman that hath had a great share in the promoting and divulging of those opinions that are causes of this trouble, and to be nearly joined not only in affinity and affections with some of those the court had taken notice of and passed censure upon, but you have spoken divers things as we have been informed very prejudicial to the honour of the churches and the ministers thereof, and you have maintained a meeting and an assembly in your house that hath been condemned by the general assembly as a thing not tolerable nor comely in the sight of God nor fitting for your sex, and notwithstanding that was cried down you have continued the same...[36]

This bitter speech, made by a man who had seen his entire career threatened by the woman now standing before him, opened a trial marked by extraordinary vindictiveness on the part of the men presiding. Why? Because their regulatory power had been, up to this point, thwarted. Hutchinson had done nothing in public, nothing that could be clearly seen and defined, nothing that could be clearly punished. The principal accusation leveled against her was failure to show proper respect to the ministers, but again, she had made no public speeches or declarations, and the court would soon find that producing evidence of her insolence was very difficult.

The assembly did not immediately strike to the heart of the matter: Hutchinson's disparagement of the ministers of the colony as under a covenant of works. Instead, the presiding ministers first accused her of disobeying the commandment to obey one's father and one's mother by not submitting to the "fathers of the commonwealth," as Winthrop termed it. Next, Hutchinson's meetings were condemned, despite her citation of a rule in Titus exhorting the elder women to teach the younger. In the debate of these points, Hutchinson's scintillating wit showed itself to best advantage; eventually, Dudley jumped in to rescue Winthrop, who was undoubtedly getting the worst of the argument, and quite simply accused Hutchinson of fomenting all discontent in the colony by deprecating the ministers as under a covenant of works. It was stated that she had aired these unacceptable views at the conference held at Cotton's house the previous December.

Hutchinson immediately bridled at this use of private remarks as evidence and argued that she had spoken in good faith, believing the ministers were genuinely interested in her opinion and her guidance. The governor responded brusquely, "This speech was not spoken in a corner but in a public assembly, and though things were spoken in private yet now coming to us, we are to deal with them as public."[37] Hutchinson then argued that she had not said the things alleged, appealing to Wilson to provide his notes of the occasion, which would vindicate her. He replied that he did not have them, and so the question was still unresolved at the conclusion of the first day's proceedings.[38]

The following day, the notes made an appearance, and Hutchinson made skillful use of them. (Exactly who provided the document is unclear. Wilson stated in the trial he had his personal copy with him on the second day and it seems likely that was the one used by the court, but Hutchinson appears to have had access to another copy overnight.) She began by saying that "I have since I went home perused some notes out of what Mr. Wilson did then write and find things not to be as hath been alleged,"[39] and then requested that all those accusing her of speaking inappropriately at the conference speak under oath. Exactly what course the trial

took in its next stages is difficult to discern from conflicting accounts and interpretations. Hutchinson was allowed to call her
own witnesses, apparently because it was considered necessary for
her to substantiate her assertion that her accusers were not telling
the truth. The disfranchised deputy Coggeshall attempted to speak
on her behalf but gave up when reprimanded by Hugh Peters,
minister of Salem and a bitter opponent of Hutchinson; Thomas
Leverett, an elder from the church of Boston, was similarly ineffective. Several ministers who volunteered then took oaths and
repeated their previous statements, asserting that Hutchinson had
told them they were under a covenant of works.

At this point, the proceedings became hopelessly tangled.
Though several ministers had taken oaths, Wilson was not among
them, and so the accuracy of his notes was still in question. Meanwhile, Hutchinson steadfastly denied that the various reports of
the occasion presented by her opponents were correct. Winthrop
thus appealed to John Cotton to "declare what you do remember
of the conference which was at that time and is now in question."[40]
Cotton had initiated and presided over the meeting; it had been
in his home; naturally, all present turned to him as the final authority on what had or had not been said.

According to his custom, he made a long and concilia-
tory speech, the sum of which was that he did not remember that
Hutchinson had said the other ministers walked in a covenant of
works. Cotton had now decisively come down on Hutchinson's
side, and he came and sat by her as well in a symbolic show of
support. Despite a blunt statement from Dudley that "They affirm
Mrs. Hutchinson did say they were not able ministers of the New
Testament," Cotton still asserted he did not remember it. At this
point, the prosecution was more or less at a standstill. Cotton
would not back up his colleague to confirm that Hutchinson had
indeed uttered that offensive statement eleven months before.
Though the court did not consider itself bound to prove guilt
within reasonable doubt or any similar notion, there was little it
could do, and had Hutchinson not spoken, she might well have
gone free.[41]

But speak she did, in a long monologue detailing the manner in which God had revealed to her the true ministry, through an "immediate revelation" she considered parallel to the divine command to Abraham to sacrifice his son. Unchecked, she continued even a step farther and claimed that powers of divine retribution were on her side.

> ...therefore I desire you that as you tender the Lord and the church and commonwealth to consider and look what you do. You have power over my body but the Lord Jesus hath power over my body and soul, and assure yourselves this much, you do as much as in you lies to put the Lord Jesus Christ from you, and if you go on in this course you begin you will bring a curse upon you and your posterity, and the mouth of the Lord hath spoken it.[42]

This speech is perhaps the most fascinating development in the entire controversy. It seems utterly incongruous that this brilliant woman should, after defending herself so deftly, play as completely into the hands of her enemies as she did when she spoke these words, and one can only wonder why she did it. Up to this point, the saving grace for Hutchinson had been the private nature of all she did; in this speech, she publicly laid claim to the one blasphemous act—receiving a direct revelation from God—that could not be proved against her because by its very nature it was private. One can imagine the stuffy magistrates first staring in astonishment and then rubbing their hands with glee. After all, revelations were the instruments of the Devil, and so there was now no evidence lacking to convict this troublesome woman. As Adams put it, "Mrs. Hutchinson accordingly had opened the vials of puritanic wrath, and they were freely emptied on her head."[43]

From then on, the court, led by Winthrop, who declared it "a marvelous providence of God to bring things to this pass that they are,"[44] rivaled each other in condemning her. Cotton's opinion was called on, and though he attempted to equivocate in Hutchinson's defense, Dudley's harsh reply—"Sir, you weary me and do not satisfy me"[45]—made it clear that the entire affair was beyond his control, and that he might well face personal danger from continuing in her aid. From this point on, Cotton gave up. The risk to his reputation and standing in the community was too great for him to stand by Hutchinson any longer. Besides, there was nothing stopping the court now, as she herself seems to have realized; she said nothing else until the very end of the trial. Impatient to be finished and home to dinner (Dudley asserted that "We shall be sick with fasting"),[46] the court hurtled toward a vote, in which only Coddington and Colburn from Boston voted against Hutchinson's banishment, with one deputy from Ipswich abstaining. Defiant to the last, Hutchinson spoke again. "I desire to know wherefore I am banished." The triumphant Winthrop retorted, "The court knows wherefore and is satisfied."[47]

Following Hutchinson's sentencing, an all-out assault on the remaining Antinomians began. On Monday, November 20, the General Court ordered those men known to be sympathetic with Hutchinson to surrender their guns, powder and ammunition at the house of Captain Robert Keayne, a wealthy merchant and John Wilson's brother-in-law. Included in the seventy-five men disarmed, (fifty-eight from Boston), were John Underhill, Thomas Oliver, and Anne's husband, son, brother-in-law, and sons-in-law. Thirty of these men recanted and had their privileges restored; others, either more loyal or more foolhardy, attempted retaliation against Winthrop in the Boston church, a challenge the governor defeated by claiming that he had been in partnership with God. (Unfortunately, the same argument had not worked for Hutchinson a week before.) And in one of the controversy's quirkiest ramifications, Harvard University was then founded at Cambridge rather than Boston because that location had not yet been contaminated by Antinomian blasphemy.[48]

Though banished, Hutchinson was not actually required to depart from the colony until the spring. She was granted time to return to Boston to provide for the care of her eight children still at home—ages seventeen, thirteen, ten, nine, seven, six, four and one; she was then placed in detainment at the Roxbury home of Joseph Weld, brother of the archconservative Reverend Thomas Weld.[49] During the winter in which she stayed in Roxbury, the vituperative Reverend Weld, along with his equally fanatical colleagues Hugh Peter and Thomas Shepard, made a point of regularly visiting their lost sheep to attempt to coax her back into the fold. Seeing that Hutchinson would not be swayed, and in fact was proceeding further down her blasphemous path by asserting that human souls were not immortal but "died like beasts,"[50] these ministers and their colleagues decided that banishment had not been enough. They called Hutchinson to an excommunication hearing in the Boston church on March 16, 1638.

In composition, the body presiding over this hearing differed little from that of the first trial. Theoretically, the magistrates had been in control before while the ministers now ran the show; however, the ministers had certainly not been passive at the judicial hearing, and Governor Winthrop and Deputy Governor Dudley, the principal political figures, were present at the excommunication hearing as members of the Boston church. This hearing—at which Hutchinson arrived late, asserting that her imprisonment had made her too weak to sit through the entire proceedings— was entirely occupied with abstruse ramblings that probably had no meaning even then to most of those present and are certainly devoid of any significance today. It seems that Puritan Boston never tired of arguing theology, especially when there was the possibility of vanquishing such a fountain of blasphemy as Hutchinson.

But something other than theological hair-splitting can be found in the account of this occasion, something more important— a picture of an energetic, brilliant and courageous woman who was at last losing strength, exhausted and ill almost beyond the point of endurance. Having been separated for months from her husband, from her children, from anyone who might look upon her with kindness, Hutchinson once again faced interrogation at the hands of an unsympathetic and bigoted board of questioners. And at the conclusion of the first day of the proceedings, the presiding ministers having decided to their satisfaction that she was not in line with the doctrines and dictates of the church, John Cotton was given the job of admonishing her. At that moment, the man Hutchinson had once looked to as her greatest source of support became the instrument for her punishment. This, more than anything, broke her spirit.

Nearly a week later, on March 22, 1638, Anne Hutchinson made her final public appearance in the Massachusetts Bay colony, and she made it in a seeming show of abject submission. She began by stating "For the first, I do acknowledge I was deeply deceived, the opinion was very dangerous," and then enumerated in detail the opinions she had wrongly held. And she finally concluded, "I spoke rashly and unadvisedly. I do not allow the slighting of ministers nor of the scriptures nor any thing that is set up by God...It was never in my heart to slight any man but only that man should be kept in his own place and not be set in the room of God."[51] For the moment at least, the ministers had won.

Yet for some reason, perhaps from sheer exuberance at the sight of this long-defiant woman at last brought to her knees, Hutchinson's opponents overreached themselves. A number of the ministers present cast doubt on the honesty of her repentance, and some suggested that she sinned simply by denying that she had ever consciously held incorrect opinions. Having abased herself, Hutchinson now found her humble appeal rejected, and so gathering her last shred of pride, she defied the men in front of her one final time. Abrogating the recantation she had just made, she proudly declared, "My judgment is not altered though my expression alters." At that moment, the outcome of the trial was decided. Dudley voiced the opinion of many when he said, "her repentance is in a paper, whether it was drawn up by herself or whether she had any help in it I know not, and will not now inquire to, but sure her repentance is not in her countenance, none can see it there I think.[52]

Now there was no hope for Hutchinson. Not only had she blasphemed, she had mocked the church by pretending a repentance she did not feel. She was from that point on the perpetrator of a new crime, lying. Cotton must have breathed a sigh of relief, since a question of doctrine was not involved, the burden of punishing the woman who had once trusted him fell not on him, the teacher, but on the pastor. When the hearing was completed, John Wilson, to his infinite satisfaction, was given the task of pronouncing the excommunication sentence against the woman who had so often scorned him.

Therefore in the name of our Lord Jesus Christ and in the name of the Church I do not only pronounce you worthy to be cast out, but I do cast you out...and I do account you from this time forth to be a heathen and a publican...Therefore I command you in the name of Christ Jesus and of this Church as a leper to withdraw yourself out of the Congregation.[53]

As Hutchinson walked out of the church, "one standing at the door said, The Lord sanctify this unto you, to whom she made answer, the Lord judgeth not as man judgeth, better to be cast out of the Church than to deny Christ."[54] And then, escorted by her good friend Mary Dyer, Anne Hutchinson departed from the Boston church for the last time. Ordered to leave the colony by the end of the month, Hutchinson (who was pregnant yet again) collected her children and her possessions and made the long journey to Rhode Island to join her husband in their new home there. Five years after that, having relocated a second time in the hope of finally escaping the grasping arm of Massachusetts authority, she along with six of her children died in New York, caught in the crossfire of a Dutch-Indian war.

When the entire history of the Antinomian rebellion is considered, an extraordinary and shocking difference in the treatment of its two leaders is immediately apparent. Wheelwright was banished. Hutchinson was banished, excommunicated, and bitterly condemned, her most personal tragedies dragged into the open (as will be later discussed) and she and her family persecuted even in Rhode Island to the point where they fled to the barely-civilized New York frontier. In attempting to somehow understand this difference, to explain why Hutchinson was continuously reviled while Wheelwright founded a respectable career as a minister in New Hampshire, it is extremely tempting to declare most, if not all, of the disparity to be the result of sexism. To a certain extent, such an analysis is valid. Undeniably, the fact that Hutchinson was a woman who had overstepped the boundaries of the kitchen and the nursery played a pivotal part in the way the public viewed her. Unlike Wheelwright, she broke a sacred rule merely in participating in any sort of political or religious controversy, and she was dealt with accordingly.

Yet to explain away the huge gulf between Hutchinson's punishment and that of Wheelwright as solely the result of sexism glosses over the deeper significance of the scandal she embodied. Above all, Anne Hutchinson was threatening not because she was a woman or a feminist, though she deserves both titles. She was threatening because she sought to topple Puritanism in private. This behavior constituted an utter rejection of the founding principle of New England society—that morality is only morality if it is in public view—and as such, it was both horrifying and terrifying. Hutchinson struck fear into the hearts of the Puritan elders by suggesting the possibility of a rebellion against the laws of God and country that could not be stopped by the mechanisms of public regulation—a rebellion that did not lie within the scope of those mechanisms. It is this unique aspect of her life, one not at all shared by that of John Wheelwright, that makes her deserving of our attention. And it was this that made her deserving of the Puritan forefathers' enmity.

There are four important aspects of Anne Hutchinson's rebellion, and they all illustrate the extent of that rebellion's private nature and the reasons why that privacy was so threatening. First, consider the meetings, the gatherings that Hutchinson held throughout her residence in Boston at which she recapitulated and commented on the sermon of the previous Sunday for the benefit of those attending. Here, any use of the word private begins to seem a little paradoxical; the whole point was that fifty women showed up. But in Puritan society, the word private did not imply a numerical limit on persons present. It simply meant that there was no designated order-keeping, morality-enforcing authority there. It is also important to note that the meetings, though not restricted to females, originated as women's meetings and usually fewer men than women attended. Men <u>were</u> the public in Puritan New England. An event at which women were the majority, held in a home and not in a meeting-house, courthouse or other building regulated by politicoreligious authority, was private.

Given that the meetings can be considered as falling within the category of revolution in the private sphere, the question is now why this private aspect made them so threatening. Quite simply, the meetings undermined the preeminent role of the appointed clergy. At first, offering such an explanation appears to be making excuses for misogyny; it seems obvious that the meetings were considered dangerous because a woman ran them. That is true. But the meetings did not just exalt women to positions of authority. More than set a woman up as a clergyperson, Hutchinson's gatherings essentially denied that the clergy was even needed; more than attacking male authority, they attacked the very principle of a religious hierarchy. Here was lay preaching long before the Baptists arrived—an assertion that a private desire to preach was just as good as public confirmation that one could, should and had the right to do so. Not only did such an idea cast aspersions on the authority of the ministers, it raised doubts as to their very necessity. Quite understandably, the men being attacked responded by attempting to quell the events that had engendered such a horrifying concept.

The second notable aspect of Hutchinson's rebellion was the importance of her conversation. Private conversation played a pivotal role in her life and in her trials to an unusual extent; the same cannot be said about John Wheelwright, or in fact about most other historical figures. Wheelwright's principal means of communicating his views to his opponents appears to have been his sermons. Not once is he recorded as directly engaging in conversation with Winthrop, Wilson, Dudley or any of the other authorities except in the context of highly formalized and public occasions such as the debate by the Boston church over his appointment and his trial and sentencing.

Hutchinson, by contrast, spoke directly to her ministerial opponents in private and face-to-face conversations twice: at the December 1636 conference in Cotton's home, and in the various discussions held over the winter of 1637-38 during her enforced stay in Roxbury. (Unfortunately, no comparable exchanges with the political figures Winthrop or Dudley were ever referred to, although since Winthrop and Hutchinson were neighbors, more private conversation between the two of them almost certainly occurred.) It is neither easy nor necessary to make a definitive statement about exactly what was said by whom during these conversations, especially given that the content of all of them was hotly debated when they were referred to in court. Suffice it to say that Hutchinson spoke clearly, even bluntly, about what she believed to the men who most believed she was wrong on both occasions.

The most important aspect of these conversations, however, is not what was said but the fact that it was said privately. In speaking in private Hutchinson was protected, an advantage she fully realized and capitalized on. When the court discussed the Fast-Day sermon, it was by no means clear if it was seditious, but Wheelwright had undeniably preached it. On the other hand, both Hutchinson and her opponents knew that it would be very difficult to prove exactly what anyone had said at these unrecorded meetings. And more importantly, by speaking in private Hutchinson highlighted the one great weakness of Puritan New England—that it could not control the unfathomable depths of the human heart, or even the unfathomable depths of the human parlor. Quite simply, she showed the ministers where their weak side was. Thus both for more technical and legal reasons and for more abstract and deeply felt ones, Hutchinson's private conversations were a much greater threat to the Puritan establishment than any comparable public declaration could have been—and the magnitude of her punishment reflected the perception of this threat.

The third way in which Hutchinson employed the concept of privacy, the doctrine of personal revelations, incorporated aspects previously seen in both the meetings and the conversations. In this case, it is clear that John Wheelwright shared in Hutchinson's philosophy at least to some extent. The doctrine that one could only know one was saved through a direct revelation from God was an important Antinomian belief, and one that Wheelwright almost certainly accepted. Hutchinson, on the other hand, was the one who really liked to talk about it; it was she who proclaimed in front of a whole ship of people that she could predict when they would land in New England, and then launched into a detailed description of similar revelations in her trial. Thus regardless of who believed in the idea of personal, private and intimate intercourse with the Divine, she bore the responsibility in the eyes of the authorities for promulgating the doctrine.

And why was her role in this case so threatening? Because the idea of revelations was yet another way in which Hutchinson challenged the public nature of Puritan society. Like the meetings, revelations denied the mediating role of the public clergy and set up a direct and private link between believers and God. And like private conversations, they defied official regulation. The content of private unrecorded conversations could not be proven. Similarly, if a believer claimed to have been told via a personal revelation that he was saved, or that his neighbor was not, who could say otherwise? Revelations and personal conversations were by nature ephemeral, unprovable, and private—and in Puritan society, those words had unspeakably negative connotations.

Finally, there is the fourth, perhaps most important and certainly most overlooked way that Hutchinson threatened the rigidly extroverted Puritan society: midwifery. This issue has rarely been discussed, primarily because it is impossible to argue that Hutchinson was a midwife in order to promote Antinomianism—her occupation preceded her radical religious sympathies by decades. Nonetheless, in the eyes of the men judging her, Hutchinson's midwifery was regarded as a weapon, another manifestation of her attempts to overturn governmental and ministerial power. Thus analysis of the Antinomian controversy that excludes midwifery ignores one of the principal reasons that Hutchinson was considered so dangerous.

Evidence that midwifery was indeed viewed as a serious threat to the Puritan hierarchy by the members of that hierarchy cannot be found in the transcripts of Hutchinson's trials, as the topic was presumably considered too indelicate for public discussion. Instead, there are two important incidents relating to her role as a midwife that prove that the authorities found that role intimidating: the birth of Mary Dyer's premature child and a severe miscarriage Hutchinson herself experienced following her move to Rhode Island. In both of these cases, the personal tragedy of an unsuccessful pregnancy was used by Hutchinson's opponents as evidence of her corruption. More than that, however, men such as Winthrop, Wilson and Dudley took an extraordinarily grotesque and voyeuristic interest in the details of the incidents, attempting to outdo each other in lurid detail and gloating all the while that God had provided them with such decisive evidence of their opponent's evil. The following quote is actually from Cotton Mather, who wrote his history of New England much later but can rightfully be considered the ideological heir of Hutchinson's opponents.

> ...there happened some very surprizing prodigies, which were looked upon as testimonies from Heaven...The erroneous gentlewoman herself, convicted of holding about thirty monstrous opinions, growing big with child, and at length coming to her time of travail, was delivered of about thirty monstrous births at once, whereof some were bigger, some were lesser; of several figures; few of any perfect, none of any humane shape...Moreover, one very nearly related unto this gentlewoman, and infected with her heresies, was on October 17, 1637 delivered of as hideous a monster as perhaps the sun ever looked upon.[54]

Mather then continued in an appalling description of what Mary Dyer's baby supposedly looked like when the baby was exhumed under Winthrop's supervision and on his orders five days after Hutchinson left Massachusetts, in March 1638. (Remember that Dyer had accompanied Hutchinson out of the church following her excommunication and thus had publicly drawn attention to herself as a supporter of the outcast.)

The public discussion of these two miscarriages highlights a crucial point about Hutchinson that is too often ignored. Her opponents knew and frequently referred to the fact that her popularity was partially due to her skill in midwifery, and that was reason enough for them to consider her occupation a threat. But equally potent was their basic fear of her control over a sphere from which they, both as men and as authorities, were completely excluded. Throughout her career in Boston, Hutchinson was prominent as a midwife and as a mother (she had an extremely large family and was pregnant several times during her residence there.) The birth of children, both her own and those of the women she attended, was a testimony to her power, and the realm of childbearing and motherhood was one in which she held unquestioned sway. And that realm was also one that was utterly private, distinctly feminine, extraordinarily mysterious—and above all, impervious to control by the political and religious hierarchy. As a midwife ministering to the wives of the most powerful men in the colony, Hutchinson made those men depend on her skill and feel helpless in the face of her power, and they feared her for that.

This visceral distrust of someone who presided over and in fact was the principal manager of an incomprehensible process that carried disquieting connotations of female sexuality was certainly important in shaping the authorities' response to her midwifery. There are also more objective aspects of Hutchinson's occupation that played a part. Remember that two other facets of her rebellion, the revelations and the conversations, possessed an inherent imperviousness to official regulation in that they were private, undocumented and unprovable. The fact that Hutchinson was somewhat protected in acting in those two spheres only led the authorities to treat her activities as correspondingly more dangerous, since in their eyes what could not be controlled was automatically suspect. In the case of midwifery, two similar defenses existed, and they resulted from the ministers' own actions. The frustration of Hutchinson's opponents when they realized that they had in fact set in place mechanisms to protect what they now sought to condemn only made Hutchinson's practice of midwifery seem more threatening. Clearly, if she had managed to so cleverly circumvent their regulating abilities to the point they actually worked against themselves, there must he something wrong with her.

The first of these defenses unwittingly set up by the authorities stems from the fact that the very exclusiveness and secrecy of midwifery, which the church decried as a cloak for unspeakable sin, had in fact been imposed by the same authority figures that now found it highly inconvenient. Squeamish and straitlaced through and through, our forefathers were hardly willing to have childbirth be anything but the most private and hushed of affairs. Thus it was difficult for them to accuse Hutchinson of deliberately working privately through midwifery to spread her evil doctrines when they had mandated that her occupation should be so private.

In the second case of embarrassing self-defeat, the politicoreligious hierarchy found itself in a position comparable to attempting to fire one's star employee. By its nature, midwifery was not only an important position, but also a responsible one. Great trust had been placed in Hutchinson's hands, and through a long series of successful births she had proven herself to be worthy of that trust, at least in the strictly medical sense. For the authorities to then accuse her of wildly irresponsible, sinful, and seditious behavior in the context of Antinomianism contradicted Hutchinson's character as a responsible and trusted member of society—a character with which they had endowed her. Thus in two separate cases, the Puritan authorities found themselves in awkward positions of self-contradiction when they attempted to attack Hutchinson's midwifery. And their embarrassment and anger at this fact can only be supposed to have made their attacks more virulent.

As radical as Anne Hutchinson's revolutionary ideas might have been, it is nearly impossible to understand them, as well as why the authorities reacted to them with such horror, without comparing Hutchinson to John Wheelwright. By seeing what Wheelwright did—and he was by no means considered a conservative—the extent to which she broke every possible societal rule becomes clear. Wheelwright lies at the opposite end of the spectrum of incendiaries; insofar as one can lead a rebellion in the prescribed manner, he did it, directing his challenge to Puritan authority through the existing channels and shaping it within the framework of social norms. Essentially, he did or was involved in three things: he sought an appointment, he gave a sermon, he was the subject of a petition. In the first case, he accepted the religious principle that being a minister was a necessary prerequisite to formulating or even commenting on theological doctrine, and he followed the accepted path towards the fulfillment of that prerequisite—a formal proposal and debate by the church in question.

Similarly, once Wheelwright received the position he did, he presented his message, however seditious, in exactly the accepted format: a sermon. Sermons during this period served as everything from homilies to political exhortations, and his was neither unduly militant nor unduly secular. It was merely supportive of the Antinomians. In the same way, the petition later presented on his behalf—in which it can reasonably be assumed he had a hand, since he was not actually imprisoned at the time—was respectful and respectable. It asked simply for public proceedings to be held and for the church to be allowed to govern its own concerns. And finally, when convicted, Wheelwright's response was predictable and not particularly radical; he requested a formal political appeal, and his request was, as we have seen, immediately quashed.

Contrast this polite and cautious behavior with Hutchinson's actions. While Wheelwright asked for appointments, she essentially denied the very principle of ordained clergy. While he gave sermons and framed respectful petitions, she used the subversive medium of private conversation to confront her enemies directly. While he asked for an appeal, she made a long speech calling the wrath of heaven down on her opponents' heads and defiantly demanded to know wherefore she was banished. And most importantly, while he played a pivotal role in events that occurred in full view of all of Boston, she acted behind the scenes, beyond the reach of the mechanisms of public regulation that were the pillars of Puritan society.

Therein lies the singularity and the value of Anne Hutchinson's legacy. There have been many religious controversies, many excommunications, and many who have fallen into the displeasure of theocracies such as the one that began the United States of America. But few people have challenged such regimes with rebellion as far-reaching and as fundamentally radical as Anne Hutchinson, who rejected the entire principle of publicity on which Puritanism had been founded, both by embracing doctrines that exalted privacy and by working in the private sphere to disseminate those doctrines. It was this rejection that earned her the virulent hatred of her opponents, and that should garner her the respect of history. More than being considered a religious or political radical who was forward-thinking enough to rebel against the oppressive Puritan system, Anne Hutchinson can be rightfully deemed the first person in American history to affirm the value of the private sphere.

Endnotes

[1] Charles H. Bell, John Wheelwright (Boston: The Prince Society, 1876) p. 4

[2] Selma R. Williams, Divine Rebel: The Life of Anne Marbury Hutchinson (New York: Holt, Rinehart and Winston, 1981) pp. 12-13

[3] Ibid., pp. 32-33

[4] Ibid., pp. 50-51

[5] Thomas Hutchinson, The History of the Colony of Massachusetts Bay, Vol. II (New York: Research Library of Colonial America, Arno Press, 1972) p. 507

[6] Williams, pp. 73-74

[7] Ibid., p. 81

[8] Charles Francis Adams, Three Episodes in the History of Massachusetts Bay (Cambridge, Massachusetts: Riverside Press, 1892) p. 397

[9] Ibid., p. 393

[10] Hutchinson, p. 484

[11] Adams, p. 400

[12] Williams, p. 96

[13] Adams, p. 398

[14] David D. Hall, The Antinomian Controversy (Middletown, Connecticut: Wesleyan University Press, 1968) p. 207

[15] The name means literally against laws, which makes reference to the belief that obeying the Old Testament's laws governing personal behavior cannot guarantee one's salvation.

[15] John Winthrop, The History of New England, Vol. 1, ed. John Savage (Boston: Phelps and Farnham, 1825) p. 200

[16] Adams, p. 407

[17] Williams, p. 111

[18] Ibid., pp. 112-113

[19] Ibid., p. 117

[20] Edward Johnson, Wonder-Working Providence ed. William Towne (Andover, Massachusetts: Warren F. Draper, 1867) p. 96

[21] Ibid., p. 413

[22] Ibid., p. 425

[23] Ibid., p. 428

[24] Winthrop/Savage, p. 211

[25] Adams, p. 444

[26] Winthrop/Savage, p. 220

[27] Williams, p. 132
[28] Ibid. pp. 132-133
[29] Winthrop/Savage, p. 240
[30] Ibid., p. 262
[31] Williams, pp. 136-137
[32] Hall, p. 259
[33] Williams, p. 141-142
[34] Hall, p. 263
[35] Hutchinson, p. 432
[36] Hall, p. 319
[37] Williams, pp. 153-155
[38] Hall, p. 317
[39] Ibid., p. 333
[40] Ibid., p. 333
[41] Hutchinson, p. 509
[42] Adams, p. 503
[43] Hutchinson, p. 513
[44] Ibid., p. 514
[45] Ibid., p. 517
[46] Ibid., p. 520
[47] Williams, pp. 168-170
[48] Ibid., p. 171
[49] Ibid., p. 175
[50] Hall, pp. 374-376
[51] Ibid., pp. 378-379
[52] Ibid., p. 388
[53] Ibid., p. 310
[54] Cotton Mather, <u>Magnalia Christi Americana or The Ecclesiastical History of New England, Vol. II</u> (Hartford: Silas Andrus & Son, 1835) p. 519

Bibliography

1. Adams, Charles Francis, <u>Three Episodes in the History of Massachusetts Bay</u> Cambridge, Massachusetts: Riverside Press, 1892

Adams devotes one of the sections of his book to the events of the Antinomian controversy, and I found his analysis to be almost uniformly illuminating. This book was a great help to me as I sought to piece together the various events of the controversy into a coherent whole.

2. Bell, Charles, John Wheelwright Boston: The Prince Society, 1876

Bell's brief biography provided some useful insights into the life of the second leader of the Antinomians, who is frequently ignored in other accounts. A transcript of the Fast-Day Sermon is also included.

3. Hall, David D., The Antinomian Controversy Middletown, Connecticut: Wesleyan University Press, 1968

This book is the ultimate source for information regarding the Antinomian controversy; it is essentially a compendium of all relevant documents and transcripts, including numerous writings by John Cotton not included or quoted in the other sources. Hall's brief notes are also helpful.

4. Hutchinson, Thomas, The History of the Colony of Massachusetts Bay, Vol. II New York: Research Library of Colonial America, Arno Press; 1972

Though the perspective of Anne's great-great-grandson (a notorious Tory during the Revolutionary War) on the events of her time is interesting, I made use of this book principally because its appendices include the first published transcript of Anne's trial.

5. Johnson, Edward, Wonder-Working Providence (ed. Towne, William) Andover, Massachusetts: Warren F. Draper, 1867

This is simply a reprinting with an index of Johnson's 1654 treatise on the history of New England. It includes a small section dealing with the events of the Antinomian controversy, which is difficult to follow but valuable in that, unlike Winthrop's diaries, it presents the view of a relatively impartial observer.

6. Mather, Cotton, Magnalia Christi Americana or The Ecclesiastical History of New England, Vol. II Hartford: Silas Andrus & Son, 1835

The section of Mather's writings dealing with the Antinomians is entitled "Hydra Decapitato," which gives a sense of his perspective on the controversy. Essentially, he presents the viewpoint of the most conservative ministers of Hutchinson's time in more modern and certainly more colorful language.

7. Rugg, Winifred, <u>Unafraid: A Life of Anne Hutchinson</u> Cambridge, Massachusetts: The Riverside Press, 1930

This book is the most unusual source I found; it is a fictionalized biography dealing with Hutchinson's life that attempts to fill in the gaps, speculating about her private and family life and exactly what she was thinking as she made history. Though it is hardly a rigorous historical study, this book enabled me to begin conceiving of Anne Hutchinson as a person who was more than the quick-witted woman revealed in the transcripts of the trials.

8. Williams, Selma R., <u>Divine Rebel: The Life of Anne Marbury Hutchinson</u> New York: Holt Rinehart and Winston, 1981

This book was by far the most valuable to me. It is a comprehensive biography of Anne Hutchinson that includes a great deal of background information about the period as well as sympathetic analyses of why she did what she did and why it is important. It was the starting point for my research as well as my interest in this topic.

9. Winthrop, John, <u>The History of New England, Vol. I</u> (ed. Savage, John) Boston: Phelps and Farnham, 1825

Winthrop's grandly named <u>History</u> is in fact simply his diary; this edition contains occasional notes. Though it clearly presents a biased viewpoint and its information is scattered throughout numerous entries on other less important topics, this book is the one surviving comprehensive account of the Antinomian controversy by a witness—in fact, a direct participant. As such, its value cannot be denied.

Ralph Waldo Emerson Prize 2010

RELIGION AND NATIONALISM IN IRELAND IN THE LATE 19TH AND EARLY 20TH CENTURIES

Jane Abbottsmith

Many analysts have noted the apparent connection between wide-spread social change, declining economic sectors, and revolutionary fervour. Such fervour is characterized by nostalgia for an older world, and in particular for an older social contract that is held to have been violated...many revolutionary movements have committed themselves to the defense of traditional cultural values and communal relations.

—Historian Tom Garvin

Introduction

In 1829, Christopher North wrote that Britain held dominions "on which the sun never sets."[1] Indeed, the 19th century witnessed British imperial expansion both within and beyond Europe. Tensions rose as British influence spread around the world, but the most significant challenge of the 19th century occurred within Great Britain itself. In Ireland, a powerful Protestant English minority ruled a predominantly Irish Catholic nation. Englishmen immigrated into Irish cities, creating new ethnic, religious, and class divides.[2] Cities progressed industrially faster than rural communities, where traditional customs persevered.[3] There was a "chronic mismatch between education and opportunity,"[4] and

The author graduated magna cum laude from Princeton and is a Gates Scholar at Cambridge University. She wrote this paper for Kelly Cronin's Advanced History Research Seminar at Summit Country Day School in Cincinnati, Ohio in the 2007/2008 academic year.

the Protestant aristocracy sought to maintain its political power over the lower classes.[5] All of these factors increased the ill feeling between English Protestants and Irish Catholics at the turn of the 20th century.

Amidst the British intrusion, the Irish Catholic majority feared the dilution of their customs, and nationalism increased as Irishmen realized the need to preserve their cultural identity to distinguish them from the rest of Great Britain. The term "Irish Irelander"[6] originated to characterize the true Irishman: Catholic and with Irish ancestry, learned in Irish folklore and competent in the speaking and reading of the Gaelic language.[7] As the national identity took hold, it became increasingly important to keep the "mere Irish,"[8] the quintessential Irish citizens, in Ireland. Irish nationalists ultimately hoped to gain Home Rule, or local autonomy from Britain. It has been said that the Home Rule Movement displayed "a blend of romantic idealism and an exaggerated moralism."[9] While that may be true, as evident in the call to return to the glorified Eire[10] of fairy tales and in the emphasis on Irish Catholic chastity, a more sweeping description is even more prescient: "Catholic nationalism made for exciting history lessons: Good versus Evil; heroic Irish Catholics defending their kind against the bottomless and inexplicable malevolence of English Protestants."[11] Indeed, the divide between Catholic and Protestant, Irish and English, in most of Ireland was wide; the nationalists, and in many cases Catholic bishops and priests, sought to make it unbridgeable. These divisions led not only to the well-known political attempts for Home Rule, but also to the creation of a national identity rooted in the Catholic religion and Irish culture. Even as a cultural identity developed, nationalists struggled with how to include Protestant Irish.

The Development Of Irish-British Tension

The Catholic nationalist movement began as early as the 17th century.[12] The conquest of Ireland resulted in a landed Protestant minority who ruled over a majority of predominantly Catholic peasants and tenants.[13] Over time, these religious differences "congealed and evolved into what were essentially ethnic or caste distinctions."[14] In fact, one small revolt was documented as early as the 1790s; these rebellious Irish were perhaps influenced by both the recent American and French Revolutions.[15] As historian Tom Garvin notes, many Irish schoolmasters "imbibed a version of French republican radicalism"[16] and passed it on to their students.

As Protestant Englishmen moved into Ireland and became more firmly rooted in Irish soil, they encouraged the spread of their customs, language, and religion.[17] Some historians believe this was a conscious attempt by the English to subdue Irish Ireland and supplant Irish customs with their own; other historians argue that the spread of minority customs was a natural and inevitable result of immigration by Englishmen into Ireland.[18] Furthermore, by the 1880s, Ireland began to experience industrial modernization, which was deemed a primarily English trend.[19] Commercial agriculture replaced subsistence farming, and rural peoples began to move toward the cities.[20] Linguistically, the influx of Englishmen and the growth of international business and trade made English an essential language for economic success. At this time, in the words of historian Tom Garvin, "millions migrated mentally from the medieval Gaelic world to the modern world of the English language."[21] Amidst all of these changes, and due to racial and religious prejudices, nationalists—and Irishmen in general—were considered to be unable to govern Ireland effectively.[22] Britain saw no reason to extend autonomy to Ireland.

Ireland's grievances against Britain intensified in 1845 with the Great Famine. Due to the failure of potato crops, Irish people were starving. Irish left their homes for America, and Irish patriotism suffered. Even as the Irish died, Ireland exported food to England. The issue increased the tension and conflict between the two regions. In the aftermath of this great conflict, the Irish people responded in two ways. Some blamed Ireland and rebelled against the customs, language, beliefs, and dress of the country [Ireland] that had allowed them to suffer so greatly.[23] According to 1860s Fenian leader James Stephens, this reaction made a separatist revolution more difficult to attain because it destroyed such a great part of the heritage of "old Ireland."[24] On the other hand, many young Catholic Irish men joined to end British rule in Ireland.[25] Irish nationalists considered themselves "defenders of the community and its values against a process of transformation threatened by alien political, economic, and cultural forces, usually perceived as emanating from the imperial government in London."[26] As historian Tom Garvin notes, "what did survive was an image of the Irish as the moral, innocent, and potentially corruptible People of God in an amoral, English-dominated world."[27]

In the 1900s, one magistrate said, "we were governed from London by people who knew little about our country but who ruled it fairly, though in the English interest, through an oligarchy in Dublin...The Irish people of all classes were perpetually up against the oligarchy in connection with their own personal affairs."[28] Some, however, did not think it fair, and many Irish people were unhappy with British rule in Ireland. Historian Emmet Larkin describes this ineffectiveness of English government in Ireland as "the breakdown in the British Constitutional System whenever it was applied to Ireland."[29] The extent of England's lack of understanding—and perhaps more significant, its perceived lack of concern—is evident in the following example: the British government kept back a sum of money from an Irish official as a punishment for poor performance; after his death, the government paid the increment, for the official's death "removed all grounds of hesitation"[30] about accepting his claim of illness as a reason for his inefficiency.

Economically, the Chief Secretary of Ireland, who had no "financial discretion,"[31] was dependent upon Britain in all fiscal matters of the State; he became an intermediary between the departments of Ireland and the Treasury in London, having no real power over either.[32] In fact, the Treasury made the final decisions in all economic issues, leaving the Irish Chief Secretary no economic authority whatsoever.[33] This was a significant problem. The Irish leaders considered England's financial system, in the words of the IRA, "wasteful and inappropriate of the needs of the country."[34] In addition, the Irish government had no control over military forces; this became increasingly difficult to tolerate during crises.[35] Another Irish grievance against Britain was religious in nature and was the result of a loss of trust in the British state. At this time, Britain feared that granting the Irish home rule would give great power to the Vatican because of its influence over the majority of Irish Catholics.[36] The taunt "home rule meant Rome rule"[37] moved England to attempt to influence Rome to help stop the nationalists. As Emmet Larkin states, "Rome was to persuade the Irish bishops to persuade the priests to persuade the people to keep the peace."[38] When the Irish people learned of these efforts, much of their remaining trust of the English government failed, and rebellious tensions only increased in strength.

Adding to the tension, Ireland underwent modernization in the 1890s; Britain was blamed for the effects by Irish people who believed England was pushing its culture on Ireland. Railways spread rapidly across Ireland and cities grew in size as rural farmers followed the European trend of urbanization and moved closer to urban centers.[39] At the same time, mass literacy in English allowed the spread of English newspapers, and a Catholic middle-class emerged and grew.[40] There were unusually significant differences between the city and the country: "towns were English, and Dublin the centre of English colonial power, whereas the countryside was Irish, Catholic, resistant to city rule, and even Gaelic."[41] As Conor Cruise O'Brien, a Catholic nationalist, notes, "formidable bastions of Protestant power and influence remained in urban life, especially in business and in education."[42] In short, cities "were less Irish."[43] Therefore, many nationalist countrymen believed they were fighting for "the Ireland of the farmland and village rather than the emerging Ireland of towns and cities with a modern Anglo-American popular culture."[44] For example, in the northern province of Ulster, industrialization had progressed quickly and the Protestant population was greater than in the rest of Ireland.[45] On the other hand, in the city of Cork in Munster, the southern province, industrialization was comparably less advanced; agrarian and separatist movements were most successful in this region.[46] With the Local Government Act of 1898, Catholic-nationalists were able to secure local authority everywhere except Ulster.[47] Significantly, after the success of the Fourth Home Rule Bill in 1920, the northern province of Ulster was so ideologically different from the rest of the nation that it remained part of the Union; the region that was Ulster in the 1900s is today Northern Ireland.

The tension that was increasing between the English government and the Irish people led to the development of the Home Rule movement. Home Rulers believed the Irish problems could only be solved when Irishmen led their own country.[48] Even British Prime Minister Arthur Balfour said in 1905, "there can be but one head of the Irish administration."[49] Many Irish people in favor of Home Rule wished to preserve the union with Britain but gain more local autonomy for Ireland. They hoped that an Irish government devoted to only Irish affairs would ensure the strength and efficiency of their nation, while the economic and diplomatic alliance with Britain would ensure the safety of Irish affairs.[50] Other more extreme nationalists, however, believed in separatism, or complete separation and independence for Ireland. The most widely appealing nationalist goal for Home Rule is summarized by historian Tom Garvin,

> Opposition to English rule attracted different people for different reasons....A reactionary might be attracted to such a stance as a means of defending the noble values of feudalism against English reformers; a pious Catholic would see it as a means of defending the religious convictions of the Irish people from English skepticism, anti-Catholicism, and indifference; a nationalist of centrist inclinations might see it as a virtuous attempt to forestall state socialism, big business, trade unions, and the malign effects the intrusion of English commerce had on the livelihood of the Irish shopkeeper, farmer, or artisan; lastly, a radical might see separatism as anti-imperialist campaign for a

socialist Irish republic. Separatism's ideological proteanism reflected the wideness of its appeal.[51]

Intense separatist-nationalists believed in the goodness, strength, and beauty of their Irish nation, and they wished to improve its condition by shaking off the chains that bound it to England. Only by breaking free of those bonds could Ireland return to its former condition as a land of piety, of folklore and legend, and of music, dance, and cheer. Beginning in the latter half of the 19th century and continuing into the second decade of the 20th century, Irish nationalists fought for the Ireland they loved.

The utterly overwhelming number of opposing political factions with their contradictory goals and proponents, however, made political progress on the Home Rule front difficult to achieve.

The main groups competing for political leadership in pre-independence Ireland were, firstly, those among the Anglo-Irish who hoped to retain some shreds of their traditional social and political ascendancy under the coming new dispensation; secondly, the new Catholic middle class, internally divided, inexperienced, and less than adequately educated; and lastly, the Catholic clergy, which wielded enormous power, mainly because of the weakness of the other two groups. A fourth group, the Ulster unionists, in effect opted not to compete but to construct another arena. A small but intense socialist movement also existed, which in many ways was to trigger the violent phase of the revolution but which was not to profit from it. Big business was mainly unionist in politics...one of the peculiarities of the Irish revolution is how small a role classic labour and bourgeois groups played in it.[52]

The sheer number of competing ideologies, when combined with the bureaucracy's dogged determination to "do as little as possible which might stir the country up,"[53] riddled the political frontier with inaction. In the Irish government itself, more than 40 departments and offices, each with its own configuration and purpose, functioned in Ireland.[54] Amidst all of the branches sat the chief secretary, responsible for "land reform, public order, economic development, and constitutional politics."[55] The political chaos among the departments and parties made the chief secretary largely unable to fulfill his responsibilities due to his limited power over all of the departments and his duty to justify their actions before the House of Commons.[56]

In the 1880s, two main political groups came to a head: the Unionists ("the party of the Constitution"[57]), and the Nationalists (frequently, "the party of the Revolution"[58]). The Unionist party held power from 1886—when the first Home Rule Bill divided the opposing Liberal party—to the end of Arthur Balfour's rule in 1905; there was only a brief, three-year hiatus with Liberal power.[59] Understanding the Catholic-nationalist opposition, Unionists feared Home Rule because they believed it would result in a Roman Catholic stronghold—and thus, greater power for Rome—in Ireland. Knowing also that the success of Unionism outside of Ulster depended upon support from Britain, Unionists enacted a campaign of appeasement to squelch rising discontent and revolutionary fervor.[60] The period from the 1880s to 1920 witnessed the Unionist policy of "killing home rule with kindness,"[61] or attempting to convince the people of Ireland—through a series of land reforms and economic restructuring laws—that they were content under the caring, watchful eye of the English Parliament.[62]

Nationalists' attempts to use the Irish Catholic peasants as a focal point for the cause ultimately failed. With the spread of the Industrial Revolution throughout continental Europe and England, railways and cities expanded and enlarged in Ireland as well. As cities grew in size, employment opportunities grew and attracted peasants from smaller Irish towns. Irish peasants, who were the traditionally pious, Catholic population that was well versed in Irish folklore, began to move to the cities seeking economic betterment, and some even left the country for America, the land of promise. Emigration, however, did not contribute to economic progress in Ireland, so it was considered an abandonment of country and a transgression against the homeland. As nationalists watched the rural Irish people, who best exemplified the characteristics of the Irish Irelander, leave their motherland, they feared the disappearance of these Irish peoples, the "mere Irish."[63] Therefore, they attempted to encourage peasants to remain in Ireland, arguing as one bishop said, "money is not everything, and the same thrift and industry and self-discipline which the Irish emigrant must exhibit abroad to hold his own in the hard race of life, if resorted to at home would give him a competency and a measure of success in his own Ireland sufficient to gratify the average human heart."[64]

The Catholic Church feared the effects of cities' moral corruption and cutthroat business, as well as their predominantly Protestant religious base, on the quiet faith of its obedient Catholic peasants.[65] The Church perceived industrial cities as destroyers of the familial order as well as of the Irishman's dignity.[66] As one priest commented,

> In the work-rooms, factories, and other places of employment, our young men are brought into daily and hourly association with people, who have either long since ceased to be even nominal believers, or who profess allegiance to a Church other than that of Rome.[67]

This interaction with non-Catholic people concerned many members of the Catholic hierarchy, including Father Joseph Guinam, who warned that cities brought to Irish Catholics "a fate worse than death—a fate compared with which the poverty, hunger and rags of an Irish hovel would be very heaven."[68] Bishop Hoare of Ardagh said in 1902 that the cities, those "hives of industry," were "huge destroyers of the morals of the people (hear, hear)."[69] The Church's certainty that cities brought about a decay of morals was only supported by news from America that many Irish emigrants, settling in the morally dangerous cities, had fallen from religion and become lapsed Catholics.[70]

To encourage Irish peasants to remain at home rather than emigrate to the cities, the Church glorified the kindness and beauty of the countryside. For example, Father Joseph Guinan said, "I felt no compunction at all in being the means of bringing about this seemingly unfavorable turn in his fortunes; for I regarded that the humble couple in their hut on the wind-swept mountain side as a valuable asset to the country."[71] He continued,

> At home in 'holy Ireland' there was an atmosphere of faith and piety; a climate 'soft as a mother's smile;' the deep, strong love of the kindly

old folks; the consoling sight of familiar faces; and the strangely sweet charm and the weird witchery of childhood's home. All these are things that wealth in a foreign land could never bring.[72]

The Church discouraged emigration to cities in all cases, even if, by remaining, the Irish people would be forced to become farmers' servants. The Church believed any lifestyle in Ireland would be preferable to life in the cities.[73] Furthermore, in light of the difficulties Irish immigrants faced finding work in America, in 1902 bishops pronounced the move to America "reckless."[74] In Kilmaley, County Clare, a few years later, one bishop said, "Don't let anyone deceive you, the average Irishman or woman is never so happy as in his Catholic Irish home, where the air is pure, and where there is a feeling of religion and sympathy around him."[75] All of these efforts were undertaken to keep the Irish people in Ireland—to root them "in the soil."[76]

To bolster the effort, nationalists attempted to make land reforms that would improve the economic condition of the peasants and, thereby, persuade them to remain in their country. A series of land acts in the late 19th century improved the condition of the peasants, transferring land from predominantly Protestant landlords to mostly Catholic tenants.[77] Catholic bishops participated in this move, feeling that they had,

> a solemn duty, in face of the unabated exodus of our population, to declare anew our deep conviction that an adequate solution of the Irish land question never can be reached until the half-neglected grazing lands of the country are made available on fair terms for the agricultural population that is still forced to emigrate in such appalling numbers to earn a livelihood.[78]

With the nationalist changes, Protestant landlords were losing power. Thus, the reform effort proved a double-edged sword; as land reforms progressed and conditions improved, revolutionary spirit died down. Discontent with the dominance of Britain over Ireland diminished, and the Home Rule movement lost momentum.[79] Throughout the period of nationalist activity, the attempt to preserve the true Irish population for the sake of culture weighed down the progress of the Home Rule movement.[80] For this reason, nationalists were forced to "take up the causes of cultural defense and religious fervor to breathe life into their political project."[81] They adhered to the rural cultural identity, the characteristic Catholic, Gaelic identity of the rural peasants, throughout the duration of the Home Rule movement.

The political deadlock, coupled with the unionist stronghold during this period, led nationalists to develop a different approach to Home Rule. Beginning in the 1880s and continuing through World War I, nationalists attempted to cultivate an Irish cultural identity based on language and religion. The Irish Ireland movement appealed mostly to young middle-class Catholics.[82] It excluded, to a large degree, Protestants, who were deemed to be allied to the British State. The Catholic Church, however, behaved ambiguously toward religion in the political world.[83] Certainly, the Church attempted to encourage peaceful, constitutional nationalism rather than the revolutionary spirit that was rising.[84] It hesitated, though, to enter the political squabble that ensued at the upper levels of the government. Nevertheless, as nationalists connected Catholicism to their movement, priests and bishops sometimes played a role in the establishment of this Irish cultural identity. The development of a Catholic cultural identity for the nationalist movement also created problems for Protestant Irish.

The Development of a Cultural Identity

For centuries, the Catholic religion had held the foremost place in many an Irish heart, and at the turn of the 20th century three quarters of the Irish population were Catholic.[85] Of course, loyalty to the Catholic Church became a hallmark of the Irish Irelander. Nationalists developed pride in the adherence to faith that had led to the martyrdom of their ancestors.[86] At the end of the 19th century, as the nationalist movement encouraged Irishmen to welcome their heritage and return to tradition, the religious history of the Irish people became a source of deep pride that cemented Catholicism as the religion of the true Irish. Men and women of Ireland looked back to their ancestors, who had held steadfast to their faith amidst persecution and proselytism, as models of courage, deservers of approbation and reverence, and examples of the tremendous piety of the Irish people.[87] Conor Cruise O'Brien remembers that his father, an active nationalist, taught him to "be proud that [his] ancestors had stuck to their religion in the centuries of persecution...when such fidelity was extremely disadvantageous."[88] Clearly, ancestral pride was an integral part of Irish nationalism at the turn of the 20th century. As Louis Paul-Dubois noted in 1907, "No one can visit Ireland without being impressed by the intensity of Catholic belief there, and by the fervour of its outward manifestations."[89] The "outward manifestations,"[90]—the Church's move to build religious universities and its publicized intolerance of Protestantism—were pivotal elements of the nationalist movement.

Catholicism in Ireland meant more than just faith; it was a "badge of nationality"[91] that identified the "mere Irish,"[92] or the natives with Irish ancestry. By the end of the century, Catholicism was doubly significant because it meant that one's ancestors had resisted the pressures of the English Reformation and remained loyal to their Catholic faith. Again, pride in one's Irish predecessors strengthened the already-firm faith of Irish men and women at the turn of the 20th century. In fact, religious affiliation became so important that it began to replace ethnic origin as the chief identifier of true Irish.[93] Catholics were both *Gaedhil,* or Gaels, and *Gaill,* foreigners with ancestors from Scandinavia, Scotland, Wales, and England who had intermarried and merged.[94] They lived together in peace and cooperation. Religious solidarity trumped ethnicity in the forming of what became an Irish Catholic nation.

The Catholic "cultural nostalgia"[95] drove the nationalist movement to establish a sort of neo-medievalism in Irish religion. The successful return to the religious values of the past, especially in the last few years of the 19th century, promised to ward off the intruding secularism associated with Britain and safeguard Irish Catholics from the malignant modernizing influences of the English-speaking world.[96] Religious nationalism at the turn of the 20th century embraced the same religious fervor as the reform movement of the 16th century Counter Reformation, which had tried to overcome the Protestant Reformation. In this modern era of religious zeal, the Catholic Church now sought to safeguard the morals and beliefs of its Irish people and secure its position at the forefront of the Irish heart. With no real political authority, the Church looked to education as a way to inculcate Catholic values in Irish children. Catholic education had traditionally occurred first in Ireland's many Catholic homes and then under the instruction of the Christian Brothers in the early years of primary and secondary school.[97] The Christian Brothers sought to solidify orthodoxy in the lower classes and emphasize the parallels between Catholicism and nationalism to curb the rising "irreligious nationalism."[98] With their encouragement, Catholic nationalism grew and began to fuel the growing power of cultural politics.[99]

Over time, religious nationalism became manifest politically, and Catholic nationalists expressed their loyalty to Ireland by proclaiming their hatred of the Anglican Church.[100] At this time, the terms "Englishman," "Anglican," and "Protestant" were interchangeable, the latter referring primarily to members of the Church of England. The aforementioned pride in the religious constancy of the first Irishmen led many modern Irish Catholics to resent the intrusion of Protestants and Protestantism in their land. They feared Protestantism, which they believed threatened to sully their nationality and faith. After all, they thought, "to be a Protestant implied that one's forebears had immigrated from Great Britain, or that they had yielded to the temptations of self-interest and foreswore the faith of their fathers."[101] Either way, Protestantism represented foreignness and betrayal that, in the Irish Catholic mind, would corrupt the morality of the faithful Catholics. In reality, Anglicanism, not Protestantism, was the primary source of these worries. The less-conservative Catholics were accepting of other religions, or at least tolerant, feeling that it was simply important "not to belong to the Church of England."[102]

The anti-British sentiment that coursed through Ireland at the turn of the century was a powerful motivator, and its influences were sincerely felt. This was especially true when radical

Protestant nationalist Maud Gonne, the object of William Butler Yeats' love poetry for almost 30 years, converted to Catholicism. She said, "I am officially a protestant [MG's lower case initial] supposed to look at it from another, a much narrower one which is moreover the English one....Our nation looks at God through one prism, The Catholic Religion [MG's initial capitals]....I prefer to look at truth through the same prism as my country people."[103] Fortunately for Gonne, Monsignor Pierre-Joseph Geay, who performed the baptism, was a lenient French nationalist who accepted her marginal reasons for conversion and tolerated her deviation from the traditional abjuration of heresy. Gonne later wrote in a letter:

> I said I hated nothing in the world but the British Empire which I looked on as the outward symbol of Satan in the world where ever it came in [in the course of the ceremony] I was to declare hatred of heresy. I declared hatred of the British Empire, on this form I made my solemn abjuration of Anglicanism, declaration of hatred of England.

As Conor Cruise O'Brien notes, "a declaration of hatred of England was an even more acceptable proof of Catholicism."[104] Gonne's hatred of England was not uncommon among nationalists at this time, but her fellow Protestant nationalists disapproved of her abandonment of Protestantism. Yeats was outraged; in a letter to Gonne, he wrote,

> It is the priest, when the day of great hazard has come who will lead the people. No, no. He will palter with the government...He will say, 'Be quiet, be good cristians [sic] do not shed blood.' It is [?is it] not the priest who has [?softened] the will of our young men—who has broken their pride. You have said all these things not so long ago. For [it] is not only the trust of your friends but your own soul that you are about to betray.

Yeats never spelled very well, but the frequency of errors in the diction and syntax of his letter suggest that he wrote hastily and angrily; as a loyal Protestant nationalist who was bravely enduring exclusion in Ireland because of his religion, he felt betrayed by Gonne's seeming act of weakness and compromise.

Like Yeats and Gonne, all Protestants faced a choice. On one hand, they could adhere to their religion and push for integration, in which case they would gain the support of the Protestant minority. On the other hand, they could abandon Protestantism and identify with the Catholic nationalist movement, thereby gaining the supportive approval of the Catholic majority, the much larger of the two populations.[105] While a few conservative Protestants, primarily in the Ulster region, fought against Catholic nationalism to maintain the Union with Britain, the majority chose to adhere privately to their religion and hope that the intensifying cultural and linguistic revival would cause the "symbol of Irish nationality"[106] to shift in favor of culture and language rather than religion. These Protestants wished for an "inclusive nationalism"[107] that would no longer isolate them. While still believing in separation from Britain, they "longed for a means of identifying with the Ireland of the Catholic majority while nurturing the hope of eventually bringing their own coreligionists into the national fold as well."[108] William Smith O'Brien, the famous radical nationalist leader of the land reform movement of the 1890s and early 1900s, hoped that this reconciliation between Catholic and Protestant could be reached.[109] In fact, as the nationalist movement progressed, Irish Home Rulers made connections with separatist movements in the other British Celtic countries, uniting around a common wish to separate from Britain and, in doing so, "softening the Catholic tinge of that identity with some Scottish Presbyterians and Welsh Methodists."[110]

As the cultural movement progressed, however, Protestants discovered the reality that the nationalist movement was still focusing primarily on Catholicism and excluding Protestantism from the Irish identity, and some Protestants lost interest in Catholic nationalism.[111] William Butler Yeats, the well-known Irish poet and dramatist, had been particularly active up to this point. Yet, he faced continued criticism from the widely-read Catholic nationalist news publication, *The Leader*. Conor Cruise O'Brien, the son of Irish Catholic nationalists, writes on this topic,

> The Church disapproved of Yeats because he was a Protestant or worse, if worse there were. So bully for Yeats! The Church disapproved of "mixed" cultural activities, because these might lead to mixed marriages or worse, if worse there were. So what? One might just go

ahead and marry a Protestant and be damned, to show those people
what you felt about them murdering Parnell! Well, maybe not go so
far as that! But there was a delightful frisson in declining to avoid
authoritatively-designed occasions of sin, and this lent sexy spice to
the whole Protestant-inspired cultural nationalist enterprise.[112]

Conor Cruise O'Brien, a Catholic nationalist, went to Sandford
Park School, a non-denominational secondary school with a
somewhat Protestant philosophy. From there he went to Trinity
College, Dublin. In these schools he became more comfortable
with liberal Protestants and former Catholics than with strict religious adherents.[113] As a Catholic himself, O'Brien was certainly
unusual for having such a tolerant acceptance of Protestantism.

Conor Cruise O'Brien was the exception; the majority of
Irish Catholics only rarely accepted Protestants into the nationalist movement, and they still believed that the true Irishman was a
Catholic Irishman. They believed that Catholicism in Ireland was
the equivalent of Protestantism in England in regard to national
identity and reputation, and they demanded that non-Catholics
recognize this fact.[114] One Irishman exemplifies the brunt of this
religious philosophy when he states, "We desire to realize an Irish
Ireland and let the non-Catholics help in the work or get out of
the system. Their kin have robbed us and enslaved us and inter-
rupted our development as a nation. They owe us restitution."[115]
Catholics were willing to accept Protestant nationalists as long as the
non-Catholics respected the facts of Irish national identity.[116] The
Leader was less forgiving: "If a non-Catholic Nationalist Irishman
does not like to live in a Catholic atmosphere, let him...give up all
pretence to being an Irish Nationalist."[117] Protestants who did not
adopt the Catholic religion or adhere to a Catholic-dominated
nationalism were labeled "Palesmen."[118] Palesmen were expected
to function "behind the Gael,"[119] and many Protestants resented
this exclusion. In reality, Britain assigned English Protestants to
positions of power; as Conor Cruise O'Brien notes, "Ireland has
two religions and the majority cannot talk about their religion
above their breath, for fear of appearing bigoted, intolerant and
offending our patonizers."[120] Yet, Catholics themselves, according
to O'Brien, believed that Protestants only, not Catholics, could

be bigots.[121] For this reason, the Catholic publication *The Leader* fostered the development of two other derogatory terms, besides Palesman, to describe Protestants: "Sourface,"[122] the more offensive and racial of the two, and "West Briton."[123] Furthermore, once a Protestant received one of these titles publicly, either through The Leader or through other news distributors, he could not shake it off.[124] It appears, to an extent, that Catholic nationalists succeeded in minimizing acceptance for Protestants, for no Protestant since Charles Stewart Parnell has ever penetrated the elite nationalist circles.[125] Of course, Parnell was easy to criticize. First, he was Protestant and, therefore, was "no fit leader for the Irish people (for 'Irish people' as used by Irish Catholics, read always 'Irish Catholic people')."[126] Second, he fell socially in a widely-publicized divorce scandal that proved that "being a Protestant, he could not share the moral values of the Irish people, or understand how fiercely they resented any offence against chastity."[127] By the early 20th century, Irish Catholicism had become a rallying point for Ireland's nationalist party.

The Church's influence on Irish values and culture rested in part on its role in the education system. The Church wished to instill Catholic values through religious instruction during childhood in the hopes that the students, when adults, would pass down the Catholic teaching to their children, the next generation of pious Irish leaders.[128] This was not a problem through secondary school, for numerous Catholic schools existed in Ireland. The problem was university education. The Church feared the decadence of morals that it believed occurred in the secular universities, but it also realized that Catholics who did not attend a university would not have adequate skills to lead the country. This issue was complicated by the "hostility in Britain to the idea of state endowment of religious foundations, and by the absolute refusal of Trinity College to change its ways."[129] Furthermore, even some jealous clerics feared the growth of an educated laity with equal or superior intellect.[130] The Catholic Church attacked the "mixed"[131] education of Protestants and Catholics that occurred outside of clerical control in "godless colleges"[132] like Trinity and the Queen's Colleges. Even schools that allowed the playing of "foreign games"[133] were deemed West British (and, by extension, Anglican in principle and philosophy) and received criticism. The Church prohibited "non-Catholic higher education,"[134] but the existing Jesuit University College in Dublin was understaffed and unable to provide an adequate education to Catholics.[135] For this reason, the Church pushed to form a new Catholic university.

The Church argued the importance of a Catholic education in several ways. First, it claimed that children who did not learn about political and cultural events from the Christian Brothers, "who taught that we were not justified in hating those who wronged us...would learn them from the newspapers."[136] Second, to secure its position in education, the Church presented an attractive pretense to England: "the textbooks inculcated the Catholic faith, which taught charity to all men and respect for the established government."[137] As one Irishman argued, "Faith thus being strengthened...tends to preserve a spirit of subjection and obedience in the people."[138] This logic was enticing to Britain, which sought to foster political subservience in an effort to quell the rising nationalist agitation.

The Catholic university question also received support from Ireland's lower classes, who viewed education as an escape from peasantry. Limerick Bishop Thomas O'Dwyer cautioned that Catholics should not be given political power without receiving opportunities for ample education, yet because so few Catholics had access to higher education, the "politically ambitious Catholic young men"[139] were deemed "intellectual[ly] inadequa[te]."[140] Chief Secretary Morley indeed noticed the scarcity of Roman Catholics in the top leadership positions, which he considered "a great standing difficulty"[141] that "will remain one until the Catholics have better educational chances."[142] When received, Catholic education was competent, albeit limited, and it provided ambitious Catholic youth a means of "ceasing to be peasantry and becoming citizens."[143] By offering a pathway to skilled, middle-class working occupations, education was a means of social and economic advancement.[144] Furthermore, education fostered the adoption of important "cultural markers"[145] such as "accent, dress, and speech...learned behaviors that can be relearned."[146] For this reason, education had the "obvious if unadmitted function of relearning social deportment for purposes of social mobility."[147] Education could align a child with the Irish cultural identity early on. Significantly, the 1878 Intermediate Education Act provided grants to aid Catholic education, and the number of Catholics seeking new occupations doubled between 1861 and 1911:[148] "They desert the country for the town; they prefer to be clerks, civil servants, schoolmasters, journalists, rather than farmers or curates...the class thus created inherits the traditional feelings of the Irish peasant; it shares in his profound racial consciousness and his antipathy to the British intruder."[149] In this way, religious education not only advanced pupils economically, but also fostered hatred of Britain. In doing so, it produced many proud Irish nationalists who were to take action in the coming years. Clearly, the Church's argument to Britain that Catholic education would teach submission was false.

The pupils of the Christian Brothers at the end of the 19th century formed what historian Tom Garvin describes as the "nucleus of the mass nationalist movements"[150] of the 20th. In fact, amidst the "intellectually inhibited discontent, total economic dependence on both Church and state combined with great local cultural influence."[151] Nationalists emerged bursting with fervor; they looked back to their education and ascribed their introduction to extreme nationalism to their teachers.[152] For example, Padraic Pearse, along with six other men killed after the 1916 Easter Rising, had been a student of the Christian Brothers.[153] Though they may have preached peace, their students learned sometimes a different lesson from Catholic nationalism.

Even amidst the political tensions of the early 20th century, the constitutional nationalists and the Christian Brothers were not really very far apart in vision; as Conor Cruise O'Brien said, they each "appealed to the same folk-memory...and so spoke a similar language."[154] One pupil described schooling under the Christian Brothers as "the heart of a holy patriotism."[155] The Brothers sought to form a force of religious, Catholic nationalists to outnumber the irreligious[156] nationalists. Their goal was to define the national-ist movement around the Catholic religion, while the irreligious nationalists sought entry into the movement through their Irish cultural identity.[157] Unlike the Brothers, many nationalists did want to see a cultural identity based on more than just religion.

By the late 19th century, nationalists had indeed chan-neled their energy into the formation of an Irish national identity beyond its connection to Catholicism.[158] From language revival to news publication to literary involvement, the nationalist effort gradually gained momentum beginning in the final decade of the 19th century. The reception of such a movement varied. Many nationalist groups were condemned as "drinking clubs for young men"[159] and the effects of an "adolescent phenomenon."[160] Indeed, the groups were composed of many young people, including former pupils of the Christian Brothers. Conor Cruise O'Brien, whose father, a nationalist, lived during this time, remembers learning to be proud of his Irish heritage and his family's history as a child.[161] At the turn of the 20th century, many children were taught to cherish their ancestry and national identity as Irishmen. The intensity of the Irish movement varied from place to place and person to person; some nationalists favored Home Rule, while others supported separatism.[162] Common to all, however, was the dream of the ideal Irishman: "He or she is passionately opposed to all forms of English influence in Ireland."[163] Such opposition was necessary to attain the nationalist dream to develop an Ireland that celebrated a heritage and language all its own.

The first step to strengthening the Irish cultural identity was to reverse the decay of the Gaelic language. Knowledge of the Irish language had diminished due to the practicality of English in economic negotiation and international business; Irish-speaking regions were quickly shrinking.[164] Some feeble efforts had been made to preserve the language in the 19th century, including the incorporation of Irish as an optional subject in school curricula in 1878.[165] Yet, not until the 1890s did the nationalist interest in Irish grow and gain momentum and support.[166] Among nation-alist circles, academic study of the Irish language was expected.

Conor Cruise O'Brien describes the Irish nationalist: "He or she is enthusiastic about the Irish language, not necessarily able to speak or write the language in the here and now, but actively engaged in learning it, or at the very least, deemed to be doing so."[167] Significantly, with the onset of this cultural movement came a new maxim, "Irish-Ireland,"[168] coined by journalist D.P. Moran, who is most well-known for his involvement with The Leader, a Catholic-nationalist journal. The celebrated Irish Irelander—the ideal citizen culturally and linguistically—was knowledgeable about Irish culture, devoted to the Gaelic language, and proud to be an Irishman.

Due to the speed of its disappearance, efforts to reverse the incoming tide of English required mobilization on a large scale. In 1893, the Conradh na Gaeilge, or Gaelic League, emerged as a nonpolitical, nonsectarian body devoted to the preservation of the Irish language and Irish culture.[169] Despite its claims to be a nonpolitical group, it was adopted as an organ of the nationalist movement in 1901, by which time the language revival movement had become just one part of the growing Irish Ireland movement.[170] Indeed, while the majority of the Irish population remained illiterate in Irish by 1910, the League was politically important because it kept Irish nationality alive until the Easter Rising of 1916.[171]

To achieve the total revival of language that the nationalists dreamed of, it was necessary to inspire linguistic interest in all the Irish people. To be successful, the Irish language, which had been for so long the language of rural peasants, could not transform into an impractical hobby of an elite, well-educated body of nationalists; it had to be used by the people, or in the words of historian David W. Miller, be taken "out of the drawing rooms and into the hundreds of villages of Ireland."[172] To do this, the League employed a number of tactics meant to reach the people. It went to communities, where it established classes in Irish and encouraged Irish "arts, crafts, and music."[173] For example, Seamus O' Maoleoin's brother Tomas remembered that his mother had traveled to rural areas to speak with the elderly villagers about Irish tradition, compiling a patched culture that she taught to her children.[174] The language revival project tended to separate Irish Catholicism and Irish nationalism. To counter this, Douglas Hyde, one of the League's founders, approached language through religion, associating the Irish language with Catholic piety to encourage clergy to support the cause.[175] Hyde wrote, "with the decay of Irish went the Gael's devotion to the rosary!"[176] Hyde's tactics were effective to an extent, and holy men such as Archbishop Walsh developed a "timely scholarly interest in fine points of Irish grammar and spelling and in techniques of language instruction."[177] The League also declared that "the Souper movement [i.e. influx of Anglicanism into Ireland] in the past did much to kill Irish."[178]

Some nationalists went so far as to claim that the Irish language was the real indicator of a true Irishman, disregarding religion and ancestry. These people tended to be Protestant in religion or Anglican in ancestry, and were seeking entry into a Catholic-Irish nationalist movement from which they felt excluded. Addressing language, Derry Protestant R. Farmer wrote, "Any man who learns a moderate amount of Gaelic may be classed as a Gael at heart, whatever his blood may be: my blood is in all probability a mixture & my wife is at least 1/2 a Gael as her mother is a Catholic."[179] He continued with a justification of race and religion: "As to race, half the Leinster Catholics have Saxon blood, and as to religion we are all just what we were born—these things are really accidents—and the true test is what is a mans (sic) attitude to Ireland."[180] Farmer's views were not uncommon at this time among Protestants who sought not to be left out of their country's movement, but Catholics did not lessen the strength of their movement. Indeed, the nationalist movement did not lose momentum, much to the credit of the Gaelic League, until after Easter 1916.

As the language revival continued, neo-medievalism and de-Anglicization became more and more common as part of the nationalist movement. Poet and author Padraic Pearse looked to the Irish language and culture as essential parts of the Irish identity; their imminent death seemed inevitable, and it was feared that the Irish nation would perish with them.[181] For this reason, nationalists began to attack English customs, phrases, and ideas that intruded into the country. Some nationalists proclaimed that an Irish-speaking Ireland would be "immune to the immoral and irreligious influences carried into Ireland by the English language."[182] It was about this time that Douglas Hyde gave a lecture before the National Literary Society called "The Necessity for De-Anglicizing the Irish Nation."[183] One priest even wrote a pamphlet entitled "Irish or Infidelity—Which?"[184] The attempt was a purging of what DP Moran called "West Britonism."[185] To spread anti-English ideas, Moran established *The Leader*, a weekly Catholic-nationalist paper, in September 1900.[186] West Britonism included "'gutter literature' and the 'imported amusements' offered in Dublin's theatres and music halls."[187] Nationalists even attacked British morals, supporting "the conception of 'the Irish mind' as 'chaste, idealistic, mystical,' sullied only by 'the invading tide of English ideas,' particularly those ideas embodied in 'trashy' periodicals."[188] These efforts were an attempt to rid Ireland of encroaching elements of English culture.

Despite many efforts to reestablish the Gaelic language in Ireland, English prevailed as the primary language, and language became, in the words of John Hogan, "only another point of difference"[189] among Irishmen. In fact, education had a significant role in the spreading of English in pre-Famine Ireland, and pupils continued to achieve high levels of literacy in English.[190] Furthermore, without support from the Catholic Church—whose religious influence in countries such as the United States and Canada, Australia and New Zealand, and India and Africa was based primarily in English—the movement lost a great amount of momentum.[191] The Church could not support the replacement of English by Irish, for by doing so it would be threatening its "Spiritual Empire" in the world for the sake of Irish nationalism. Furthermore, the success of the nationalist movement depended on the use of English; nationalists expressed their hatred of the English language, which they deemed "poisonous" in the English language.[192] As Conor Cruise O'Brien notes, "None felt it necessary to explain why they themselves were using this putatively toxic medium of communication. Nor did *The Leader* itself admit any concern about its own responsibility in distributing poisonous material, week after week, to all its readers."[193] In fact, *The Leader* remained entirely English-speaking throughout its existence, and it only published one or two occasional articles in Gaelic.[194] While it published several articles in 1909 entitled "Is the English language poisonous?"[195] to faith and patriotism, Conor Cruise O'Brien mockingly writes, "If it was poisonous to Faith, the bishops and priests of Ireland must have been poisoning the faithful, for the language of the Catholic Church in Ireland was then English, as it remains today."[196] The Irish language revival was not spreading, and only a few Irish Irelanders, like Conor Cruise O'Brien's mother, actually studied and traveled until they could speak, read, and write the language easily.[197] In terms of language revival, the nationalist effort did not succeed.

At the same time as nationalists were struggling to save the Irish language, others were spreading nationalist propaganda to the people by developing printed journals. Ironically, increased literacy in English allowed Irish nationalists to distribute the "mass literature of nationalism"[198] to the Irish people, advocating the supplanting of English by Gaelic. Furthermore, many members of the Irish Parliament lived in London, and they entered professions such as journalism in order to pay for their stay.[199] The Sullivan brothers published *Nation*, which targeted the Catholic lower-middle class of Irishmen.[200] Publishers Duffy of Dublin and Cameron and Ferguson of Glasgow published popular nationalist literature, and Richard Pigott wrote anti-British papers. In addition, the Fenian United Irishman published a mocking letter from William Butler Yeats regarding Edward VII's visit to Maynooth.[201] *The Freeman's Journal* presented a more lukewarm nationalism and even claimed that religion was a private choice. It claimed that nationalism was a completely separate issue. Not surprisingly, moderate upper-class nationalists read this journal.[202]

While each of these journals contributed to the success of the nationalist movement, *The Leader* was the most widely-read and the most "lively,"[203] according to O'Brien. It has been called "the journalistic flagship of Irish Ireland"[204] for its clear descriptions of the ideal characteristics of the Irish Irelander. The first issue of *The Leader*, founded by journalist and Catholic-nationalist DP Moran, was published on September 1, 1900.[205] It served as the distributor of nationalist news from and to nationalists themselves. Eminent radical nationalists such as Padraic Pearse, O'Brien's father, and William Butler Yeats read, wrote for, and advertised in the journal.[206] Indeed, the Catholic nationalism as defined and expressed by *The Leader* became the national ideal.[207] Because it spoke for itself only, it had more freedom and fewer restrictions on the information it published.[208] For historians, archives of the articles are essential in understanding the national consciousness and the actions and motives of Catholic nationalists.[209]

The Leader gained the approval of the Church for its Catholic outlook and its publication of Catholic ideals.[210] Moran himself, albeit eccentric, was a strong Catholic and a strong nationalist, or in the words of O'Brien, a "thoroughgoing 'Faith and Fatherland' person."[211] Through his journal, he hoped to squelch Protestant power by proposing the trueness of Catholicism; he frequently mentioned the importance of "fear of God" and judgment in the hopes that Protestants would turn from their religion, which he believed was false, in favor of the Catholic religion.[212] For example, in the October 1903 article, "The Philosophy of an Irish Theatre," *The Leader* published, "The Irish people are Christian, they believe in the morality of the Catholic Church, and they will not suffer any attempt to pervert their opinions on such matters, or to misrepresent their attitudes toward such problems [of religion]."[213] It is no wonder that many Catholic priests supported the paper, and that Catholic supporters began to believe that Ireland belonged to them, and that Protestants should only be allowed in if they agreed to be ruled by Catholics.[214]

In addition to declaring the goodness and truth of Catholicism, Moran attempted to produce hatred of irreligious persons and encourage their isolation and exclusion from political life.[215] To do so, he invented insulting, derogatory terms for Protestants and for Catholic Unionists. For example, the word "shoneen"[216] was an

insult that referred to Catholic unionists, or "Castle Catholics."[217]
For Protestants, the term "West Briton"[218] was a mild label that could
only be rescinded if the Protestant studied the Irish language. The
more intense insult was to be called "Sourface,"[219] which referred
to a person with English background and, therefore, genetically-
inherited English ideas, attitudes, and opinions. In addition, the
word "bigot"[220] usually referred to a Protestant. Moran's hatred of
Protestants and distrust of English parliamentarians is a form of
Anglophobia that he tried to spread in the name of his country.[221]
Moran even criticized the Woman's Suffrage movement as a West
British development; he believed, in the words of O'Brien, that
it was part of a "fiendish British conspiracy against the chastity of
Irish womanhood."[222]

The conflict between *The Leader* and Protestantism can be
seen specifically with William Butler Yeats. Yeats frequently read and
contributed to *The Leader*, not for its Catholic identity (indeed, he
was Protestant) but for its efforts to reestablish the Irish cultural
identity through language and literature.[223] For a devoted supporter
of the nationalist literary movement, approval and acceptance by
The Leader, the most widely-read and respected nationalist journal,
was important.[224] Since he could not receive acceptance based on
religion, nationalist acceptance was very important to him. Since
he was not Catholic, creating a super-nationalist identity was important to allow entrance into the nationalist circles. In the words
of his mentor, nationalist John O'Leary, "in Ireland a man must
have either the Church or the Fenians [nationalists] on his side
and you [Yeats] will never have the Church."[225] Moran, however,
disapproved of Yeats' lack of Catholicism and argued that a non-
Catholic was not truly nationalist.[226] Moran demanded that Yeats
"go back to the Gael"[227] and find his place "behind the Gael,"[228]
where he would learn how to be a true Irishman under Catholic
instruction.

At the same time as the literary journals were spreading,
nationalist poets and playwrights were also making their marks
in the world of literature. Poets who studied the Gaelic language
published works in Irish.[229] Other poets, either unable to write

in Gaelic or aware of the dominance of English-speaking Irish-men, wrote in English. They wrote criticizing British actions and glorifying Ireland.[230] Both the Catholic Church and nationalist groups condemned British immorality through plays, theater, and reviews.[231] In an article called "The English Mind in Ireland," *The Leader* claimed, "Most of the heroines of modern British drama are prostitutes."[232] Overall, the renunciation of Britain and the glorification of Ireland in early 20th century prose and poetry contributed positively to the cultural revival. William Butler Yeats' relationship with *The Leader* represents the interaction between religion and nationalism in the cultural arena quite well.[233] *The Leader* wrote attacks on Yeats without directly naming him, but the target was clear:

> He [not named] sometimes writes poetry which no Irishman under-stands, or rather which no Irishman troubles his head to read; he thinks Catholics are superstitious and he believes in spooks himself; he thinks they are priest-ridden and he would like to go back to Paganism; he is a bigot who thinks he is broadminded, a prig who thinks he is cultured; he does not understand Ireland.[234]

Yeats was deemed a West British Sourface attempting to be called a nationalist.[235] The attack was strong, and in fact was too much for some sincere Irish Irelanders. For example, Father J. O'Donovan of Loughrea, who wrote often for *The Leader*, responded gently to the attack, "even Mr. Yeats does not understand us, he has yet to write one line that will strike a chord of the Irish heart."[236] Father O'Donovan wrote about an instance to the contrary: "I have a dainty volume of Mr. Yeats' collected poems. I asked my housekeeper if she saw it. In some confusion she said it was in the kitchen where she had taken it to read one of the poems—*The Ballad of Peter Gilligan*—to a neighbour. 'To tell you the truth, sir, the two of us cried over it.'"[237] Attitudes toward Yeats were often mixed in this way, but *The Leader* was determined to purge nationalism of all traces of Protestantism.

While Yeats endured these attacks on the religious front, culturally he made great nationalist literary contributions. Nevertheless, his productions received mixed reviews as well. In his drama *Cathleen ni Houlihan*, Yeats revived the age-old Cathleen,

nearly lost in ancient poems and folk stories.[238] Through her, he
imparted an irresistible hope for the return to all that had been
loved about Ireland. Some Catholic nationalists saw in *Cathleen ni
Houlihan* a sort of religion, and they believed in it as if it were a
"sacrament" or gospel.[239] In his play Countess Cathleen, she was
"an Irishwoman of exceptional, if eccentric, virtue. Her chastity is
above suspicion."[240] In Yeats' play, in a great nationalist call, Michael
leaves his bride-to-be to follow the call of Ireland, personified as
the Old Woman:

> Old Woman: It is not a man going to his marriage that I look to for
> help.... Michael breaks away from Delia.[241]

Similarly, James Joyce, who grew up in a Catholic-nationalist
world, contributed to this literature movement.[242] Grainne, the
star of James Joyce's drama, was condemned as "the vile woman
of this coarse English play....let the English mind in the future
write plays for itself. We will have none of them."[243] Like Yeats,
however, Joyce did follow cultural revival trends. The editor of
the Penguin Classics edition of *Dubliners* commented on Joyce's
words, "she did not wear a low-cut bodice...the large brooch...an
Irish device"[244] with the following annotation: "The Celtic Revival
of the 1880s onwards encouraged the self-conscious adoption of
the Celtic design in fashions and costume jewellery. Individuals
who espoused the separatist cause and the Irish Ireland movement were often notably puritanical in sexual matters, which may
account for Miss Ivors' modest evening wear."[245] Conor Cruise
O'Brien claims that the character Miss Ivors was modeled after
his own mother, who had "a strong sense of mission about the
language and its culture."[246] Joyce clearly retained the cultural
patterns in his plays, even if the religious overtone left much for
Irish Catholics to desire. O'Brien's mother studied Irish seriously
and even traveled to the Aran Islands until she could speak and
write fluently in Irish.[247] Joyce's story shows how hard it was for a
nationalist to separate from nationalism.[248]

In fact, despite their focus on building a cultural identity,
they had not given up their political goal. Throughout this period,
nationalists had attempted two Home Rule Bills, but each had

been knocked down. The Third Home Rule Bill was finally passed in 1914, but enactment had been postponed upon the outbreak of World War I. War mobilization in 1914 caused an abrupt shift in national focus, and the war took precedence over domestic concerns. Sinn Fein, the most prominent Irish nationalist group today, argues that the Irish people supported the war effort because they had been fooled by the promise of enactment of post-war Home Rule.[249] In fact, the Catholic Church did not oppose the war, and both nationalist and unionist Irishmen enlisted in support of Great Britain. For the first time, nationalists and unionists were on the same side, though the tension still continued.[250] Nationalists, however, did not forget about Home Rule entirely. As implementation of the Third Home Rule Bill was pushed aside again and again, nationalists became frustrated. Finally, in 1916, nationalists, including Padraic Pearse, led the violent Dublin Easter Rising. In the words of Conor Cruise O'Brien,

> Even in the minds of moderate nationalists, in 1914, there must have been an atavistic undercurrent, that could not be all that favourable to Britain. Inside any given Irish nationalist, in the moment of according support to the British war effort, or enlisting in the British Army, there must have been, as it were, a little Christian Brother, screaming to be let out. Two years later, he did get out, and he is still at large.[251]

The Third Home Rule Bill was never implemented, and not until 1920 was it replaced by the Fourth Home Rule Bill, or the Government of Ireland Act. The war had ended the political deadlock, and the nationalists pushed their bill through Parliament. The bill officially extended Home Rule to Ireland and divided the region into Northern Ireland—the Protestant Ulster region that would not be nationalized—and Southern Ireland. Thus, the Catholic-Protestant conflict that had plagued the nationalist movement ended not with compromise, but with division.

Conclusion: Ireland Today

The events at the turn of the 20th century in Ireland were driven by the desire to develop a cultural identity in Ireland, and they reveal the aligned interests of the Catholic Church and political nationalists. The Catholic Church feared for the morality of its people, who were leaving their country and traveling to cities to work in factories, believing that they would become morally corrupt under the harmful influences of an insensitive world away from home. Industrialization was a symbol of British influence, so the Church sought to keep the Irish people in Ireland and discourage emigration. The Catholic Church also wished to maintain its hold on education so that it could further save the religion and morality of the children and young adults of Ireland. To accomplish this ambition, the Church aligned itself with nationalists in support of the development of a stronger national pride.

Initially, nationalists fought for home rule, for Irish control of local affairs. Over time, however, the nationalists discovered that the Irish Unionists and the British Conservatives in the House of Lords would not agree to such a radical proposal immediately. Therefore, while the Home Rule Bill sat amid the standstill of unrelenting opposition, nationalists looked to cultural revival to further strengthen Irish nationalism. Uniting the Irish around their shared heritage and encouraging Irish people to embrace their roots and return with pride to tradition, they encouraged the study and use of the Irish language. While the language movement failed to supplant English with Gaelic, it did remind people of their Irish heritage. More successful was literary nationalism. Publishing plays and poetry and participating in literary battles between news journals, Irish nationalists connected people to their Irish heritage. At no time, however, was the nationalist movement able to successfully solve the inherent conflict. A cultural identity connected to Catholicism could never fully include Protestants.

After the enactment of Home Rule in Ireland in 1920 and the subsequent creation of the Irish Free State in 1922, the nationalist struggle did not end; Anglicization of Ireland continued, and nationalist efforts fought to keep up.[252] Significantly, even though Irish was made the first official language in 1937 in the Irish Constitution, English remained the most widely used language in Ireland.[253] In fact, the *Fianna Fail*, the most influential nationalist group today, even use the second official language in everyday life.[254] Recognizing the unacknowledged failure of the language revival movement, the *Fianna Fail* currently seeks to achieve political reunification of Northern Ireland and Ireland.[255] Since 1922, nationalist struggles have attempted to unite the Catholics in Ireland and Protestants in Northern Ireland.[256] Efforts to achieve reunification and peace still continue today.

[1] Alex Tyrrell, "Paternalism, Public Memory and National Identity in Early Victorian Scotland: The Robert Burns Festival at Ayr in 1844," History 90, no. 297 (2005) p. 42

[2] Tom Garvin, Nationalist Revolutionaries in Ireland: 1858-1928 (New York: Oxford University Press, 1987) pp. 18-19

[3] Ibid., pp. 18-19

[4] Ibid., pp. 18-19

[5] Ibid., pp. 18-19

[6] Conor Cruise O'Brien, Ancestral Voices: Religion and Nationalism in Ireland (Dublin: The University of Chicago Press, 1994) p. 33

[7] Ibid., p. 33

[8] David W. Miller, Church, State, and Nation in Ireland 1898-1921 (Dublin: Richview Press, 1973) p. 1

[9] Garvin, p. 23

[10] Ireland was called "Eire" in Gaelic.

[11] O'Brien, p. 25

[12] Patrick Maume, The Long Gestation: Irish Nationalist Life 1891-1918 (Dublin: Gill & Macmillan Ltd., 1999) p. 10

[13] Garvin, p. 5

[14] Ibid., p. 5

[15] Maume, p. 13

[16] Garvin, p. 28

[17] O'Brien, p. 43

[18] Ibid., p. 43

[19] Garvin, p. 2

[20] Ibid., p. 2

[21] Ibid., p. 2

[22] Maume, p. 10

[23] Garvin, p. 3

[24] Ibid., p. 8

[25] Ibid., p. 5

[26] Ibid., p. 8

[27] Ibid., p. 8

[28] Quoted in Eunan O'Halpin, The Decline of the Union: British Government in Ireland, 1892-1920 (Syracuse: Syracuse University Press, 1987) p. 8

[29] Emmet Larkin, "Church and State in Ireland in the Nineteenth Century," Church History 31, no. 3 (1962) p. 306

[30] Quoted in O'Halpin, p. 9

[31] O'Halpin, p. 9

[32] Ibid., p. 9

[33] Ibid., p. 7

[34] Quoted in John Kendle, <u>Ireland and the Federal Solution: The Debate over the United Kingdom Constitution, 1870-1921</u> (Kingston: McGill-Queen's University Press, 1989) p. 92

[35] O'Halpin, p. 5

[36] Larkin, p. 306

[37] Ibid., p. 306

[38] Ibid., p. 306

[39] Maume, p. 7

[40] Ibid., p. 7

[41] Garvin, p. 12

[42] O'Brien, p. 35

[43] Garvin, pp. 11-12

[44] Ibid., p. 37

[45] Ibid., p. 37

[46] Ibid., p. 7

[47] O'Brien, p. 35

[48] Kendle, p. 105

[49] O'Halpin, p. 6

[50] Kendle, p. 95

[51] Garvin, p. 4

[52] Ibid., p. 23

[53] O'Halpin, p. 2

[54] Ibid., p. 5

[55] Ibid., p. 10

[56] Ibid., p. 7

[57] Larkin, p. 305

[58] Ibid., p. 305

[59] Miller, p. 8

[60] Maume, p. 10

[61] O'Halpin, p. 14

[62] Ibid., p. 14

[63] Miller, p. 1

[64] Ibid., p. 72

[65] Ibid., p. 70

[66] Ibid., p. 73

[67] Ibid., p. 72

[68] Quoted in Ibid., p. 72

[69] Ibid., p. 72

[70] Ibid., p. 18

[71] Ibid., p. 18

[72] Quoted in Ibid., p. 18

[73] Ibid., p. 70

74 Quoted in Ibid., p. 71
75 Quoted in Ibid., p. 72
76 Quoted in Ibid., p. 73
77 Garvin, p. 2
78 Quoted in Miller, p. 1
79 Garvin, p. 1
80 Ibid., p. 1
81 Ibid., p. 11
82 O'Brien, pp. 50-51
83 Ibid., p. 26
84 Larkin, p. 305
85 Miller, p. 1
86 Maume, p. 9
87 Ibid., p. 9
88 O'Brien, p. 51
89 Miller, p. 1
90 Ibid., p. 1
91 Ibid., p. 1
92 Ibid., p. 1
93 Maume, p. 11
94 Ibid., p. 11
95 Garvin, p. 10
96 Ibid., p. 10
97 Maume, p. 10
98 O'Brien, p. 27
99 Ibid., p. 30
100 Maume, p. 11
101 Miller, p. 1
102 O'Brien, p. 72
103 Ibid., p. 72
104 Ibid., p. 73
105 Miller, p. 40
106 Ibid., p. 39
107 Maume, p. 5
108 Miller, p. 39
109 Ibid., p. 40
110 Ibid., pp. 39-40
111 Ibid., p. 42
112 O'Brien, p. 30
113 Ibid., p. 51
114 Ibid., p. 59
115 Ibid., p. 59
116 Miller, p. 42

[117] Ibid., pp. 41-42

[118] O'Brien, p. 41

[119] Ibid., p. 41

[120] Ibid., p. 41

[121] Ibid., p. 43

[122] Ibid., p. 57

[123] Ibid., p. 57

[124] Ibid., p. 57

[125] Ibid., p. 29

[126] Ibid., p. 29

[127] Ibid., p. 29

[128] Miller, p. 80

[129] O'Halpin, p. 22

[130] Garvin, p. 44

[131] Miller, p. 67

[132] Quoted in Ibid., p. 63

[133] O'Brien, p. 41

[134] Garvin, p. 44

[135] Ibid., p. 44

[136] O'Brien, p. 25

[137] Ibid., p. 25

[138] Quoted in Ibid., p. 25

[139] Garvin, p. 41

[140] Ibid., p. 41

[141] O'Halpin, p. 21

[142] Ibid., p. 21

[143] Garvin, p. 43

[144] Ibid., p. 16

[145] Ibid., p. 40

[146] Ibid., p. 40

[147] Ibid., p. 40

[148] Ibid., p. 44

[149] Quoted in Ibid., p. 45

[150] Ibid., p. 44

[151] Ibid., p. 27

[152] Ibid., p. 27

[153] Maume, p. 10

[154] O'Brien, p. 27

[155] Quoted in Maume, p. 9

[156] In the late 19th and early 20th centuries, the term "irreligious" was most broadly applied to all nationalists who were not obedient Catholics, even if they were religious in the sense that they adhered to another religion. Over time, the

term was used more and more frequently to refer to Protestant nationalists.

[157] O'Brien, p. 25
[158] Miller, p. 39
[159] Maume, p. 6
[160] Ibid., p. 6
[161] O'Brien, p. 51
[162] Maume, p. 2
[163] O'Brien, p. 33
[164] Miller, p. 34
[165] Ibid., p. 34
[166] Ibid., p. 34
[167] O'Brien, p. 33
[168] Ibid., p. 32
[169] Miller, p. 39
[170] Ibid., p. 42
[171] Maume, p. 1
[172] Miller, p. 35
[173] Ibid., p. 35
[174] Garvin, p. 27
[175] Miller, p. 41
[176] Quoted in Ibid., p. 41
[177] Miller, p. 36
[178] Quoted in O'Brien, p. 57
[179] Quoted in Miller, p. 40
[180] Quoted in Ibid., p. 40
[181] Garvin, p. 9
[182] O'Brien, p. 88
[183] Miller, p. 35
[184] O'Brien, p. 88
[185] Miller, p. 41
[186] Ibid., p. 41
[187] Ibid., p. 41
[188] Ibid., p. 41
[189] Ibid., p. 40
[190] Garvin, p. 28
[191] O'Brien, p. 88
[192] Ibid., p. 88
[193] Ibid., p. 87
[194] Ibid., p. 86
[195] Ibid., p. 87
[196] Ibid., p. 87
[197] Ibid., pp. 85, 86

[198] Maume, p. 6
[199] Ibid., p. 9
[200] Ibid., p. 5
[201] O'Brien, p. 75
[202] Ibid., p. 43
[203] Ibid., pp. 58-59
[204] Ibid., p. 44
[205] Ibid., p. 34
[206] Ibid., p. 58
[207] Ibid., p. 43
[208] Ibid., p. 37
[209] Ibid., p. 36
[210] Ibid., p. 58
[211] Ibid., p. 32
[212] Ibid., p. 35
[213] Ibid., p. 76
[214] Ibid., p. 35
[215] Ibid., p. 52
[216] Ibid., p. 41
[217] Ibid., p. 41
[218] Ibid., p. 41
[219] Ibid., p. 41
[220] Ibid., p. 49
[221] Ibid., p. 54
[222] Ibid., p. 50
[223] Ibid., p. 38
[224] Ibid., p. 38
[225] Quoted in Ibid., p. 58
[226] Ibid., p. 54
[227] Quoted in Ibid., p. 54
[228] Quoted in Ibid., p. 54
[229] Maume, p. 12
[230] Ibid., p. 12
[231] Ibid., p. 39
[232] Ibid., p. 39
[233] Ibid., p. 6
[234] Quoted in O'Brien, 58
[235] Ibid., p. 57
[236] Quoted in O'Brien, p. 56
[237] Ibid., p. 56
[238] O'Brien, p. 70
[239] Quoted in Ibid., p. 70
[240] Ibid., p. 70

[241] Ibid., p. 70

[242] Ibid., pp. 48-49

[243] Quoted in Ibid., pp. 48-49

[244] Ibid., pp. 48-49

[246] Ibid., p. 44

[247] Ibid., p. 44

[248] Ibid., pp. 48-49

[249] Ibid., p. 94

[250] Ibid., p. 93

[251] Ibid., p. 95

[252] Garvin, p. 11

[253] Ironically, the Constitution was written in English and translated into Irish, but the translated version takes precedent over the original English version if there is ever a discrepancy.

[254] O'Brien, p. 86

[255] Ibid., p. 89

[256] Ibid., p. 41

Works Cited

Garvin, Tom, <u>Nationalist Revolutionaries in Ireland 1858-1928</u> New York: Oxford University Press, 1987

Kendle, John, <u>Ireland and the Federal Solution: The Debate over the United Kingdom Constitution, 1870-1921</u> Kingston: McGill-Queen's University Press, 1989

Larkin, Emmet, "Church and State in Ireland in the Nineteenth Century," <u>Church History</u> 31, no. 3 (1962) pp. 294-306

Maume, Patrick, <u>The Long Gestation: Irish Nationalist Life 1891-1918</u> Dublin: Gill & Macmillan Ltd., 1999

Miller, David W., <u>Church, State, and Nation in Ireland 1898-1921</u> Dublin: Richview Press, 1973

O'Brien, Conor Cruise, <u>Ancestral Voices: Religion and Nationalism in Ireland</u> Dublin: The University of Chicago Press, 1994

O'Halpin, Eunan, <u>The Decline of the Union: British Government in Ireland, 1892-1920</u> Syracuse: Syracuse University Press, 1987

Tyrrell, Alex, "Paternalism, Public Memory and National Identity in Early Victorian Scotland: The Robert Burns Festival at Ayr in 1844," <u>History</u> 90 no. 297 (2005) pp. 42-61

Fred Anderson
*Crucible of War: The Seven Years' War and
the Fate of Empire in British North America, 1754-1766*
New York: Vintage, 2000, pp. 289-291

George Washington had been at war more or less continuously for five years. Now, with the expulsion of the French from the Forks and presumably the restoration of peace to the Virginia frontier, he believed he had done enough [1758]. Although he had told almost no one that he intended to resign if the campaign reached a successful conclusion, he had prepared carefully for his reentry into civilian life. The previous spring he had proposed marriage to the richest and most eligible widow in New Kent County, Martha Dandridge Custis, and she had accepted; they were to be married on January 6. By joining their lands, slaves, and wealth they would position the family (for Martha was already the mother of two small children) well up in the ranks of northern Virginia's planter elite. Shortly after Martha agreed to marry him, Washington had decided to confirm his new standing by seeking election to the House of Burgesses as a representative of Frederick County. The freeholders had elected him to the seat, by a wide margin, in late July, and he would take his place in the House when the winter session began in February. Any interested observer might reasonably have concluded that Washington's military career—inauspiciously begun with with defeat in 1754 and marked thereafter by increasing competence, if not glory—had been no more than a preliminary and perhaps calculated stage in the rise of an unusually ambitious man. But Washington's career as commander of the 1st Virginia Regiment had in fact been much more.

Most of all the war had been a kind of education, in many aspects of life, for a man who had undergone very little formal instruction. Most obviously, his military experience had taught him a variety of technical and practical lessons. In defending the Virginia frontier from 1754 through 1757, he had learned how to make the most of manpower that was never adequate to the task, how to lay out and build forts and blockhouses, organize supply and transport services, dispense military justice, drill and train soldiers, and manage the manifold tasks of administration and paperwork that the service required. He had learned less palpable but equally important skills of command as well: how to earn the respect and maintain the loyalty of his subordinate officers, how to issue clear and concise orders, how to keep his distance, how to control his temper. He had acquired these skills in part by study—he had been an indefatigable reader of military manuals and treatises, devouring everything from Caesar's *Commentaries* to Colonel Humphrey Bland's *Treatise of Military Discipline*—and in part by observing experienced officers in action. He had transcribed the orders issued by the regular officers, Braddock and Forbes and Bouquet, under whom he had served, and studied them carefully. unlike the New Englanders, who had generally recoiled from redcoat discipline and clung the more strongly to their region's contractualist military traditions, Washington had observed how the regulars conducted themselves in order to emulate them. Thus he acquired their attitudes, copied their habits of command, and absorbed their prejudices to the point that he became one of them in virtually every respect but the color of his coat and the provenance of his commission. As fully and as self-consciously as possible, Washington made himself a professional military officer between 1754 and 1758 and learned how to handle regimental affairs with a proficiency not inferior to that of many colonels in the British army.

Ralph Waldo Emerson Prize 2011

CONVIVENCIA IN MEDIEVAL SPAIN:
CULTURAL AND INTELLECTUAL ADAPTATION AND
INTERACTIONS AMONG MUSLIMS, JEWS,
AND CHRISTIANS

Wei Li

Introduction

In the city of Cordoba in the heartlands of southern Spain,
there stands a magnificent mosque known as the Mezquita. It is
hailed as one of finest examples of Arab-Islamic architecture in
the Umayyad style, with its characteristic look of horseshoe arches
that sit piggybacked on one another, in dizzying alternating colors
of red and white and over 1,000 columns of jasper, onyx, marble,
and granite.[1] These columns and the capitals were all reused frag-
ments from the ruins of Gothic churches and Roman buildings
that used to sit in its place.[2] The look of the mosque itself also
holds many echoes of the earlier forms and styles of this land: the
horseshoe arch was used in the indigenous churches of pre-Muslim
Spain and its signature doubled-up arches can be found in Roman
aqueducts, like the one in Merida, not far away.[3] The Mezquita
was held in exalted status, once the second largest mosque in the
Muslim world, and connected directly to the Caliph's palace.[4] After
the capture of the Moorish capital in 1236, it was converted into

---

The author is at Williams College. She wrote this paper as a Junior at
Singapore American School in Singapore, for Rick Bisset's AP European
History course in the 2008-2009 academic year.

a Cathedral by King Ferdinand II of Castile.[5] Today it houses the main church of the diocese of Cordoba in Spain.[6]

The Mezquita of Cordoba is, in a way, an allegory of the history of the Iberian Peninsula from about 711 C.E., when some 10,000 Muslim invaders from North Africa toppled the Visigoth rulers, to 1492 C.E., when the Catholic Monarchs, Ferdinand and Isabella, expelled all the Jews and Moors from the newly-unified Spain in the end of the Reconquista.[7] Though originally a Christian Visigothic church of St. Vincent,[8] it was bought by the first Muslim emir of the Umayyad line, Abd al-Rahman, who began its construction, and in the tradition of his Syrian forefathers, rebuilt the mosque on the site of and with pieces of ancient Roman and Gothic ruins,[9] reflecting the myriad, mixing cultures that resided alongside one another in medieval Moorish Spain. Its eventual conversion back into a cathedral by King Ferdinand heralded the end of the Muslim rule over medieval Spain, with its rich flourishing of sophisticated culture and learning, even while the rest of Europe was mired in the dark ignorance of the Middle Ages. It is to this span of some 800 years that we must return in order to analyze and formulate a conclusion about a single word: convivencia.

In 1948, the famed Spanish cultural historian and philologist Américo Castro proposed a controversial thesis about Spanish identity in his paper, *The Spaniards: an Introduction to their History*.[10] Among its various arguments was the first appearance of the term *convivencia*, or "coexistence." The word itself covers many aspects. It is generally used to describe the period of Muslim rule of the Iberian Peninsula in medieval times. *Convivencia* can alternately refer to the relatively peaceful social "living-togetherness" among the Muslim, Christian, and Jewish communities, the common interplay of cultural and intellectual ideas among these three groups, or the idea that a widespread religious tolerance generally existed among them. This essay will be investigating the second of the three aspects mentioned above as it deems this area most important with regards to its contributions. It will examine the *convivencia* in al-Andalus with regard to the intellectual and cultural interactions, contributions, and adaptations among the different religious groups. To achieve this, this essay will carefully study the background history and the evidence present for the period from Abd al-Rahman's arrival in 755 C.E., to the invasion of the peninsula by the Almoravids in 1090. It will observe the unique environment provided by the *convivencia*—defined for such purposes as "the marked degree of peaceful interaction present among the different religions during this time, which although not a complete 'golden age' of respect, harmony, and tolerance, was quite enlightened compared to other places"—with special regard to the influence and importance of the years of the Caliphate of Cordoba, the *dhimmi* status, the specific achievements of the various religious groups, and entrenchment of Islamic practices— "Arabization"—among the religious minorities. It will conclude that there was a common interplay of cultural and intellectual ideas among the three religious groups and that the unique, rich climate of learning and culture that flourished in al-Andalus at this time was the main reason for such cultural and intellectual adaptation, interaction, and absorption.

Background Information

In 755 C.E., a young man named Abd al-Rahman arrived in the then already Muslim-dominated Iberian Peninsula, also commonly known as "Al-Andalus."[11] He brought with him much political turmoil. Abd al-Rahman was the sole survivor of the massacre of his family, the Umayyads, a dynasty based out of Damascus that had ruled the global Islamic empire—the "House of Islam"—for 100 years.[12] He was the legitimate heir to the Syrian Arabic House of Umayya as well as the son of a Berber tribeswoman, making it easy for him to claim the loyalty of the Berber settlers and soldiers already settled in the fertile region.[13] Rebuffing the emir of al-Andalus's offer of permanent refuge and the hand of his daughter, Abd al-Rahman easily defeated him outside of Cordoba in May of 756 C.E.[14] He established himself as the new emir of the region, although his authority was technically no more than the governor of the westernmost, "backwater" province on the edge of the caliphate, which was now controlled by his enemies the Abbasids, the very rival house that had decimated his line.[15] They had moved the capital of the caliphate from Damascus to Baghdad, away from any traces of Umayyad legitimacy.[16] Although they were, in all probability, undoubtedly disturbed by Abd al-Rahman's reemergence as a viable leader, it is just as likely that they deemed him as good as dead in his permanent "exile" to the Iberian Peninsula—also known variously as Hispania, Iberia, and later al-Andalus—which was at the time a mere frontier outpost of their empire.

The Iberian Peninsula before the Muslim conquest had been much like the rest of Europe in the post-Roman Empire period in the 8th century. Rome had governed the area for about 600 years, beginning around 200 B.C.E.[17] Previously, a long string of Mediterranean settlers and cultures had ruled the land—Phoenicians, Carthaginians, and Greeks.[18] After the fall of Rome and its northern and eastern frontiers, the peninsula was taken over by the Visigoths, infamous for their sack of Rome in 401 C.E.[19] Due to the rather imperfect adoption of Christianity by the Visigoth overlords, paganism was still prominent in the countryside, where the once Romanized rural population had little to do with either their new overlords or Christianity.[20] On the other hand, the Jewish communities that had come with the Romans lived in almost enslaved squalor.[21] The vacuum left behind by the collapse of the Roman civil institutions was far too vast to be filled by the new Visigoth overlords, despite the best efforts of Archbishop Isidore of Seville—a respected but admittedly partisan scholar in the 6th century—to portray them as a regime worthy of succeeding the Romans, most notably in his influential political work, *In Praise of Spain*.[22] Centuries spent battling over the peninsula, first with the Vandals and then among themselves, before establishing themselves as overlords, did not contribute positively to the matter either. The utter political disarray, moral corruption, and decadence of the last Visigoth kings ensured that the region was fragmented and unstable, politically, culturally, and religiously, making it an easy conquest for the Muslims from North Africa, who had always coveted the region, in 711 C.E.[23]

If the Muslim conquest of Iberia signaled the start of the long Muslim reign in the region, spanning about 800 years, then Abd al-Rahman's arrival about 50 years later was the beginning of the great phase of Islamic al-Andalus. Instead of fulfilling his enemies' hopes and spending the rest of his life in embittered exile, this young man, recognized by almost everyone in the outer Islamic provinces as the rightful caliph, established a tenuous rule over most of Iberia over his 30-year reign. He set the groundwork for the golden age of al-Andalus, as the stability of the orderly successions of his descendants brought peace to the lands as well as an immense economic revival and a population boom, among other indications of increasing prosperity. Nowhere was as representative of this golden age as the city of Cordoba—"the ornament of the world" and capital of the Caliphate in al-Andalus.

Cordoba and the Caliphate

The brilliant ornament of the world shone in the West, a noble city newly known for the military prowess that its Hispanic colonizers had brought. Cordoba was its name and it was wealthy and famous and known for its pleasures and resplendent in all things and especially for its seven streams of wisdom [the *trivium* and *quadrivium*] as much as for its constant victories.[24]

These are the words written by the cultured nun Hroswitha of Gandersheim in her glowing account of the capital of the Caliphate, based on her conversations with an emissary sent by caliph Abd al-Rahman III, grandson of his namesake, to the court of Otto I, Holy Roman Emperor, in 955.[25] The city itself symbolized an intellectual opulence that was the result of a rare and widespread meshing of its material and intellectual wealth. This is best represented by the caliphal library, one of the 70 in the city, which contained by some accounts, 400,000 volumes at a time when the largest library in Europe had no more than 400.[26] The literacy rate was also far higher than in other Western countries at the time.[27] This was in part due to the desire of the ruling Umayyads to have Cordoba rival Baghdad in terms of libraries and educational institutions and to be seen as intellectual rivals to the Abbasids. The libraries of Cordoba also contained volumes of crucial traditions of the ancients, including the ones that Hroswitha mentions above, due to their frequent contact with Baghdad, which had made translation of Greek works a prized project.[28] These were long lost to the rest of Europe and unknown still to them in the 10th century;[29] indeed, when Europe rediscovered these classic works at the beginning of the Renaissance, many of the manuscripts they found had come originally through Islamic Spain. Such eager hunger for knowledge and deep-seated desire for Cordoba to rival Baghdad—still under the rule of the Abbasids who had usurped Abd al-Rhaman's family's position—contributed greatly to the rich cultural and intellectual atmosphere of the Caliphate.

The Caliphate of Cordoba was proclaimed in 929 C.E.,[30] when a declaration that had been understood or acknowledged by the rest of the Islamic world was announced for the first time. In every mosque in al-Andalus, the following declaration was read: "Abd al-Rahman III was the true Defender of the Faith, the legitimate caliph of the whole Islamic world, and the religious leader of all Muslims."[31] Essentially, he was pronouncing himself caliph and declaring his lands independent from the Abbasid caliphate at Baghdad. This was largely due to the political chaos that erupted in Baghdad in 909 C.E., when a breakaway group of Shiites—an Islamic sect that saw themselves as descendants of Muhammad's son-in-law, Ali—seized control of the Islamic empire's western provinces and declared their state to be the caliphate in Tunis, not far from al-Andalus.[32] To the Umayyads in Iberia, it was one thing to pay lip service to the far-off Abbasids in Baghdad, but Tunis was closer and the Fatimids (as the new sect called themselves) represented a real threat of rival authority.[33] Thus, the decision was made to declare independence. Although this act triggered many hostile reactions and would eventually return to haunt the fledgling caliphate,[34] those consequences are not within our scope of discussion. What the establishment of the Caliphate does signify is the political strength and unity that al-Andalus possessed at the time. This period of relative political stability played a large role in the thriving cultural and intellectual activity of the region.

This period of the Caliphate of Cordoba was seen by many Muslim writers as the golden age of al-Andalus. It had by far the most advanced agricultural economic sector in all of Europe due to advanced irrigation and food imports from the Middle East.[35] It is not a coincidence that Spanish agricultural and water terminology is filled with words derived from Arabic: *acequias* (irrigation canals), *azudes* (sluices or floodgates), and *acenas* (water mills).[36] Moorish Spain engineered some of Europe's most sophisticated technology at the time for tapping, channeling, and distributing water.[37] With their complex irrigation system, they grew crops introduced from the Islamic East like oranges, lemons, spinach, and watermelon that added greatly to the European diet.[38] As an added benefit, the surplus production freed laborers from farming so that they could focus on learning more specialized crafts, creating an artisan workforce; these manufactured crafts and surplus produce became vital to a burgeoning foreign trade that grew at a tremendous rate.[39] Andalusian traders conducted their commerce across the Mediterranean Sea, which had effectively become a "Muslim lake" with the Muslims controlling land on virtually all sides.[40] One medieval commentator boasted that by the 10th century, "not a single Christian board floated on [the Mediterranean]."[41] Compare this level of economic activity to the stagnant, self-sufficient system of feudalism in place in medieval Europe at the same time. Their flourishing economy gave the Iberian community the economic means to devote time to cultural and intellectual pursuits. Cordoba under the Caliphate grew immensely, to a population of 500,000, and eventually overtook Constantinople in the Byzantine Empire as the largest and most prosperous city in Europe, a clear testament to the region's prosperity under Muslim rule.[42]

Status of Minorities

Having examined the unique conditions and circumstances of al-Andalus at the time that contributed to its flourishing of cultural and intellectual pursuits, we will now proceed to examine the three main religious groups—Muslims, Jews, and Christians—all of whom participated in such pursuits in their own manner. Before we begin discussion of the cultural and intellectual exchange and adoption between them, we must first understand the socio-political status of the minority groups in al-Andalus at the time, which opened up the possibility of creating such an interactive atmosphere.

The status of the Christians and Jews under Muslim rule in al-Andalus during this time was quite different than under Roman or Visigoth rule. Islam offered them a sort of restricted tolerance as second-class citizens, requiring them to pay a special poll tax called a *jizya* for such a privilege (Muslims didn't pay taxes).[43] The Prophet Muhammad had taught that both Christians and Jews were *Ahl al-Kitab*—"People of the Book"—for although they 'unfortunately' followed their own 'mistaken' dogma, they still worshipped the same God of Abraham as the Muslim faithful.[44] The *Quran* itself states, "And dispute ye not with the People of the Book...but say, 'We believe in the revelation which has come down to us and in that which came down to you; our God and your God is One.'"[45]

So while pagans were forcibly converted by the Muslims, Jews and Christians were dealt with separately under the special terms of a *dhimma*, a "pact" or "covenant" between the ruling Muslims and the various 'book' communities that now found themselves in Muslim territory and subject to their laws.[46] The "People of the Book" thus received the status of *dhimmi*, entitling them to limited legal and social rights, including the right to practice their religion and generally participate in much of Muslim social and economic life, with the exceptions of the military and agriculture. They did face a number of imposed regulations, including being forbidden to build new places of worship, toll church bells, and any other public displays of worship,[47] but even Bernard Lewis, a proponent of the view that the modern use of *convivencia* is both ahistorical and apologetic, acknowledged that while *dhimmis* held an inferior status under Islamic rule, their position "was very much easier than that of non-Christians or even of heretical Christians in medieval Europe."[48] This was because *dhimmis* rarely faced martyrdom (at least unwillingly), exile, or forced conversion and were generally free in their choices. And no religious group benefited more from this semi-protected status of *dhimmi* than the Jews.

Jews

The impact of the *dhimmi* status on the Jews and their opinion on Muslim rule was a stark contrast with the Christians. While the Christians were impacted very negatively by the establishment of Muslim rule, as it meant a dramatic decline from the status of the ruling majority to second-class citizen, the Jews' social and political status actually improved.[49] The Jews had been persecuted by the Christian majority in Spain since the 4th century B.C. with Spanish bishops forbidding any interfaith relations or contact. The Visigoths that followed had been fervently anti-Semitic and heaped oppressive legislation on them, outlawing observance of Jewish holy days and circumcision and enforcing these with severe punishments, usually the mutilation of some organ.[50] Thus, it is understandable that the Jews of Iberia were both stunned and delighted by the Muslims' attitude towards them when they arrived in 711, especially in Cordoba where, after gathering their community, the Muslim conqueror "left them in charge...trusting them in preference to the Christians, on account of their hatred and animosity toward the latter."[51] This practice was apparently a general trend, as it is clear in the chronicler al-Makkari's report, "This practice became almost general in the succeeding years, for whenever the Moslems conquered a town, it was left in the custody of the Jews, with only a few Moslems, the rest of the army proceeding to new conquests."[52]

This practice did fit in with the pattern of Muslim conquest in which, unwilling to be encumbered by administration, armies generally left governing to the locals.[53] In Iberia, the Jews were the logical choice as they remained the minority and therefore presented far less of a threat than did the rebellious and resentful conquered Christians.[54] However, this same minority status would also always render the Jews vulnerable and dependent on the whims of the current ruler, whether Muslim or (later) Christian. That said, during the golden age of al-Andalus, the Umayyad rulers were fairly liberal in their treatment of the Jews, although the same cannot be said of later times. Thus, the Andalusian Jews happily took advantage of their elevated status and joined the educated classes as well as the booming commercial environment; they assimilated into the Islamo-Arabic culture of the ruling class all the while preserving their religious, cultural, and linguistic traditions and identity.[55] It was during the time of the Caliphate of Cordoba (929-1030 C.E.) that a creative and highly independent Andalusian Jewish culture began to emerge and flourish. The sheer scope of their accomplishments is reflected in a generous assessment by one historian that "Spanish Jews were the greatest luminaries of Hebrew civilization since Biblical times."[56] The Jewish civilization of al-Andalus produced several luminaries in all fields, from politician to philosopher. Two of these stand out, due to both their personal achievements and the times they represented.

The first luminary was Hasdai ibn Shaprut, a prominent Jewish physician, diplomat, and statesman who lived during the Caliphate, the zenith of al-Andalus. He served as *vizier*, the right-hand man, to both the caliph Abd al-Rahman III and his son, Al-Hakam II.[57] He was the *nasi*, or "prince," of the Spanish Jewry as well as being their secular head, and his rise to power was a major factor in the emergence of an Andalusian Jewish culture. Hasdai acted as the minister of foreign affairs, controlling shipping and customs, negotiating alliances, and receiving envoys.[58] In 949, he served as the head of a delegation representing the caliphate that carried out delicate negotiations with the Byzantine Empire; among the gifts brought by the Emperor's envoys was an original Greek medical work, Dioscorides' *On Medicine*.[59] This was eagerly received as Cordoba had been reliant on Baghdad for Arabic translations of Greek manuscripts due to the dearth of Greek readers in Europe.[60] Hasdai was the one who organized the translation of this valued text and being a highly gifted physician and stylist, reportedly even had a hand in crafting the final Arabic version. This translation into Arabic enabled this important work to be shared in the Arab world and later, medieval Europe, but it was doubly significant in that it signified a further symbolic claim of independence of Cordoba from Baghdad,[61] in a time when general Andalusian self-assurance and self-realization began to surface across the kingdom.[62] He also engineered another symbolic gesture of independence, this time among his own Jewish community, by declaring that Andalusian Jewry would mark its own new moons and holy days rather than following the lead of the goan, the leader of the traditional seat of Jewish authority situated in Baghdad.[63] Hasdai's participation in these events demonstrated his brilliance as a key Jewish figure of his age.

The second luminary was Samuel ha-Nagid, who came to prominence in the First Taifa Period from about 1031 to 1090. The Cordoba Caliphate had effectively collapsed in 1031, when the capital itself was sacked by Berber mercenaries.[64] The previously politically strong and unified al-Andalus broke up into small, independent states called taifas, which fought constantly among themselves.[65] In addition to being the grand *vizier* of King Badis of Granada, Samuel ha-Nagid was also the leader of the military forces making his power unmatched by any other medieval Jew.[66] Many Muslim rival states and Granadans alike were unhappy that Granada's military answered to a Jew and that this Jew was Badis's most powerful courtier. "Turn your eyes to other countries and you will find the Jews are outcast dogs. Why should you alone [Granada] be different."[67] Yet although they continued to begrudge his faith, even they conceded Samuel's greatness, claiming that, "This cursed man was a superior man, although God did not inform him of the right religion."[68] Samuel proclaimed himself "the David of my age." Under his leadership, Granada won bold victories over rival Muslim states, even defeating the powerful state of Seville, expanding its influence and prestige.[69] His military

success showered him in glory and at the same time, it protected
Granada's Jewish community, as Samuel was also *nagid*, the civic
leader of the Jewish community appointed by the Muslims.[70]
Historian Chris Lowney says of Samuel ha-Nagid, "This courtier
and poet called the David of his Age may well have been the most
extraordinarily accomplished Jew not only in Spain but anywhere
in medieval Christendom, and one of the most accomplished of
any era in European history."[71]

Samuel's influence was not restricted to the battlefield.
Among his many accomplishments, he was also the first poet and
founding father of the new Hebrew poetry. In fact, his poetry
remains today the most visible cornerstone of a crucial chapter
in Hebrew poetry known as the Golden Age.[72] In part due to
his influence and in part due to their exile from the conquered
Cordoba, the Jewish intellectuals embraced their mother tongue
and transformed it back once again into the language of a living,
vibrant, secular poetry, transcending the limited devotional and
theological uses it had been confined to.[73] This new Hebrew poetry
was metered and rhymed like the Arabic poetry it was modeled
after, was open to non-religious themes, and often contained wit
and paradoxes (which quickly became favorites) that older religious
poetry had lacked.[74] This revolution spurred on the development of
Jewish literature and it was during the First Taifa Period with Jewish
literature in full bloom that many masterpieces were produced.[75]
This transformation of the use of Hebrew in poetry was heavily
influenced by the Muslim's versatile use of Arabic, which was both
the sacred language of the *Quran* and the sensuous language of
love poetry. Ironically, it was also this versatile use of Arabic and
the power and elegance that it carried that attracted the other
religious minority in al-Andalus during Islamic rule—Christians.

Christians

We have already mentioned that the Muslim conquest of Hispania affected the Christians negatively as they were forced from the elevated status of the ruling class to that of second-class citizens. Yet this change was reality and in time, the Christian community adapted to their new surroundings and rulers. However, there were certain stubborn pockets of resistance from a small but highly visible group of Christians, such as Paul Alvarus, who lived in Cordoba in the mid-9th century and observed with horror the growing Arabization of the Christian communities:

> The Christians love to read the poems and romances of the Arabs; they study the Arab theologians and philosophers, not to refute them but to form a correct and elegant Arabic. Where is the layman who now reads the Latin commentaries on the Holy Scriptures, or who studies the Gospels, prophets or apostles? Alas! All talented young Christians read and study with enthusiasm the Arab books; they gather immense libraries at great expense; they despise the Christian language as unworthy of attention. They have forgotten their own language. For every one who can write a letter in Latin to a friend, there are a thousand who can express themselves in Arabic with elegance, and write better poems in this language than the Arabs themselves.[76]

These transformations that Alvarus was so disgusted by were part of a larger trend of assimilation into Islamic culture by the Christian communities. Firstly, the number of conversions to Islam was growing rapidly, many from the once dominant Christians, resulting in an expansion of the Muslim population. When the Muslims had invaded Iberia in 711, there were only 20,000 or 30,000 Muslims among more than 5 million Christians.[77] However, by the turn of the millennium, Iberia was at least 80 percent Muslim.[78] Many of those lost to Islam were the children of mixed marriages, because even if the Christian brides did not convert and their children grew up speaking their mother tongue—the curious old vernacular of Hispania that was no longer Latin yet still without a name at the time of Alvarus—the children were inevitably raised as Muslims.[79] The most prominent examples of such children were the Umayyad princes themselves, who were often fair-haired and quite visibly their mothers' sons, descended from both the caliphs of old of Arabia and Syria and the old Christian families of Iberia.[80] The other half of the reason for this growing trend of Arabization among Christians had nothing to do with religion and everything to do with secular culture and the language that accompanied it.

The people of old Hispania had spoken Latin in the days of the Roman Empire, but that had evolved over the years until it had become an unnamed language of its own. Latin existed only in religious texts and it was this tradition of commentaries on the Scriptures that the young people of the Christian communities were now abandoning in favor of Arabic. The contrast between these two languages could not be greater. Like Hebrew before Samuel ha-Nagid, Latin had become stagnant and dead: people no longer spoke it in the streets, nor did they use it in poetry or literature. It had become strictly a religious language. Arabic on the other hand was both the language of Islamic prayer and the one that allowed Abd al-Rahman to express his loneliness in exile in an ode to his native palm tree.[81] Arabic was still what Latin and Hebrew had been centuries ago, a language both religious and secular that sparkled with vigor and life and allowed men to say, read, and write of all the thousands of things that lay outside of religion—philosophy, songs, and poetry among others. Most of the Christian community embraced it eagerly, feeling like the Jews that the adoption of Arabic was in no way a betrayal of their faith. Indeed, eventually all of the Christian liturgy—the Gospels, the Prophets, the Apostles—would also exist in Arabic[82] and scholars of all three religions would study it in this common language shared by them. However, the Christians were different from the Jews in that the Jews were used to adapting to others' cultures in order to survive. The Christians still had a core group of radicals, including Alvarus, who resisted the mixing of religions and cultures and rejected the conversions in these as they thought these would prove to be disastrous for their community's future.[83] The most famous action taken by these radicals was the martyr movement that began in Cordoba in 855 by the "Mozarab martyrs."[84] One by one, over the span of a decade, a group of some 50 Christians, both male and female, some with Muslim heritage—two of the

women, Maria and Flora, were children of mixed marriages[85]—
publicly and conspicuously denounced Islam and the Prophet
Muhammad:

> Now hand down the sentence, multiply your cruelty, be kindled with
> complete fury in vengeance for your prophet. We profess Christ to be
> truly God and your prophet to be a precursor of antichrist.[86]

Although the Muslim rulers (then still the Emirate of Cordoba)
were fairly lenient with regards to doctrine and especially Christians, the one single intolerable offense that was most certainly
punished with capital punishment was blasphemy of the Prophet.[87]
All were beheaded. The emir tried to pressure and dissuade the
Christians from attempting such actions through less severe means:
churches were demolished, pensions withheld, and taxes raised.[88]
The opinion of Cordoba's Muslim authorities on the martyr movement is clearly reflected in the reaction of one court official to
a tirade by Eulogius, last of the martyr movement and its leader:

> If stupid and idiotic individuals have been carried away to such lam-
> entable ruin, what is it that compels you...to commit yourself to this
> deadly ruin, suppressing the natural love of life? Hear me, I beseech
> you, I beg you, lest you fall headlong to destruction. Say something
> in this hour of your need, so that afterwards you may be able to
> practice your faith.[89]

Fortunately, these cases proved to be the exception rather than the
rule. Most Cordobans, both Christian and Muslim, viewed these
"Mozarab martyrs" as wild-eyed, out-of-control radicals. Although
they would eventually receive very good press (Eulogius was later
made a Saint),[90] their actions did little to stem the embrace of Islam and subsequent tide of conversions. Assimilation had already
begun taking place at the highest levels of Christian society, within
the clergy and even the Church hierarchy.[91] Ironically and tellingly,
after the fall of Muslim rule in Iberia, the group that would be the
most resistant to any kind of reform was the Arabized Christians
of Cordoba—the "Mozarabs."[92]

The term "Mozarab" originally meant "wanna-be Arab"[93]
and was used as a derogatory term, most probably by the radicals
that Alvarus belonged to, to refer to Christians who embraced

Arabic and Islamic culture. However, the name stuck and evolved to refer to all Christians living under Muslim rule and became a symbol of the endurance of Christianity alongside Islam.[94] After the fall of Islam in Spain, the term Mozarab referred to the group of Iberian Christians who had adopted elements of Arabic culture and language, followed their own Mozarabic rite (which was the conserved Visigothic rite of Mass), and used the Mozarabic language—the collective name of the set of closely-related languages that were the early stages of the development of Romance languages in Iberia (Spanish and Portuguese).[95] Today, there is still a thriving community of 1,300 Mozarab families in Toledo, all of whom can trace their ancestry back to the ancient Mozarabs of al-Andalus.[96]

Conclusion

This essay has examined the adaptation of the religious minorities to Islamic rule in al-Andalus, specifically the cultural and intellectual aspects. It has covered their background history to better understand the reasons and motives for certain actions. The various instances of cultural exchange and absorption, like the Arabization of Jews and Christians and the evolution of Hebrew poetry, among different religious groups have been explored as well as specific achievements pertaining to different religions.

But perhaps there is one last thing to mention in order to comprehend the captivating culture of al-Andalus and the interactions of its diverse people. Among the most lasting of the influences of the native Iberians—Christians and Jews—on their Muslim rulers was the invention of "ring songs."[97] The singing of songs was a treasured art and widely cultivated by the Andalusians. The origins of these "ring songs" can be traced as far back as the Mozarab martyrs in the mid-9th century as there is ample evidence that songs in vernacularized and part-Romanized Arabic had been sung alongside Arabized Romance for at least that long.[98] These "ring songs" were a kind of song that linked each stanza in continuous "rings" using highly complex rhyme schemes.[99] What was unique about these songs, however, was the simple little refrain to be repeated after each stanza.[100] These refrains were the music of the streets, sung by women in a cheeky vernacular. Thus, the brilliant synthesis of cultures is presented once again, similar to the red and white horseshoe arches of the Mezquita. The refined poetry of the Muslim courts intertwined with the vivacious voices of the women who sang their refrain in Mozarabic—the mother tongue of the native Christian Iberians—reflecting once more the rich tradition of cultural and intellectual adaptations and interactions among religious groups in al-Andalus. Alas, that glorious golden world is lost to us today, although one can still catch fleeting glimpses of it: inside the Mezquita of Cordoba, lost among its dizzying colors; within the splendors of the Alhambra in Granada, among the temples of water shaded with slender, swaying myrtle trees; and lastly, in the echoes of a vanished world in the words of Spaniards every time they utter a wish, for their idiom *Ojalá* is derived from the familiar Arabic phrase that still rolls off the tongues of the descendants of the Muslims of al-Andalus and their brethren: *En shaa Allah*, "If God wills..."

References

[1] Carlos Fuentes, <u>The buried mirror: reflections on Spain and the New World</u> (Boston: Houghton Mifflin, 1999) p. 53

[2] Maria R. Menocal, <u>The Ornament of the World: how Muslims, Jews, and Christians Created a Culture of Tolerance in Medieval Spain</u> (Boston: Little, Brown, 2002) p. 60

[3] Ibid., p. 60

[4] Ibid., p. 60

[5] Chris Lowney, <u>A Vanished World: Muslims, Christians, and Jews in Medieval Spain</u> (New York: Oxford University Press, 2006) p. 193

[6] "Cordoba Spain, the Mezquita Cordoba Mosque," <u>Andalucia information, tourism holiday destinations, accommodation, property, travel and culture, Andalucia Spain</u> (18 May 2009) <http://www.andalucia.com/cities/cordoba/mosque.htm>

[7] Menocal, p. 49

[8] "Cordoba Spain, the Mezquita Cordoba Mosque"

[9] Ibid., p. 60

[10] "Américo Castro," <u>Encyclopaedia Britannica</u> (2009) Encyclopaedia Britannica Online (18 May 2009) <http://www.britannica.com/EBchecked/topic/98815/Americo-Castro>

[11] Menocal, p. 6

[12] Ibid., p. 5

[13] Ibid., p. 8

[14] Ibid., p. 8

[15] Ibid., p. 8

[16] Ibid., p. 8

[17] Ibid., p. 24

[18] Ibid., p. 25

[19] Ibid., p. 25

[20] Ibid., p. 25

[21] Ibid., p. 25

[22] Ibid., p. 26

[23] Ibid., p. 26

[24] Ibid., p. 32

[25] Ibid., p. 32

[26] Ibid., p. 33

[27] Ibid., p. 33

[28] Ibid., p. 34

[29] Ibid., p. 34

[30] Ibid., p. 80

[31] Ibid., p. 81

[32] Ibid., p. 82

[33] Ibid., p. 83

[34] Ibid., p. 83

[35] Lowney, p. 67

[36] Ibid., p. 67

[37] Ibid., p. 67

[38] Ibid., p. 67

[39] Ibid., p. 67

[40] Ibid., p. 68

[41] Ibid., p. 68

[42] Tertius Chandler, <u>Four Thousand Years of Urban Growth: an Historical Census</u> (Lewiston, New York, U.S.A.: St. David's University Press, 1987)

[43] Lowney, p. 60

[44] Menocal, p. 72

[45] Lowney, p. 48

[46] Menocal, p. 72

[47] Ibid., p. 73

[48] Bernard Lewis, <u>The Jews of Islam</u> (Princeton: Princeton University Press, 1984) p. 62

[49] Lowney, p. 95

[50] Ibid., p. 26

[51] Ibid., p. 96

[52] Ibid., p. 96

[53] Ibid., p. 96

[54] Ibid., p. 96

[55] Menocal, p. 85

[56] Lowney, p. 96

[57] "Jews in Muslim Spain," <u>History Resource Center</u> Thomson Gale, Khoo Teck Puat Library, Singapore (12 January 2009) <http://galenet.galegroup.com/servlet/History/>

[58] Menocal, p. 80

[59] Ibid., p. 89

[60] Ibid., p. 89

[61] Ibid., p. 90

[62] Ibid., p. 90

[63] Ibid., p. 90

[64] Ibid., p. 100

[65] Ibid., p. 103

[66] Lowney, p. 97

[67] Ibid., p. 97

[68] Ibid., p. 97

[69] Ibid., p. 97

[70] Ibid., p. 99

[71] Ibid., p. 95

[72] Menocal, p. 106

[73] Ibid., p. 109

[74] Hillel Halkin, "Hebrew Poets in Old Spain,"
Commentary 124 (2007) pp. 46-52 History Resource Center
Thomson Gale, Khoo Teck Puat Library, Singapore (10 May
2009) Keyword: Medieval Spain

[75] "Jews in Muslim Spain"

[76] Menocal, p. 66

[77] Lowney, p. 63

[78] Ibid., p. 63

[79] Menocal, p. 67

[80] Ibid., p. 67

[81] Ibid., p. 68

[82] Ibid., p. 69

[83] Ibid., p. 71

[84] Lowney, p. 58

[85] Ibid., p. 58

[86] Ibid., p. 58

[87] Menocal, p. 70

[88] Lowney, p. 59

[89] Ibid., p. 59

[90] Menocal, p. 71

[91] Ibid., p. 69

[92] Ibid., p. 69

[93] Ibid., p. 69

[94] Ibid., p. 69

[95] "Mozarab. Who is Mozarab? What is Mozarab? Where
is Mozarab? Definition of Mozarab. Meaning of Mozarab."
Knowledgerush (18 May 2009) <http://knowledgerush.com/
kr/encyclopedia/Mozarab/>

[96] Ibid.

[97] Menocal, p. 126

[98] Ibid., p. 128

[99] Ibid., p. 127

[100] Ibid., p. 127

Annotated Bibliography

Abate, Mark T., ed., "Christian-Muslim Relations in Medieval Spain," History Resource Center Thomson Gale, Khoo Teck Puat Library, Singapore, 12 January 2009 <http://galenet. galegroup.com/servlet/History/>
   This is a viewpoint essay examining if the word convivencia (coexistence) can be used to describe Christian-Muslim relations in medieval Spain. This was very helpful as it presents a key point from opposing sides and provides much insightful evidence, mostly on the more negative side, which is less covered in other sources.

"Abd-Al-Rahman, III," Historic World Leaders Farmington Hills, MI: Gale Research, 1996, History Resource Center Thomson Gale, Khoo Teck Puat Library, Singapore, 24 March 2009. Keyword: Muslim Spain
   This is a pretty detailed biography of Abd al-Rahman III, the Andalusian leader who proclaimed the Caliphate of Cordoba. This source was used to cross-reference certain facts from other sources.

"Américo Castro," Encyclopaedia Britannica 2009, Encyclopaedia Britannica Online, 18 May 2009 <http://www. britannica.com/EBchecked/topic/98815/Americo-Castro>
   This is an encyclopedia article about Américo Castro. It was mainly used to provide information about the paper he wrote regarding convivencia.

Chandler, Mario A., "The Moors of Spain," Wow.UAB. edu The University of Alabama at Birmingham, 12 Jan. 2009 <http//wow.uab.edu/spain/show.asp?durki=29701>
   This is the personal site of a professor from the University of Alabama. It gives a good overview of the rise and fall of the Moorish empire and is light and easy to read.

Chandler, Tertius, Four Thousand Years of Urban Growth: an Historical Census Lewiston, New York, U.S.A.: St. David's University Press, 1987
   The only information taken from this book is the fact about Cordoba's growth in population in relation to Constantinople.

Collins, Roger, " Christians in Al-Andalus, 711-1000," The English Historical Review 118 (2006) pp. 468-470 History Resource Center Thomson Gale, Khoo Teck Puat Library, Singapore, 23 March 2009, Keyword: al-Andalus
This was a review of a work by another author on this topic. The article provided little information and what was provided was very basic and often mentioned in other sources.

"Convivencia in Medieval Spain: A Brief History of an Idea: Religion Compass," 02 Apr. 2009 <http://www.blackwell-compass.com/subject/religion/article_view?article_id =reco_articles_bpl119>
This is an abstract on a paper about convivencia. It was used to cross-reference facts on Americo Castro from a previous source.

"Cordoba," Spanish-Living.com 12 January 2008 <http://www.spanishliving.com/regional/Andalucia_Cordoba.php>
Cordoba was a highly important city in Muslim Spain and this tourist attraction site gives some good background information on the period. The most helpful part was the list of several places of interest in the city, most with a historic connection to medieval Spain under the Moors.

"Cordoba Spain, the Mezquita Cordoba Mosque," Andalucia information, tourism holiday destinations, accommodation, property, travel and culture, Andalucia Spain 18 May 2009 <http://www.andalucia.com/cities/cordoba/mosque.htm>
This was a tourism article on the Mezquita, and it provided a background history, descriptions, and ticket prices. This was used to augment existing information on this topic.

"Europe and Islam: The Centuries of al-Andalus," The Economist 353 (1999) p. 32 History Resource Center Thomson Gale, Khoo Teck Puat Library, Singapore, 23 March 2009, Keyword: al-Andalus
This is an article in The Economist. It covers more modern aspects of Muslim-Christian relations in Spain, like the Madrid bombs. It was not used due to the difference in time period, but is an interesting look at change over time for this essay.

Fuentes, Carlos, <u>The Buried Mirror: Reflections on Spain and the New World</u> Boston: Houghton Mifflin, 1999
This book provides a detailed account of Spain's culture and history from medieval to modern times and also examines its impact on the New World. The parts on Moorish Spain are very elaborate and thorough and the color pictures are a plus, but the parts on Latin America were not relevant to this essay.

Halkin, Hillel, "Hebrew Poets in old Spain," <u>Commentary</u> 124 (2007) pp. 46-52 <u>History Resource Center</u> Thomson Gale, Khoo Teck Puat Library, Singapore, 10 May 2009. Keyword: medieval Spain
This was an article on Hebrew poetry and poets in al-Andalus. It was very helpful with regard to the sections on the revolution in Hebrew poetry, as it provided specific examples.

"Islam in Spain and Western Europe," <u>The Muslim Almanac</u> Farmington Hills, Michigan: Gale Research, 1996, <u>History Resource Center</u> Thomson Gale, Khoo Teck Puat Library, Singapore, 8 April 2009, Keyword: Muslim Spain
This is an article on the evolution of Islam during different periods of European history. It has some good information and covers topics that are not touched on in this essay like the Christian conquest of Muslim Spain. Overall, this is a very comprehensive look at Islam in Europe.

"Islamic History in Arabia and Middle East," <u>Islamicity. com—Islam & The Global Muslim eCommunity</u> 02 May 2009 <http://www.islamicity.com/Mosque/IHAME/Ref4.htm>
This is a website dedicated to Islamic History. Its sections on al-Andalus have some good information, especially on technological and scientific advancements, but most of this information was not mentioned in this essay.

"Jews in Muslim Spain," <u>History Resource Center</u> Thomson Gale, Khoo Teck Puat Library, Singapore, 12 January 2009 <http://galenet.galegroup.com/servlet/History/>
This article focuses specifically on the rise and fall of the fortunes of the Jews in medieval Spain. It was helpful in providing specific details about the Jews that other sources may have missed, especially specific details about Jewish literature.

Lewis, Bernard, <u>The Arabs in History</u> Oxford: Oxford University Press, 2002

The only information used from this book was about the dhimmi status and the choices the dhimmi had under it. It is by a renowned expert in the field though, so the book should be quite comprehensive.

Lewis, Bernard, <u>The Jews of Islam</u> Princeton: Princeton University Press, 1984

The only information used from this book was Lewis's quote on the status and treatment of dhimmi in al-Andalus in comparison with the rest of Europe at the time. Again, it should be a comprehensive look at Jews throughout Islamic history, as it is one of Lewis's fields of expertise.

Lowney, Chris, <u>A Vanished World: Muslims, Christians, and Jews in Medieval Spain</u> New York: Oxford University Press, 2006

This book was one of the two main sources of information for this essay. The author covers the period from 711 to 1492 very thoroughly and although firmly in the camp of convivencia, he also records the darker ironies of the time. He is especially thorough in his information on the situation of the Jews in al-Andalus and Samuel ha-Nagid.

Menocal, Maria R., <u>The Ornament of the World: how Muslims, Jews, and Christians Created a Culture of Tolerance in Medieval Spain</u> Boston: Little, Brown, 2002

This book was the other main source of information for this essay. The author stresses the intellectual and cultural achievements of the time and states that the Renaissance was strongly foreshadowed by the intellectual climate of Muslim Spain. She is very much in support of the view that there was a convivencia present in al-Andalus during this time and presents ample evidence to back this claim up.

"Mozarab. Who is Mozarab? What is Mozarab? Where is Mozarab? Definition of Mozarab. Meaning of Mozarab," <u>Knowledgerush</u> 18 May 2009 <http://knowledgerush.com/kr/encyclopedia/Mozarab/>

This website covers all the basic knowledge on Mozarabs, including their language, religious rites, and a brief history. This source was used in this essay with regards to anything about the Mozarabs.

Pepin, Paulette L., "Conflict and Coexistence: Archbishop Rodrigo and the Muslims and Jews of Medieval Spain," The Historian 68 (2006) pp. 890-892, History Resource Center Thomson Gale, Khoo Teck Puat Library, Singapore, 23 March 2009, Keyword: Muslim Spain

This is a book review on the book named in the title. This source was not helpful, as it contained more opinions and very little information. What information there was pertained to a different time period.

Chris Bellamy
Absolute War
New York, Vintage Books, 2007, pp. 388-389

In the Spring [1942], 300,000 survivors of the terrible first winter [in Leningrad] began a massive clearing-up operation. Once the snow and ice thawed, the million tonnes of refuse that had accumulated during the winter would become a health hazard. Enormous efforts were made to restore and maintain morale, and to reintroduce a semblance of normality after a winter in which nearly a million might have died. The Soviet authorities also tried to project an image of normality to the rest of the country, and its allies. To convince the Leningraders, the country, the allies and the Germans that Leningrad was unbowed, they hit upon a wonderfully Russian, superbly flamboyant piece of psychological warfare. To stage and broadcast around the world a performance of Shostakovich's new Seventh Leningrad Symphony, which had first been staged far away in central Asia. The score was flown into the besieged city in late June. After six weeks of rehearsal, on 9 August, the Leningrad Philharmonic opened for the performance. There were some lights in chandeliers although the windows were all boarded up with plywood. [Soviet] Lieutenant General of Artillery Govorov, commanding the Leningrad Front, was there in his best uniform, with Kuznetsov, the Party Secretary. Many soldiers and sailors had tickets, and they wore uniform, but everyone else was in their best suit or silk dress. As the chords, like workmen hammering to construct a vast edifice, became louder, in a slow but inexorable build-up of strength and intensity, [German] General Friedrich Ferch, Eighteenth Army's Chief-of-Staff, started getting reports that his troops were listening on the radio. The performance was being relayed across the Soviet Union and by short-wave radio to the rest of Europe and the United States. The Germans later banned the symphony from being played in any territory they occupied. But for now, Ferch sensed an opportunity. He ordered his long-range artillery to zero in on the Philharmonic.

But Govorov had anticipated him. The siege of Leningrad was very much an artillery battle and the Germans knew the whereabouts of any significant buildings in the city. Their bombardment timetable had always targeted people who might be going to the theatre. However, the Russians had always been very good gunners, and Govorov, a specialist in counter-battery fire—silencing the enemy's artillery with your own—knew where the German batteries were. As the majestic symphony played on, a massive and precisely targeted Russian artillery strike paralysed the German guns. There is no doubt about this. Ferch ordered the initial German strike, but all the witnesses—and the elite of Leningrad were all there—confirm that no German shells landed anywhere near the concert hall. As the entire orchestra in the Philharmonic joined in, building the volume of the symphony, other parts of the wider 'orchestra', Leningrad's guns, joined in too. Land-based artillery, and the grey Baltic fleet battleships, their fire superbly directed, belched shell at the German positions. The moral and physical components of a nation's soul and fighting power fused in harmony, and the German guns were silenced...

Ralph Waldo Emerson Prize 2012

MATTEO RICCI AND THE JESUIT MISSION
IN CHINA 1583-1610

Caitlin Lu

Abstract

This essay considers the question: What strategies did Matteo Ricci (1552-1610) employ in his mission to spread Catholicism in China, and how effective were they? Matteo Ricci was an Italian Jesuit scholar and priest who entered China in 1583 to lead the Jesuit missionary movement. After mastering the Chinese language and the Confucian classics, he became the first foreigner allowed by the Ming Emperor into the Forbidden City in Peking. He died there in 1610 and was the first non-Chinese to be officially allowed burial in the capital city, an immense honor to this day. This essay will document Ricci's pioneering work in bridging Chinese and Western culture, critically analyze his strategy of evangelism, and conclude that while he largely failed in his proselytizing mission, his secular and spiritual works hold lasting significance in China and the outside world. They represent the highest form of scholarship, scientific exchange and cross-cultural understanding. In short, this remarkable East-West scholar succeeded in opening China to the West and vice-versa as no man has done before or after. His distinctively humanistic legacy endures four centuries after his death, as strongly in China as it does in Europe.

The author is a Freshman at Stanford. She was a Senior at the Chinese International School in Hong Kong, when she wrote this paper for Mr. Christopher Caves' IB Higher Level History course in the 2010/2011 academic year.

Introduction

Matteo Ricci (1552-1610) was a brilliant and learned Italian scholar-priest who led the Jesuit missionary movement in China at the end of the 16th century. He was a formidable pioneer, bridging Chinese and Western culture through Jesuit proselytism. Although he largely failed in his evangelical mission, his secular and spiritual works hold lasting significance in China and the outside world. A remarkable train of events inspired this astonishing man to leave Italy, serve in Goa and Macao, and spend the last quarter century of his life as Superior of the Jesuit mission in China. The path of his life, and his impact on the Eastern Hemisphere in particular, is fascinating to analyze.

The year 2010 marks the 400th anniversary of Ricci's death. Celebrations were held in Macerata, his birthplace, and in Rome, where Pope Benedict XVI hailed Ricci as "a Jesuit endowed with extraordinary cultural and intellectual gifts, and a daring and intelligent messenger of Christ's Gospel...in China."[1] The most elaborate festivities, however, took place across China: in Beijing, where he lived for the last decade of his life and is buried; and in Macao, Zhaoqing, Nanchang, Nanjing and Shanghai, places where he lived, worked and left an enduring legacy. Thousands of Chinese each year make the pilgrimage to the Zhalan Cemetery in Beijing to pay their respects to the man they call Li Madou Xi Tai, or "The Scholar from the West."[2]

The Chinese revere Matteo Ricci, and many consider him the foreigner who did the most to open up China to the Western world and vice-versa. In the fall of 2009, the official Xin Hua News Agency wrote that Ricci was "beloved by all Chinese—Catholics and non alike. He is a 'model of exchange between East and West'...a pioneer seeking a common basis for dialogue and scientific and cultural exchange. With his extraordinary, timeless cultural and theological talent, he indicated an alternative route of incorporation of culture and science for all."[3] Westerners similarly laud his life and work. According to Sinologist Wolfgang Franke, Ricci was "the most outstanding cultural mediator between China and the West of all time."[4] Historian and Ricci biographer Jonathan Spence experienced Ricci's impact first-hand:

> From the first moment I went to China as a student, the one Chinese name of a Westerner that I found recognized by everyone was Li Madou, Matteo Ricci. To say I was interested in Li Madou evoked smiles and nods all over China. This Italian Jesuit, who went to China in 1583, has a kind of special resonance in the hearts of the Chinese even now...a remarkable tribute to one particular missionary.[5]

As a testimony to his stature, Ricci became the first non-Chinese visitor to be allowed entry into the Forbidden City in 1601, by the Ming Emperor Wan Li. Wan Li was so impressed with Ricci's vast intellect and command of the Chinese classics that he provided lifelong housing and a generous stipend for Ricci and his mission. He then accorded Ricci the highest tribute by permitting his body to be buried in Peking, the first such honor for any foreigner.

Ricci's intellectual prowess and scholarly achievements are legendary. Schooled in the Jesuit tradition, he mastered mathematics, astronomy, philosophy, geography and cartography, in addition to the Catholic canon. He studied classical Chinese to the point where he could converse intelligently with the most accomplished Chinese scholars and literati, who formed the pinnacle of Ming Dynasty society. His command of Chinese was so great that he translated the Confucian classics, *The Four Books*, into Latin, and co-translated six books of Euclid's *Elements* into Chinese.[6] He devised the first Portuguese-Chinese dictionary, inventing his own system of romanization. He developed and taught a special mnemonic memory system, which enabled him to memorize voluminous amounts of information in Latin, Italian, Portuguese, Spanish and Chinese. In addition, he produced many world maps, some of enormous scale and complexity, with full annotations in Chinese. He did this intensive intellectual work while tirelessly endeavoring to spread Catholicism and the revelations of the Gospel across Confucian China.

Education

Ricci was born to an affluent noble family in 1552 in Macerata, a town in central Italy overlooking the Adriatic. In 1572, he went to Rome to study law at the Jesuit Roman College. He came under the tutelage of three mentors, each a distinguished scholar who would have a lifelong influence on him. Alessandro Valignano (1539-1606) was master of novices and imbued Ricci with an appreciation for the importance of cultural sensitivity and adaptability. Ricci would later apply these principles with creativity and devotion to his mission in China. Christopher Clavius (1538-1612) was a noted German astronomer and mathematician in the movement to reform the Gregorian calendar. His seminal books on astronomy were used by missionaries for much of the late 16th and early 17th centuries. Clavius inspired in Ricci a lifelong passion for mathematics and astronomy, which he would later use to great benefit in impressing Chinese scholars, mandarins and, ultimately, the Ming Emperor.[7] Roberto Bellarmino (1542-1621) was an Italian Jesuit Cardinal in Rome. His teachings on dogmatics and his revisionist catechisms made him one of the most influential Cardinals of the Catholic Church during that period. Under Bellarmino's tutelage, Ricci would develop the formidable apologetics skills of reason, persuasion and dialogue which would prove invaluable in his intellectual and spiritual interchanges with his Chinese counterparts.[8] Apprenticing under this trio of mentors gave Ricci the religious, scientific and intellectual foundation that would deeply impress the highest echelons of Chinese society—and ultimately open the doors to dialogue with the imperial court.

In 1577, Ricci was sent to the Portuguese mission in Goa to teach Latin and Greek. He was ordained priest in 1581, and stayed there for almost six years. In 1583, Valignano, by then head of the Jesuit mission for all of Asia, instructed him to go to Macao. His task was to assist Father Michele Ruggieri (1543-1607), the Superior of the mission in the Portuguese enclave, who had been struggling to gain entry into China. Ricci arrived in the middle of that year and promptly immersed himself in studying Chinese. As a testament to his brilliance, he succeeded in mastering the language in a few years. Cambridge historian of science and Sinologist Joseph Needham considered Ricci "one of the most remarkable and brilliant men in history," and noted the enormity of the task:[9]

> There was of course the almost insuperable difficulty of language at a time when sinology hardly existed and no good dictionaries had been made.[10]

At the end of 1583, Ricci moved with Ruggieri to Zhaoqing, a small city near Canton where the Governor-General of Guangdong and Guangxi provinces had his official residence. Ricci would never again return to Europe or leave China.

Historical Context

It is important to understand the historical, ecumenical, geopolitical and intellectual context of Ricci's entry into the Middle Kingdom, and how these factors impacted the nature of his mission. In Europe, the Counter Reformation had commenced four decades earlier with the Council of Trent (1545-1563). By 1583, the Catholic revival was in full force, most notably led by the Jesuit movement. The Society of Jesus, as the Jesuits were officially known, had been formed in 1540 by St. Ignatius Loyola (1491-1556), a Spanish nobleman and former soldier. As disciplined and devoted as he was charismatic and organized, Loyola quickly established the Jesuit order as a quasi-military brotherhood, almost fanatical in their zeal to restore the reputation of the Catholic church and stem the Protestant tide. Beyond the monastic vows of poverty, chastity and absolute obedience, St. Ignatius placed great emphasis on careful selection, iron discipline and rigorous educational training for his members.[11]

St. Ignatius's overarching mission was to spread the Gospel of Catholicism into the new worlds being opened by the explorers, armadas and traders of Europe, and convert as many non-Christians as possible.[12] St. Francis Xavier (1506-1552), one of the Jesuits' more forceful founders, assumed responsibility for spreading Catholicism in the Far Eastern dominions. After a brief sojourn in India, he settled in Japan and made some headway in converting non-Christians. In 1552, he determined that China held more importance to the evangelical cause, and proceeded to its southern coast. He died late that year on Shangchuan, an island off the coast of Guangdong, failing in his quest to enter the mainland. Before his death, however, he wrote several exhortations to the Jesuit leadership on the strategic importance of establishing a Catholic mission in China.[13]

In the late 1500s, the Mediterranean world was split by the economic, political and military rivalry between Portugal and Spain.[14] Each nation was trying to assert its dominion over the New World, mainly the central and southern Americas, and the territories to the east of the Mediterranean. The Treaty of Tordesillas (1494), mediated by Pope Alexander VI, divided this expanse longitudinally west of Africa at the Cape Verde Islands.[15] With the exception of the Philippine Islands, the Asian domains fell under the auspices of the Portuguese. Out of consideration for the Pope's peacemaking role, the Vatican missions in these territories were to receive safe haven from their Portuguese and Spanish settlers. The Jesuit missions in Asia toward the end of the century focused on Portuguese-controlled India, Japan, Korea, Taiwan and China. The rival Dominican and Franciscan missions used the Philippines, under Spanish protection, as their base to enter China. This rivalry was to cause much trouble for Ricci later on during the so-called Chinese Rites Controversy.

In China, the end of the 16th century marked the apex of the Ming Dynasty (1368-1644). Spence notes:

> In the year AD 1600, the empire of China was the largest and most sophisticated of all the united realms on earth....the Ming Dynasty seemed at the height of its glory. Its achievements in culture and the arts were remarkable, urban and commercial life were spreading new levels of prosperity, while Chinese skills in printing and the manufacture of porcelain and silk exceeded anything that could be found in Europe at the time.[16]

Moreover, the Chinese had for centuries considered themselves the Middle Kingdom, a civilization superior to all other societies, and they were particularly dismissive of Europeans, whom they considered barbarians. Buccaneering Spanish and Portuguese traders only reinforced this stereotype through their behavior in coastal China. As Immanuel Hsu writes:

> On the whole, foreign traders in China, who were mostly profit-seeking adventurers and uncouth men of little culture, made a poor show of themselves. Their violent and reckless conduct confirmed the Chinese view of foreigners as barbarians. They were not welcomed but tolerated.[17]

Ricci was entering a country whose rulers and people were leery of foreign evangelists and traders alike.

Intellectual and Religious Background

Intellectually, Europe stood at the dawn of the Age of Reason. Perhaps the greatest intellectual controversy involving the Catholic Church in the late 1500s was the debate between faith and science sparked by the Copernican revolution. Nicolas Copernicus's (1473-1543) heliocentric theory of the universe was blasted as heretical by Catholic doctrinaires. At the same time, pressures to reform the Julian calendar were intensifying, particularly given the need for dioceses around the Catholic world to coordinate festivals and rituals.[18] Events were leading to the trial of Galileo, who would be denounced just two decades later during the Roman Inquisition. The Gregorian calendar was officially adopted by Rome in 1582, just one year before Matteo Ricci embarked on his journey into China. Ricci, trained not only in the Catholic canon but also in mathematics, the physical sciences, astronomy and rhetoric, must have felt torn by these competing intellectual forces. Representing the best of the Jesuit apologetist tradition, he remained loyal to both the theological catechisms and the principles of rationalism, debate and scientific evidence.

Christianity in China can be traced back to the Tang Dynasty (618-907), with the arrival around 635 of the first missionaries from Persia (the so-called "Jinhjau") in the capital city of Chang-

an, or present day X'ian.[19] But there is little documented activity
thereafter until the 13th century, when several Mongol tribes were
thought to have adopted Nestorian Christianity.[20] There is also
evidence of Papal representatives making contact with officials in
the Yuan Dynasty capital of Khanbaliq, current-day Beijing.[21] In
1289, Franciscan friars from Europe initiated missionary work in
China, often in tandem with the Nestorians. The Christian movement was halted, however, in 1369, when the incoming Ming rulers
moved to expel all foreign influences, including Buddhism.[22]

The Ricci Mission and Method

It was against this two centuries' void that Matteo Ricci set
forth on his journey into China. His mission was clear: to determine
and implement an effective strategy to evangelize the country and
bring China into the Catholic realm.

As he was new to China, Ricci did not have a well-formulated
strategy at the outset of his odyssey. He was influenced by the
thinking of St. Ignatius and the practices of St. Francis Xavier. St.
Ignatius advised his missionaries:

> Show that you conform, as far as the Institute of the Society permits,
> to the customs of the people there....teach matters of faith and morals
> in a way that is accommodated to those people...without taking away
> from them anything in which they especially value, try to get them to
> accept the truths of Catholicism...do everything gently.[23]

Valignano, Ricci's longtime mentor, also had great influence on his
thinking. All three emphasized the importance of respect, tolerance
and pragmatic accommodation of local customs where necessary,
so Ricci adopted a flexible, rather than doctrinaire approach.

After living in the southern city of Zhaoqing for two years
and immersing himself in local life, Ricci decided on an evangelical strategy with four guiding principles: achieving linguistic and
cultural mastery; focusing on how to influence the top echelons
of Chinese society, rather than the masses; impressing Chinese
literati and officials with the science and technology of the West

as a means to pique curiosity in and acceptance of Christianity; and finally, accommodating Chinese values, rituals and customs in an attempt to harmonize them with Christian teachings.[24]

These guiding principles became known as "The Ricci Method" and showed Ricci's informed, pragmatic and nuanced style. Ricci's strategies were also remarkably sensitive for the era. Undoubtedly, the historical, theological and intellectual context of the Counter Reformation (and its attendant primary mission of recapturing lay members), the emergence of the zealous Jesuit movement, the Church's ambivalence about yielding to science and adopting the Gregorian calendar, and St. Francis Xavier's dying wish to enter China, spurred Ricci to formulate and deploy a strategy which would best realize his mission's objectives. He would need to be pragmatic, given the opaque and complex nature of China. At the time, China was an insular, intensely proud and inherently conservative culture that prized intellectual accomplishment. Ricci realized that he would need to employ finesse, cultural sensitivity and accommodation along with intellectual "shock and awe" to gain trust, respect and ultimately acceptance by the powers in question.

Valignano's thinking formed the foundation for Ricci's initial guiding principle of linguistic mastery. The former's first official act upon arriving in Japan was to require all new missionaries to spend at least two years in intensive language study.[25] In China, he instructed the Jesuits to find the best teachers and learn to read, write and speak Chinese so as to "Sinicize" themselves rather than to "Portugalize" their converts:

> The work of evangelization, of making Christians, should be carried on both in Peking and in the provinces...following the methods of pacific penetration and cultural adaptation. Europeanism is to be shunned.[26]

Valignano preferred to see progress in furthering Jesuit influence over blind adherence to Christian principles. His strategies stood in marked contrast to those of the Dominican and Franciscan missionaries, who pursued a more rigid, Eurocentric and less culturally sensitive approach to the conversion process.

Ricci's thoughtful method of linguistic immersion and acculturation was unique at the time in China. He understood that the bureaucratic and scholarly elite were largely suspicious of foreigners, whom they generally considered to be uncivilized and mercenary. He took on the role of learner rather than proselytizer, judiciously choosing to present Christ in Chinese terms and not in European ones.[27]

Ricci not only immersed himself in the study of Chinese, but he also adopted the dress of Buddhist clerics upon entering China. Probably inspired by Valignano and his experience in Japan, Ricci felt that this appearance would allow him and his companion Ruggieri to blend in as men of the spirit, rather than be seen as foreign aggressors.[28] He replaced this attire with the robes of the Confucian literati around 1595, when he modified his method to concentrate on influencing the top echelons of the elite.[29]

Ricci was politically savvy enough to realize that acceptance and approval at the highest level of Chinese society would greatly enhance his cause. This approach ran counter to the conventional evangelical method at the time, which was to attract the masses. He understood that China was a profoundly hierarchical society and that at the apex stood the Emperor. Accordingly, he worked hard to find ways to approach and influence Wan Li, the Ming Emperor. The basic assumption behind the strategy was that if the Emperor and his mandarins accepted Christianity, then conversion of the masses would follow in due course. Indeed, the Jesuits "dreamed of a new Constantine for China."[30] Ricci cleverly sent gifts to the Forbidden City, including beautiful Italian clocks, a clavichord, astronomical measuring devices and oil paintings to entice a meeting with the Wan Li Emperor.[31]

As noted, Ricci was a man of extraordinary intellectual versatility. It was his skill in cartography, however, that led him to Beijing and a direct contact with the ruler. Starting in 1584, Ricci created a series of sixteen world maps, all annotated in Chinese. The Western concept of a world map was alien to the Chinese at the time, who envisaged their country and its civilization as the Middle Kingdom that lay between Heaven and Earth. The rest of the world's land and sea masses were of little concern to them. Typical indigenous maps of the time showed the 15 Chinese provinces surrounded by a small area of sea, with a seemingly random group of foreign countries often misidentified.[32] Ricci's maps opened Chinese eyes to the outside world. Building on his growing reputation as a memory expert, mathematician, astronomical genius and accomplished Confucian scholar, Ricci supervised the drawing and production of a series of large scale maps which accurately positioned the Middle Kingdom in relation to countries in Europe, the subcontinent, and the New World. As he noted in his diaries:

> This was the most useful work that could be done at that time to dispose China to give credence to the things of our Holy Faith...their conception of the greatness of their country and of the insignificance of other lands made them so proud that the whole world seemed to them savage and barbarous compared with themselves.[33]

He astutely placed China in the center of his maps, and made sure to feature it larger than scale. He annotated his drawings with fascinating facts, figures and allegories about specific regions, particularly those important in Christian scriptures. This maneuver proved highly effective on two fronts: it piqued the interest of the Emperor and the Ming Court, resulting in an official invitation to visit the Forbidden City in 1601; and it allowed Ricci to insert into each map the location of Rome and the Holy Land, with stories, verses, psalms and other Church teachings to hint that behind the grandeur and beauty of the world lay the divine Christian God and his teachings.[34] He revealed the real significance of this endeavor in a journal entry: "Making the maps was not only an instrument of missionary strategy, but it involved a religious world view....Understanding the universe precisely scientifically means to know God and Creation."[35]

   Ricci was also successful at impressing the top tier of the influential Confucian elite. The system of power and patronage at that time was meritocratic, centering on performance in grueling imperial civil service examinations. Excelling at these brought power, prestige and economic security. Examination success required mastery of the Confucian classics. The core curriculum comprised "The Four Books of Confucianism" (*si shu*), namely *The Great Learning, The Doctrine of the Mean, The Analects of Confucius,* and *The Book of Mencius*.[36] Mastering these texts involved rigorous rote memorization and regurgitation.

Ricci spotted an opportunity and shrewdly capitalized on his prodigious memory techniques. He made every effort to demonstrate his carefully developed mnemonic system, which he referred to as his "memory palace," and was happy to impart this skill to the scholar-elites he wished to cultivate. According to Spence, "Ricci was able to recite long passages from Chinese texts after only a fleeting glance."[37] Ricci noted in his diaries: "In order to increase their wonder, I began to recite the characters all by memory backwards in the same manner, beginning with the very last until reaching the first. By which they all became utterly astonished as if beside themselves."[38]

During the Ming Dynasty, scholars sat imperial examinations on average once every three years. Eager prospective mandarins soon made their way in increasing numbers to Ricci's door to acquire this key to scholastic and career advancement.

Beyond phenomenal memory techniques and dazzling world maps, Ricci enthusiastically showcased his formidable arsenal of intellectual ideas, teachings, scientific and rhetorical skills to demonstrate the sophistication and beauty of Western civilization. He participated in open debates with Confucian scholars, Taoist and Buddhist monks, and high officials, engaging these masters in themes ranging from science, mathematics and technology to ethics, theology and philosophy. In 1603, he published *The True Meaning of the Lord of Heaven* (*tianzhu shiyi*), a brilliant dialogue between a fictitious Chinese scholar (*zhongshi*) and his Western counterpart (*xishi*) in which the Chinese scholar is won over to the Westerner's views on the existence of a Celestial God, Creation, and Christian ethics and teachings.[39] Ricci's brilliance and humility attracted three renowned top scholars, Xu Guangqi, Li Zhicao and Yang Tingyun, who soon converted to Catholicism and became Ricci's most trusted and influential disciples. They are known as the "Three Great Pillars of Chinese Catholicism."[40]

Xu proved to be the most illustrious of these early converts. He was celebrated for having attained *jinshi*, the highest possible ranking in the imperial civil service examinations, and was a member of the elite Hanlin Academy, a very prestigious think-tank patronized by the Emperor.[41] Baptized by Ricci with the name Paul, Xu studied under Ricci from 1604 to 1607 before returning to his native Shanghai. There, he established the famous Xujiahui Church, literally meaning "Xu Family Church." It stands today as a Shanghai landmark and still holds regular services. Among their many important collaborations, Xu and Ricci translated the first six books of Euclid's *Elements of Geometry* into Chinese, further cementing both men's sterling academic reputations.

Overall, the first three principles of the The Ricci Method proved highly effective. Ricci endeared himself to the literary elite as he slowly made his way from Zhaoqing in southern China and travelled north through the cities of Nanchang, Nanjing and Shanghai. He successfully established missions in each of these cities, although the number of Christian converts remained painfully small—less than 600 in the entire country in the year 1600, according to Jesuit mission estimates.[42] He achieved his greatest success when in 1601, after nearly two decades of relentless effort, he won an audience with the imperial court and was permitted entry into the Forbidden City. This invitation marked the first time any foreigner had penetrated the inner sanctum of the Chinese empire. It was at this point that Ricci began to implement his fourth principle, that of cultural accommodation. In the short run, his choice proved a highly successful addition to The Ricci Method. In the long run, however, cultural accommodation precipitated the Chinese Rites Controversy, which proved disastrous to his mission and the entire Catholic and Christian movement in China.

The Chinese Rites Controversy

Creatively adapting Valignano's accommodation method, Ricci showed tolerance for the traditional Chinese rituals of ancestor worship and the veneration of Confucius. Ricci considered these practices to be civil rites and not religious ones, arguing that Confucianism was not a religion per se, but rather a code of ethics residing within the human person. He referred to it in his writings as governed by a form of "natural law."[43] However, conservative elements within the Church, particularly the Dominicans and Franciscans who were also actively proselytizing in China, blasted this accommodation policy as a breach of Catholic orthodoxy. They argued that Confucian rites and rituals smacked of idolatry and paganism, and were wholly inconsistent with the notion of a Heavenly Father and Holy Spirit.[44] This dispute gave rise to the Chinese Rites Controversy, which was to consume the Papal office and the missionary movement for centuries to come.

The controversy centered on three issues: a semantic issue relating to whether the Chinese classical terms for "Heaven" (*tian shang*), "Master of Heaven" (*tian zhu*) and "Most High" (*shang di*) should, as Ricci advocated, also be construed to represent the Christian God; a procedural issue relating to whether Christians should prohibit ceremonies and rituals worshipping ancestors and venerating Confucius; and finally an interfaith issue relating to whether or not Chinese Christians should be allowed to participate in festivals honoring non-Christian deities.[45]

Ricci wrote elaborately and eloquently on all three topics, and provided several reasoned, nuanced and well-researched defenses of his positions. In his most celebrated Chinese book, *The True Meaning of the Lord of Heaven* (*tianzhu shiyi*), he masterfully crafted a fictional dialogue between a Western scholar and his Chinese counterpart. The book was designed to harmonize the basic Christian tenets of Divinity, the Holy Trinity, redemption and eternal life with the essential concepts of Confucianism. However, the Dominicans and Franciscans were intransigent, and escalated the controversy all the way to the Vatican. Their missionaries, supported by rival Spanish colonial interests in the Philippines, approached evangelism in China in an uncompromising, Europeanist manner. They viewed non-Christian cultures as the work of the devil and tolerance of these cultures as a betrayal of Christian principles.[46] Dominican and Franciscan methods in every aspect opposed the subtle, culturally sensitive, and integrative approach of St. Ignatius.

Notwithstanding this vehement attack on Ricci's method, a succession of Popes did nothing following Ricci's death to overturn the accommodation method in dealing with the Chinese rites issue. Jesuits continued to administer papally-approved Chinese rites, and also embraced ancestor worship and veneration of Confucius on the grounds that these practices were civic and not religious in nature. It was not until the time of Pope Clement XI (1700-1721) that the internecine dispute reached its most bitter—and ultimately destructive—turning point. In 1704, the Holy See issued an edict forbidding all missionaries in China from sanctioning Chinese rites; Clement XI reaffirmed this judgment in 1715.[47]

These actions proved disastrous not only to the Jesuit mission in China but to all Christian evangelism. Confused and angered by the Church's internal dissension, and by mixed messages and loss of Chinese face, the Qing Kangxi Emperor ordered all missions closed in 1721 and Church officials banished.[48] Chinese Catholics were persecuted and books burned. This prohibition was to last for two centuries until Pope Pius XII (1939-1958) reversed Clement XI's decrees in 1939.[49] But the Chinese Rites Controversy had already caused irreparable damage to the Jesuit and Catholic missions.

Ricci was finally vindicated by Pope John XXIII in 1958, when by decree in the encyclical *Princeps Pastorum* he declared that "Matteo Ricci would become the model of missionaries."[50] But as historian Arnold Toynbee lamented, "Christianity had during Ricci's time and after the chance to become a true world religion—but rejected it over internal squabbles over semantics and local customs. Never again would history present itself on such favorable terms."[51] Had Ricci's method of accommodation been embraced and supported by Rome, the religious history of China might well have been quite different.

Conclusion

If judged by the metric of Catholic conversions, one might easily conclude that Ricci's mission in China was a failure. By 1600, after nearly two decades of effort, there were barely 600 Chinese Catholics on record and only five missions operating in the entire country.[52] By the time of Ricci's death another decade later, the number had grown to only 2,000.[53] This statistic compares with 17,000 converts to Catholicism in Taiwan, 300,000 in Japan, and 350,000 in the Philippines around the same period.[54]

The infighting that was precipitated by the Chinese Rites Controversy and which undermined the Catholic movement was certainly a major impediment to Ricci's efforts during his lifetime. However, by 1640, the total converts to Catholicism in China had grown to almost 70,000; by 1651, the number had reached 150,000.[55] By any measure, the Jesuit endeavors in China must be seen as having been highly successful over the longer run.

With the hindsight of four centuries, it is far easier to appreciate Ricci's immense significance. Chinese and Western thinkers hold him in equally high regard. Even the Chinese Communist Party respects Li Madou Xi Tai as "the greatest and least predatory of the culture bearers from the West."[56] He was the first Western scholar to immerse himself completely within local Chinese communities. In so doing, he became an accepted and admired member of the literary elite. He had considerable personal influence over the Emperor. He introduced European mathematics, science, philosophy and technology to the Chinese and likewise opened the West to the exquisite richness of Chinese civilization through his voluminous translations of key texts, poetry, his reflections on life in China, and his astounding maps of the world—with the Middle Kingdom, of course, at the center.

The obstacles Ricci faced were daunting, and included physical hardship, danger, loneliness, linguistic and cultural differences, xenophobia, and attacks by Dominican and Franciscan rivals. It was a testimony to his extraordinary will and intellect that Ricci was able to overcome these hardships, to such a degree that many of his writings in Chinese are considered classics of Chinese literature, moral philosophy, mathematics and science.

Toynbee accords Ricci the highest place in Eastern and Western civilization, and frames his life's work in the larger Jesuit perspective:

> The Jesuits' approach to their enterprise of propagating Christianity in China was so different and so promising in itself, and is so much to the point today, that our discussion of Asian peoples' encounter with the West would be incomplete if we did not take into consideration the line which the Jesuits in China and India opened out.[57]

In Beijing today, where Christianity is tightly controlled, there is a stunning monument to Ricci's legacy. In 1601, Emperor Wan Li issued an imperial decree bestowing upon Ricci the land and funds to erect a chapel and permanent residence in central Peking.[58] Built in 1605, the Cathedral of the Immaculate Conception (popularly known as the "South Cathedral") stands in the busy Wang Fu Jing district of the capital. Two tablets inside the east and west walls at the front of the cathedral were gifts from the Emperor himself, and bear tribute to Ricci's standing in late Ming China.[59]

Before Ricci's death, all Jesuit priests who died in China had to be carried to Macao for burial. Ricci was the first foreigner allowed to be buried in Peking. In a country where symbolism often speaks louder than words, Ricci's entombment in China is proof of the respect and reverence he is accorded to this day.

Father Luis Sequeira, former head of the Jesuit order in Macao, wrote poignantly about Ricci: "He showed respect for the other. His mission was to show the humanity of Christ and open the door to all, and not behave as in Europe, where people were killing each other over religion."[60]

Ricci's gentle, culturally embracing, nuanced and tolerant methods, embodying the ethos of St. Ignatius, stood in sharp contrast to the belligerent, arrogant and contemptuous disregard shown by many foreigners who followed in his footsteps. The history of Western interaction with China in the 17th, 18th, and early 19th centuries is marked by predatory mercantilism, gunboat diplomacy, the opium trade, unequal treaties, and war. Rather than peaceful accommodation, mutual respect and inculturation, this epoch was characterized by colonial aggression, subjugation and humiliation.

Chinese memories are long, and the life and work of Matteo Ricci, the Scholar from the West, go some way to assuage the resentment Chinese people still harbor about foreign aggression. More importantly, the deeply humanistic values that underlay his approach transcend religion, theology, customs and rituals. They speak to the glory not so much of God as of the human spirit. This is the essence of what makes Ricci's example one for the ages; an indomitable, tolerant, accepting and accommodating spirit that reached out to the best in people irrespective of race, creed or faith. This is what makes Matteo Ricci's life, with its lasting impact over four centuries, so important and inspiring to humankind.

[1] Benedict XVI, "Message of His Holiness Benedict XVI on the Occasion of the Fourth Centenary of the Death of Fr. Matteo Ricci," Libreria Editrice Vaticana (6 May 2009) http://www.vatican.va/holy_father/benedict_xvi/messages/pont-messages/2009/documents/hf_ben xvi_mes_20090506_ricci_en.html (accessed 9 August 2010)

[2] Vincent Cronin, The Wise Man from the West: Matteo Ricci and his Mission to China (New York: E.P. Dutton, 1955) p. 3

[3] "Matteo Ricci: Sage of the West," Xinhua News Agency (23 November 2009)

[4] L. Carrington Goodrich and Chaoying Fang, eds., Dictionary of Ming Biography, 1368-1644 (New York: Columbia University Press, 1976) p. 1144

[5] Jonathan D. Spence, "Claims and Counter-Claims: The Kangxi Emperor and the Europeans (1661-1722)," The Chinese Rites Controversy: Its History and Meaning (Nettetal: Styler Verlag, 1944) p. 16

[6] Jean-Pierre Charbonnier, Christians in China, AD 600-2000 (San Francisco: Ignatius Press, 2007) p. 152

[7] Cronin, p. 22

[8] Charbonnier, p. 143

[9] Joseph Needham, Science and Civilization in China Vol. 1 (Cambridge: Cambridge University Press, 1954) p. 148

[10] Ibid., Vol. 3, p. 173

[11] Rene Fulop-Miller, The Power and Secret of the Jesuits (London: G.P. Putnam's Sons, 1930) pp. 78-79

[12] John P. Donnelly, Ignatius of Loyola, Founder of the Jesuits (New York: Pearson, 2004) p. 90

[13] Fulop-Miller, pp. 221-222

[14] Yves Camus, SJ, "Matteo Ricci's Legacy: A Loving Patience," Thinking Faith (11 May 2010) p. 2, http://www.thinkingfaith.org/articles/20100511_1.htm (accessed 10 August 2010)

[15] Ibid., p.2

[16] Jonathan D. Spence, The Search for Modern China (New York: W.W. Norton, 1990) pp. 3, 7

[17] Immanuel C.Y. Hsu, The Rise of Modern China (New York: Oxford University Press, 2000) p. 96

[18] John W. O'Malley, SJ, et al., The Jesuits: Cultures, Sciences and the Arts, 1540-1773 (Toronto: University of Toronto Press, 1999) p. 117

[19] Bob Whyte, <u>Unfinished Encounter: China and Christianity</u> (London: Collins, 1988) p. 35

[20] Ibid., p. 41

[21] Ibid., p. 42

[22] Ibid., pp. 46-47

[23] Camus, p. 2

[24] Anthony E. Clark, SJ, "Matteo Ricci, SJ: An Apologist for Dialogue," <u>This Rock</u> (November-December 2009) pp. 1-2, http://www.catholic.com/thisrock/2009/0911fea3.asp (accessed 9 August 2010)

[25] Hsu, p. 97

[26] George H. Dunne, <u>Generation of Giants: The Story of the Jesuits in China in the Last Decades of the Ming Dynasty</u> (Notre Dame: University of Notre Dame Press, 1962) p. 44

[27] Steve Hu, "Newbigin, Syncretism and the Emerging Church," <u>Morehead's Musings</u> (17 April 2008) p. 10, http://johnwmorehead.blogspot.com/2008/04/steve-hu-newbigin-syncretism-and.html (accessed 12 August 2010)

[28] Andrew C. Ross, "Alessandro Valignano: The Jesuits and Culture in the East," in O'Malley et al., pp. 343-345

[29] Charbonnier, p. 151

[30] Ibid., p. 194

[31] Whyte, p. 61

[32] Dunne, p. 117

[33] "Matteo Ricci," <u>Catholic Encyclopedia</u> Vol. 3 (1913) p. 56

[34] Dunne, p. 119

[35] Gianni Criveller, "China: Hong Kong: Matteo Ricci maps did not put China at the centre of the world," <u>Spero News</u> (26 January 2010) http://www.speroforum.com/a/26207/China–Hong-Kong–Matteo-Ricci-maps-did-not-put-China-at-centre-of-the-world (accessed 9 August, 2010)

[36] Hsu, pp. 75-76

[37] Spence, p. 138

[38] Ibid., p. 139

[39] Charbonnier, pp. 154-155

[40] Ibid., p. 161

[41] Ibid., pp. 161-162

[42] Ibid., p. 168

[43] William T. DeBary, "Reflections on the Chinese Rites Controversy," in O'Malley et al., pp. 301

[44] John D. Young, <u>Confucianism and Christianity: The First Encounter</u> (Hong Kong: Hong Kong University Press, 1983) p. 118

[45] Beverly Foulks, "Duplicitous Thieves: Ouyi Zhixu's Criticism of Jesuit Missionaries in Late Imperial China," in The Chung-Hwa Buddhist Journal (Taipei: Chung-Hwa Institute of Buddhist Studies, 2008) p. 58

[46] Hsu, p. 101

[47] Cronin, p. 281

[48] Young, Confucianism and Christianity, p. 122

[49] John D. Young, "Chinese Views of the Rites Controversy, 18th-20th Centuries," The Chinese Rites Controversy: Its History and Meaning ed. David E. Mungello (Nettetal: Styler Verlag, 1994) p. 106

[50] Gianni Criveller, The Parable of Inculturation of the Gospel in China: A Catholic Viewpoint (Hong Kong: Chinese University Press, 2003) p. 32

[51] Arnold Toynbee, The World and the West (New York: Oxford University Press, 1953) p. 65

[52] David B. Barrett, World Christian Trends, AD 30-AD 2200: Interpreting the Annual Christian Megacensus (California: William Carey Library, 2001) p. 132

[53] Ibid., p. 132

[54] Ibid., p. 132

[55] Dunne, pp. 212, 314

[56] Kenneth Rexroth, "Matteo Ricci's China Journals," The New Republic (21 December 1953)

[57] Toynbee, p. 64

[58] Gianni Criveller and Cesar Guilen Nunez, Portrait of a Jesuit: Matteo Ricci (Macau: Matteo Ricci Institute, 2010) p. 38

[59] Ibid., p. 39

[60] Mark O'Neill, "Matteo Ricci," Macau Magazine (October 2010)

Bibliography

Primary Sources

Benedict XVI, "Message of His Holiness Benedict XVI on the Occasion of the Fourth Centenary of the Death of Fr. Matteo Ricci," Libreria Editrice Vaticana (6 May 2009) http://www.vatican.va/holy_father/benedict_xvi/messages/pont-messages/2009/documents/hf_ben xvi_mes_20090506_ricci_en.html (accessed 9 August 2010)

John Paul II, Pope, "Message on the Fourth Centenary of the Arrival in Beijing of Matteo Ricci," http://www.schillerinstitute.org/dialogue_cultures/pope_ricci_102401.html (accessed 9 August 2010)

Ricci, Matteo, China in the Sixteenth Century: The Journals of Matteo Ricci: 1583-1610 trans. by Louis J. Gallagher, SJ, New York: Random House, 1970

Ricci, Matteo, The True Meaning of the Lord of Heaven ed. Edward J. Malatesta, trans. by Douglas Lancashire and Peter Hu Kuo-chen, Taipei: Ricci Institute, 1985

Trigault, SJ, Nicolas, China in the Sixteenth Century: The Journals of Matteo Ricci, 1583-1610 trans. by Louis J. Gallagher, SJ, New York: Random House, 1953

Secondary Sources

Barrett, David B., World Christian Trends AD 30-AD 2200: Interpreting the Annual Christian Megacensus California: William Carey Library, 2001

Camus SJ, Yves, "Matteo Ricci's Legacy: A Loving Patience," Thinking Faith, 11 May 2010 http://www.thinkingfaith.org/articles/20100511_1.htm (accessed 10 August 2010)

Catholic Encyclopedia Vol. 3 (1913), s.v. "Matteo Ricci"

Charbonnier, Jean-Pierre, Christians in China, AD 600-2000 Trans. by M.N.L. Couve de Murville, San Francisco: Ignatius Press, 2007

Clark SJ, Anthony E., "Matteo Ricci, SJ: An Apologist for Dialogue," This Rock, November-December 2009, http://www.catholic.com/thisrock/2009/0911fea3.asp (accessed 9 August 2010)

Cohen, Paul A., China and Christianity Cambridge, Massachusetts: Harvard University Press, 1963

Criveller, Gianni, The Parable of Inculturation of the Gospel in China: A Catholic Viewpoint Hong Kong: Chinese University Press, 2003

Criveller, Gianni, "Matteo Ricci Maps Did Not Put China at the Centre of the World," Spero News, 26 January 2010, http://www.speroforum.com/a/26207/China-Hong-Kong–Matteo-Ricci-maps-did-not-put-China-at-the-centre-of-the-world (accessed 9 August 2010)

Criveller, Gianni, and Cesar Guilen Nunez, Portrait of a Jesuit: Matteo Ricci Macau: Matteo Ricci Institute, 2010

Cronin, Vincent, The Wise Man From the West: Matteo Ricci and His Mission to China New York: E.P. Dutton & Co., Inc., 1955

Donnelly, John P., Ignatius of Loyola, Founder of the Jesuits New York: Pearson, 2004

Dunne, George H., Generation of Giants: The Story of the Jesuits in China in the Last Decades of the Ming Dynasty Notre Dame: University of Notre Dame Press, 1962

Foulks, Beverly, "Duplicitous Thieves: Ouyi Zhixu's Criticism of Jesuit Missionaries in Late Imperial China," The Chung-Hwa Buddhist Journal Taipei: Chung-Hwa Institute of Buddhist Studies, 2008

Fulop-Miller, Rene, The Power and Secret of the Jesuits London: G.P. Putnam's Sons, 1930

Gernet, Jacques, China and the Christian Impact: A Conflict of Cultures Trans. by Janet Lloyd, Cambridge: Cambridge University Press, 1985

Goodrich, L. Carrington, and Chaoying Fang, Eds., Dictionary of Ming Biography, 1368-1644 New York: Columbia University Press, 1976

Harris, SJ, George, "The Mission of Matteo Ricci, SJ: A Case Study of an Effort at Guided Cultural Change in the Sixteenth Century," Monumenta Serica 25 1968

Hsu, Immanuel C.Y., The Rise of Modern China New York: Oxford University Press, 2000

Hu, Steve, "Newbigin, Syncretism and the Emerging Church," <u>Morehead's Musings</u> 17 April 2008, http://johnwmorehead.blogspot.com/2008/04/steve-hu-newbigin-syncretism-and.html (accessed 12 August 2010)

McBrien, Richard P., "Matteo Ricci After 400 Years" <u>National Catholic Reporter</u> 1 June 2010, http://www/ncronline.org/essays-theology/matteo-ricci-after-400-years (accessed 10 August 2010)

Mungello, David E., <u>Curious Land: Jesuit Accommodation and the Origins of Sinology</u> Honolulu: University of Hawaii Press, 1989

Mungello, David E., Ed., <u>The Chinese Rites Controversy: Its History and Meaning</u> Nettetal: Styler Verlag, 1994

Mungello, David E., <u>The Great Encounter of China and the West, 1500-1800</u> Lanham, Maryland: Rowan & Littlefield, 2009

Needham, Joseph, <u>Science and Civilization in China</u> Vols. 1 and 3, Cambridge: Cambridge University Press, 1954, 1959

O'Connell, Marvin R., <u>The Counter Reformation, 1559-1610</u> New York: Harper & Row, 1974

O'Neill, Mark, "Matteo Ricci," <u>Macau Magazine</u> October 2010

Rexroth, Kenneth, "Matteo Ricci's China Journals," <u>The New Republic</u> 21 December 1953

Ross, Andrew C., <u>A Vision Betrayed: The Jesuits in Japan and China, 1542-1742</u> Maryknoll, New York: Orbis Books, 1994

Ross, Andrew C., "Alessandro Valignano: The Jesuits and Culture in the East," <u>The Jesuits: Cultures, Sciences and the Arts, 1540-1773</u> Eds. John W. O'Malley, SJ et al., Toronto: University of Toronto Press, 1999

Spence, Jonathan D., <u>The Memory Palace of Matteo Ricci</u> New York: Penguin, 1984

Spence, Jonathan D., <u>The Search for Modern China</u> New York: W.W. Norton, 1990

Spence, Jonathan D., "Claims and Counter-Claims: The Kangxi Emperor and the Europeans (1661-1722)," <u>The Chinese Rites Controversy: Its History and Meaning</u> Ed. David E. Mungello, Nettetal: Styler Verlag, 1994

Standaert, Nicolas, "Jesuit Corporate Culture as Shaped by the Chinese," <u>The Jesuits: Cultures, Sciences, and The Arts, 1540-1773</u> Ed. John W. O'Malley et al., Toronto: University of Toronto Press, 1999

Standaert, Nicolas, "Christianity in the Late Ming and Early Qing as a Case of Cultural Transmission," <u>China and Christianity: Burdened Past, Hopeful Future</u> Ed. Stephen Uhalley and Xiaoxin Wu, Armonk, New York: M.E. Sharpe, 2001

Toynbee, Arnold, <u>The World and the West</u> New York: Oxford University Press, 1953

Whyte, Bob, <u>Unfinished Encounter: China and Christianity</u> London: Collins, 1988

Young, John D., <u>East-West Synthesis: Matteo Ricci and Confucianism</u> Hong Kong: University of Hong Kong, 1980

Young, John D., <u>Confucianism and Christianity: The First Encounter</u> Hong Kong: Hong Kong University Press, 1983

Zurcher, Erik, "Jesuit Accommodation and the Chinese Cultural Imperative," <u>The Chinese Rites Controversy: Its History and Meaning</u> Ed. David E. Mungello, Nettetal: Steyler Verlag, 1994

Paul Johnson
Pages 47–48 of "A Relativistic World" in
Modern Times, The World from the Twenties to the Eighties
New York: Harper & Row Colophon edition, 1985

The disturbances in Europe and the world which followed the seismic shock of the Great War and its unsatisfactory peace were, in one sense, only to be expected. The old order had gone. Plainly it could not be fully restored, perhaps not restored at all. A new order would eventually take its place. But would this be an 'order' in the sense the pre-1914 world had understood the term? There were, as we have seen, disquieting currents of thought which suggested the image of a world adrift, having left its moorings in traditional law and morality. There was too a new hesitancy on the part of established and legitimate authority to get the global vessel back under control by the accustomed means, or any means. It constituted an invitation, unwilled and unissued but nonetheless implicit, to others to take over. Of the great trio of German imaginative scholars who offered explanations of human behavior in the nineteenth century, and whose corpus of thought the post-1918 world inherited, only two have so far been mentioned. Marx described a world in which the central dynamic was economic interest. To Freud, the principal thrust was sexual. Both assumed that religion, the old impulse which moved men and masses, was a fantasy and always had been. Friedrich Nietzsche, the third of the trio, was also an atheist. But he saw God not as an invention but as a casualty, and his demise as in some important sense an historical event, which would have dramatic consequences. He wrote in 1886: "The greatest event of recent times—that 'God is Dead,' that the belief in the Christian God is no longer tenable—is beginning to cast its first shadows over Europe." Among the advanced races, the decline and ultimately the collapse of the religious impulse would leave a huge vacuum. The history of modern times is in great part the history of how that vacuum had been filled. Nietzsche rightly perceived that the most likely candidate would be what he called the "Will to Power," which offered a far more comprehensive and in the end more plausible explanation of human behaviour than either Marx or Freud. In place of religious belief, there would be secular ideology. Those who had once filled the ranks of the totalitarian clergy would become totalitarian politicians. And, above all, the Will to Power would produce a new kind of messiah, uninhibited by any religious sanctions whatever, and with an unappeasable appetite for controlling mankind. The end of the old order, with an unguided world adrift in a relativistic universe, was a summons to such gangster–statesmen to emerge. They were not slow to make their appearance.

Ralph Waldo Emerson Prize 2011

TRADE BETWEEN THE AINU OF EZO AND THE *WAJIN* FROM MAINLAND JAPAN (1650-1720)

Kaya Nagayo

Abstract

The research question is: How did trade between the Ainu and the *wajin* evolve from 1650 to 1720, and how did it affect the lifestyle of the Ainu? The Ainu are the indigenous people of the Japanese archipelago. Their history sheds light on how the Japanese polity was constructed and how a minority group was subjugated in that structure. During the Tokugawa period, two *wajin* forces (the merchants in the economic arena and the Matsumae vassals in the political arena) extended their influence over Ezo, the home island of the Ainu. Their expansion was instigated by the need for trade and labour that would support the burgeoning economy of the Tokugawa polity. Ironically, in Ezo, an island on the periphery of the polity, the merchants gained an upper hand over the vassals, overturning the Confucian-inspired paradigm of a world in which the vassals are at the top and the merchants are at the bottom. By acquiring trade fiefs from indebted vassals and taking control over trade with local Ainu, merchants became what we would now call capitalists, cultivating the seeds of capitalism in the soil of feudalism.

The author is at Waseda University. As a Senior at St. Maur International School in Yokohama, Japan, she wrote this IB Extended Essay in history for Mr. Glenn Scoggins in the 2008-2009 academic year.

Meanwhile, the Ainu's relationship to the *wajin* changed drastically. In the late 17th century, the Ainu were engaging in trade with major retainers of the Matsumae domain whereas in the early 18th century, they were working as labourers at *wajin*-controlled fisheries. Decentralized Ainu communities became increasingly dependent on trade with *wajin* merchants for their subsistence, a trend that changed the Ainu's relationship with their spiritual environment and created competition between Ainu communities. In conclusion, the two *wajin* forces had put the Ainu under their control by 1720 and capitalism had begun to develop in Ezo by the 18th century.

Introduction

The Ainu are the indigenous people of the Japanese archipelago. For a long time they have made their home on the northern island of Ezo, now called Hokkaido.[1] This paper will attempt to answer the research question: How did trade between the Ainu and the *wajin*[2] evolve from 1650 to 1720, and how did it affect the lifestyle of the Ainu? The hypothesis is: the subjugation of the Ainu had already begun by the middle of the Tokugawa period[3] through trade, which allowed two *wajin* forces (the merchants in the economic arena and the Matsumae vassals in the political arena) to extend their power over decentralized Ainu communities.

During the time period chosen for this research, the Ainu's relationship to the *wajin* changed drastically, moving from an equal trade-partner relationship to an unequal relationship in which the Ainu laboured in *wajin*-controlled fisheries operated by merchants from mainland Japan. The centralized Tokugawa polity, to some extent represented by the Matsumae vassals in Ezo, took control over decentralized Ainu communities in the form of ceremonies, known as *omusha*. The merchants, meanwhile, promoted commercialism and entrepreneurship. They took over the management of trading posts from the Matsumae vassals, thus taking complete control over trade with local Ainu. The trading posts became a local monopoly, and some trade fiefs in eastern Ezo included not just the trading posts, but also travel inns, storehouses, and shrines. This shows that capitalism had already begun to develop during the Tokugawa period. The Ainu, on the other hand, became dependent on trade with the *wajin* for their subsistence. Their growing dependency on the *wajin* led to loss of independence.

Today, in 2009, the question of the Ainu people's rights is steadily gaining ground in mainstream politics. Prime Minister Hatoyama Yukio has said that the government will take into consideration the advancement of the political rights of the Ainu. In addition, a report issued on 29 July 2009 by Ainu experts will become the basis for the New Council of Ainu Specialists.[5]

Trade at the Beginning of the Tokugawa period

At the beginning of the Tokugawa period, the trade between the Ainu and *wajin* was conducted on a small scale (in the form of item exchange) at Fukuyama Castle in the town of Matsumae, the seat of the Matsumae Daimyo. This took place only once a year. The Ainu traveled to Matsumae to pay tribute and received gifts in return in the presence of traders from mainland Japan. This ceremonial trade was known as *uimam*. Through *uimam,* the Ainu and *wajin* were able to nurture bonds of friendship and receive from one another items that were not easily accessible in their own society. The Ainu would also acquire fresh knowledge from the *wajin*. In terms of items, the Ainu would receive from the *wajin* such goods as lacquerware bowls, weapons, armour, and *sake,* whilst the *wajin* received from the Ainu such goods as Chinese silk and eagle feathers. Some of the Japanese lacquerware bowls found their way to Sakhalin, and later on to the continent.[6]

The practice of yearly item exchange in Matsumae was convenient for both the Ainu and *wajin*, because in the early 17th century the Ainu still formed the majority of the population in

Ezo. It was safer for them to travel than for the *wajin* minority to travel.[7] At this time, Ainu traders still visited the Tohoku region in mainland Japan, as well as Sakhalin Island and the Amur region to the north. As it was up to Ainu communities to produce a trade surplus and take the decision to travel, the trading initiative was firmly in their hands.[8]

The Emergence of the Trading Posts

This situation was reversed when the *wajin* set up a number of trading posts, known as *akinaiba,* along coastal rivers in the late 17th century. The trade network expanded rapidly with the emergence of the trading posts, which quickly developed into large marketplaces where Ainu and *wajin* exchanged goods on a daily basis. Since the trading posts were located near rivers, they brought the trade system closer to traditional Ainu fishing and hunting grounds. Japanese items were readily accessible at the trading posts, and they were swiftly integrated into the domestic lives of the Ainu. This engendered Ainu dependence on Japanese goods and items.[9]

The trading posts were owned by major retainers in the Matsumae domain, known as *chigyonushi.* The *chigyonushi* possessed monopoly-trading rights in these trading posts, and they also owned the trading territories around the trading posts. Products from the trading posts were exchanged with traders from mainland Japan who were limited to the port of Matsumae. The traders were subject to control and taxation, a system that helped increase trade volume and domain profits. Later on, Hakodate and Esashi were opened with similar restrictions.[10]

The Matsumae domain laid great emphasis on trade because it was the only means by which it could obtain economic prestige. Whereas the other domains attained their economic status through the amount of rice they produced, the Matsumae domain had to develop its economy on the trade with the Ainu because of poor agricultural potential in Ezo. Trade substituted for agriculture in the Matsumae domain. Because of the domain's inability to produce rice, the Daimyo of Matsumae was referred to as "mudaka-Daimyo," which roughly translates to "Daimyo with no-rice production." Owning monopoly-trading rights in the trading posts was therefore a great privilege. In the year 1761, for example, the number of *chigyonushi* among the total of 200 retainers was 59.[11] The rest of the retainers received their stipends in rice.

Merchants from Mainland Japan

In the early 18th century, the trading post system under the *chigyonushi* went heavily into debt to merchants from mainland Japan. There was a steep decline in the number of products acquired by the trading posts from the surrounding environment. The number of ships that Matsumae dispatched to its trading posts fell from eight to six, and the *chigyonushi* found that they no longer profited from trade with the Ainu. They therefore began to place the trade monopoly under merchants from mainland Japan, people who would pay them in order to travel to the trading posts and conduct trade. Soon, the trade monopoly was wholly in the hands of the merchants.[12]

In time, *chigyonushi* became so indebted to merchants, who advanced them on credit the goods that they traded in Ezochi,[13] that their trade fiefs became "pawned lands" to the merchants. The merchants were given a free hand to shape trade, and the trading posts became permanent marketplaces where the merchants exploited the Ainu labour force in year-round trade.[14] The duration of the terms during which the merchants were free to control trade at the trading posts were three, five, seven, or 10 years respectively, but it appears that seven-year terms were the most common. Once the term ran out, the merchants did anything they could to continue their career at the trading post. The contract was signed between the *chigyonushi* and the merchant, and even if the *chigyonushi* wanted to replace the merchant with a different one at the end of a term, he was prevented from doing so if, as was often the case, he was indebted to the merchant financially. This was a common case because the *chigyonushi* did not have enough money to buy products from mainland Japan for trade with the Ainu, and he was forced to borrow money from the merchants in advance. The merchants also frequently paid for the living of the *chigyonushi*'s family, which bound the *chigyonushi* and merchants firmly together.[15]

Impact of Trade on the Ainu's Subsistence Practice

With the advent of merchant-controlled trading posts located near Ainu communities, the acquisition of animal skins and fish products for trade with the *wajin* became essential in the subsistence practice of the Ainu. Since the animal skins and fish products were now for trade and not for feeding and clothing the Ainu community itself, the Ainu became dependent on trade with the *wajin* for their survival. Also, the hunt, which had once dramatized the spiritual relationship between Ainu communities and their local environment, took on commercial connotations. The Ainu began to appreciate resources not simply for their utilitarian value, but also for the prices they brought at the trading posts.[16]

The *wajin* sought to profit more from trade by cheating on the Ainu. Some Ainu lamented that rice bales that had once contained nearly 10 gallons now contained only about four gallons.[17] Merchants added water to their *sake* so that they could get more for less. At the trading posts, the merchants began lending Japanese fishing tools to the Ainu. The merchants taught the Ainu how to fish in the Japanese style, and gradually the Ainu were incorporated as labourers into *wajin*-controlled fisheries. In order to ensure order and security at the trading posts, *wajin* merchants placed Ainu chiefs in charge of some of the trading posts.

Weakening of the Ainu's Autonomy

In the first half of the Tokugawa period, the Ainu saw themselves as figures at the centre of the flourishing North Pacific network.[18] Ainu from eastern Ezo acquired Russian merchandise on Urup and brought them to trading posts in eastern Ezo[19] for trade with the *wajin* and other Ainu. Since the *wajin* had not established trading posts on the Kurils, the Ainu in this area had more independence. They had the right to sail freely between Ezo and the Kurils. This situation changed, however, when the Shogunate took over jurisdiction to make political and commercial decisions related to the Kurils in the late 18th century.[20]

Once the Ainu's autonomy had weakened, many Ainu found themselves resigned to labouring in *wajin*-controlled fisheries. With Ainu increasingly unable to travel to Kamchatka because they were labouring in local fisheries, they became reliant on *wajin* merchants for daily necessities, such as rice and tobacco. Ainu chiefs still found some time to hunt and trade on Urup, but younger Ainu could not afford to leave the fisheries. By the 18th century, fisheries in eastern Ezo had come under the sway of powerful *wajin* merchants, among them one Hidayao Kybei.[21]

Hidayao Kybei's Influence in Ezo

Lumber merchant Hidayao Kybei was from Hida Province in mainland Japan. In 1702, he left Japan for Ezo in the hope of gaining access to rich timber supplies on Rishiri Island in the north, as well as in eastern and western Ezo. By gaining access to timber, Hidayao could offer a fresh source of lumber to supplement increasingly depleted stands near Japanese cities. During the 17th century, intense castle-building occurred throughout Japan, causing rapid deforestation. The Meireki fires of the 1660s had also focused shogunal attention on remaining timber supplies to rebuild Japan's wooden cities. The Shogunate had stripped Hida Province, the home of Hidayao Kybei, of its vast timber supplies, forcing local lumbermen to fend for themselves with little compensation. Landed in this situation, shrewd merchants such as Hidayao turned their attention to Ezo in search for virgin woodlands.[22]

When Hidayao arrived in Ezo, he quickly extended his influence over the Matsumae family. The Matsumae family went into debt to the Hidayao household, and it extended Hidayao contracts to use trading posts in eastern Ezo and Kunashir Island. Hidayao, in order to collect on his investment in the Matsumae family, extracted hard prices from the Ainu living in the vicinity in the form of unfair trade exchange rates and harsh working conditions at fisheries. It was rumoured that, under Hidayao control, Ainu living in eastern Ezo were beaten to death with firewood, raped, and their prized hunting dogs tossed in the rivers to drown.[23] It is interesting to note that a merchant from the lowest social stratum gained power over a Daimyo clan, an event which shows that capitalism had already begun to develop during the Tokugawa period.

The Ainu become the Labour Force at *wajin*-controlled Fisheries

Thus, the Ainu became the labour force at *wajin*-controlled fisheries. They were driven hard to catch herring for the growing demands from mainland Japan. The herring were shipped off to the mainland to be used as fertilizer for growing crops in newly-cultivated land. With the growth of a market economy, consumers continually called for agricultural products, which could only be produced at a constant rate with the help of fertilizers. In order to meet these demands, merchants at *wajin*-controlled fisheries in Ezo made the Ainu work long hours with little pay.[24] Kayano Shigeru writes that Kaizawa Sirapeno, an Ainu, had received one lacquer wine cup as payment for a year's labour at a fishery in Atsukeshi.[25]

Ainu labourers at fisheries worked all year round. Their schedules were so tight that often they did not have time to pro-

vide their family with food for the long winter months. Young
Ainu men were recruited from Ainu villages to work in fisheries, so that villages became deserted with only the children, the
sick and elderly remaining.[26] According to Matsuura Takeshiro's
"Saru Journal,"[27] of the total of 116 Ainu villagers who made up
the population in Niputani, Pipaus, and Kankan in 1858, 43 men
and women had been drafted for forced labour.[28] Ainu who had
been recruited sometimes did not return for years, which led to
a decrease in the Ainu population.[29]

The maltreatment of Ainu at *wajin*-controlled trading
posts should not be over-emphasized, however. Among the Ainu
labouring at fisheries, some owned their own ships for catching
herring and other fish. They would go fishing on their own without *wajin* supervision. Also, the hunt for bearskin, bear bladder,
and eagle feathers was a job done solely by the Ainu. It would be
misleading to visualize the Ainu as constantly slaving under the
whip. It is true, however, that products obtained through fishing
and hunting went to the *wajin* merchant who ran the fishery, that
there were no open markets, and that the environment in which
the Ainu worked was in some cases extremely harsh.[30]

Japanese Items—Their Role in the Ritual Culture and Domestic
Life of the Ainu

As trade between the Ainu and Japanese intensified, Japanese goods were incorporated into the ritual culture of the Ainu
people. Japanese items, among, them small lacquerware bowls
and cups, sword guards and hilts, and large lacquerware contain-
ers, adorned the ritual area of Ainu ceremonies. *Sake* were used
as offerings to the gods and ancestors. Because the Ainu held a
certain fascination for these 'exotic' items, they developed into
symbols that mediated between the Ainu and the vast spiritual
world that surrounded them. Within the Ainu community, there
were a number of rituals for different purposes, for example
kamuy-nomi, a ritual honouring a certain *kamuy,* or god, and the

iomante, the "sending away" of the *kamuy* of a bear, an owl, or even a wolf, whom the Ainu believed they liberated from the body of the animal at the moment of the kill.[31] In all of these festivities, the presence of Japanese items became an indispensable element that contributed to the Ainu's relationship with their spiritual environment.[32]

The integration of Japanese goods also had a deep impact on the domestic life of the Ainu. Since the Ainu did not manufacture their own iron products, the increased use of metal items contributed to their growing dependence, even as it led to decreased production of their native earthenware products. Goods such as lacquer cups and iron pots and kettles were incorporated into the daily domestic lives of the Ainu.[33] In the words of Walker, "The acquisition and use of Japanese goods became integrated into the very fabric of Ainu society."[34]

Prestige in Ainu Society

The acquisition of Japanese items also meant the attainment of wealth. In Ainu communities, Japanese goods determined the economic and political status of an Ainu. An Ainu who had acquired many Japanese items, as well as Russian items and Chinese cloth obtained from trade with the Russians, was considered rich. He would be revered by the other Ainu in his community and by other Ainu communities. In these instances, Japanese items shed their earlier utilitarian value and became, in the hands of the Ainu, objects with a completely different value; value that legitimized authority. It should be noted that wealthy Ainu lived in areas where there was active trade with the Japanese. Such wealthy Ainu possessed numerous servants, known as *utar,* and anywhere from three to five wives. Thus, the attainment of wealth translated to good fortune in trade with the Japanese, a paradigm which appears in Ainu folktales, some of which emphasize that properly conducting rituals and preparing *inaw* augers well for the Ainu in trade with the Japanese.

As we have seen, the trade with the *wajin* produced powerful chiefs within the Ainu community. Matsumae vassals worked
through some of these influential chiefs to organize and consolidate
Ainu communities in a certain area. By being given Japanese names
and titles, as well as Japanese goods, the chiefs gained respect from
Ainu communities. The presence of influential chiefs strengthened
the role of leadership to an extent unknown in traditional Ainu
society.[35] The Matsumae domain held audiences with these chiefs
in ceremonies known as *omusha,* an event during which Japanese
rules and regulations were communicated to the Ainu. *Omusha*
was literally a political tool with which the Matsumae managed the
trading posts and fisheries in Ezo. It allowed Matsumae vassals to
influence the Ainu on a local level and also gave the Matsumae
legitimacy over the Ainu. This was confirmed through the practice
in which Matsumae vassals nominally approved the chief selected
by the Ainu community,[36] a practice that legitimized Matsumae
authority over the Ainu community and incorporated the Ainu
chief into the Matsumae administrative structure.

The Changing Relationship between the Ainu and their Natural
Environment

The integration of trade and Japanese goods into Ainu
society changed the relationship between the Ainu and their surrounding natural environment. Since animal skins could be traded
for rice, tobacco, sake, and other Japanese items that had become
indispensable or valuable in the lives of the Ainu, they began to
hunt for commercial profit rather than for spiritual values, or
food and skins. The Ainu believed that the moral righteousness
of the hunter determined whether he would successfully catch a
bear or deer. Animals were considered to be gods in temporary
guise, which meant that they would choose the most righteous and
good-natured hunter, not necessarily the most skilled, by whom
they wished to be killed.[37] Once the arrows pierced the animal,
the god would be released from the body of the animal to join the

world of the gods, or *kamuy-mosir*. However, the advent of trade forced the hunt to take on commercial connotations.

The Rise of *Casi*—Border Conflicts between Ainu Communities

By the 18th century, trade had become an indispensable part of the Ainu's daily life. The amount of natural resources to which Ainu communities had access became crucial to their wellbeing. This led to conflicts between Ainu communities over land and rivers where their boundaries overlapped, and where plenty of fish and animals could be caught.[38] Ainu communities located along river systems began coalescing into larger groups led by powerful chiefs. The chiefs possessed firearms and they raised raiding parties to fight one another's groups.[39]

Ainu-constructed fortifications, known as *casi* (*chashi* in Japanese) were built in order to defend resources that were necessary for subsistence and access to trade from other competing Ainu communities. About 530 *casi* have been identified throughout Ezo, most of them located in eastern Ezo where hunting for animal skins took place and where competition over resources was most acute. It is important to note that *casi* were mainly constructed in the 17th century (1600-1667) which is at about the same time as when the *wajin* expanded their trade network across Ezo. Such evidence suggests a direct link between the growth of trade between the Ainu and the *wajin* and the increase in rivalry between Ainu communities.[40] Historians such as Kaiho Mineo assert that the *casi* were constructed by Ainu who either wanted to resist or encourage regional expansion under a charismatic chief. Kaiho suggests that these chiefs, such as Shakushain and Onishibi,[41] organized trade networks to accumulate valuable commodities from mainland Japan.[42]

The intensification of trade caused increased hunting and the depletion of natural resources. Trade also created disparities between the economic wellbeing of Ainu communities. For instance, a community located in an area with a rich supply of natural resources acquired a lot of items from the *wajin*, whereas communities located in areas with a poor supply of natural resources obtained very little from the *wajin*. Since the Ainu had become dependent on trade to a large extent, the inability to gain access to natural resources sometimes led to starvation.[43]

Conclusion

In conclusion, the two *wajin* forces (the merchants in the economic arena and the Matsumae vassals in the political arena) had extended their influence over decentralized Ainu communities through trade by the middle of the Tokugawa period. The Ainu were subjugated under the *wajin*, people whose economic and political motivations incited them to expand their trading sphere and incorporate the Ainu into their trade structure as labourers. The merchants took over management of the trading posts, which meant that they had complete control over trade with the local Ainu. Ambitious merchants such as Hidayao Kybei ran fisheries where Ainu were employed as labourers all year round. The trading posts became a local monopoly, and some trade fiefs in eastern Ezo included not just the trading posts but also travel inns, storehouses, and shrines. This shows that capitalism had already started to develop during the Tokugawa period. As we have seen, the merchants acquired these fiefs because the *chigyonushi* had become indebted to them. This demonstrates that the merchants in Ezo were capitalists who needed feudalism to survive.

The Matsumae vassals, meanwhile, extended their power and influence through ceremonies known as *omusha*. During these ceremonies, rules and regulations were read out to the assembled Ainu chiefs. This symbolized Matsumae power. It also allowed Matsumae vassals to influence the Ainu on a local level and gave the Matsumae legitimacy over the Ainu. This was confirmed through the practice in which Matsumae vassals nominally approved the chief selected by the Ainu community,[44] a practice that legitimized Matsumae authority over the Ainu community.

What is interesting to note, however, is the fact that the Matsumae family blurred the social distinction between merchants and vassals in Ezo. The Confucian-inspired ideology that raised the vassals to the top rank in society and degraded the merchants to the bottom rung on the social ladder, an ideology that had helped consolidate the Tokugawa polity under the Shogunate, was neglected. Walker quotes from records set down by Sato Genrokuro the words, "in Matsumae, what vassals do and what merchants do is, of course, the same thing."[45] Apparently, vassals on their trade fiefs did basically the same things as the merchants, and town magistrates (such as Kudo Heizaemon) collected their income from a nearby trading post.[46] This fuzzy distinction between the merchants and vassals became the target for those who wanted the Shogunate to take direct control over Ezo.[47] They argued that vassals who engaged in trade were hardly in a position to govern the northern boundary properly.

The Ainu, meanwhile, became dependent on trade with the *wajin* for their subsistence. Japanese goods were incorporated into the ritual culture of the Ainu people, there was an increase in the use of metal items gained from trade with the *wajin,* and Japanese goods began to determine the economic and political status of an Ainu. In addition, powerful chiefs were created through contact with the Matsumae vassals, people who sought to channel their authority through these local chiefs. All of these factors contributed to the Ainu's growing dependency on the *wajin.*

My hypothesis was fairly correct. The subjugation of the Ainu had already begun by the middle of the Tokugawa period through trade, which allowed two *wajin* forces (the merchants in the economic arena and the Matsumae vassals in the political arena) to extend their power over decentralized Ainu communities. What was lacking in my hypothesis was the fact that the two *wajin* forces (the merchants and the vassals) were merging together and that the social distinction between them was becoming unclear. By investigating the ways in which these two forces extended their influence over decentralized Ainu communities, I discovered that both economic and political factors played an important role in the conquest of the Ainu in Ezo.

[1] Japanese words (personal names, place names, and other historical terms) are written according to the standard system of Romanization for Japanese, known as "Hebon-shiki", named after its founder, Dr James Hepburn. In the Hebon-shiki ("Hepburn system"), double vowels that are held for twice as long as single vowels and which occur frequently in "O" and "U' sounds are written with a macron on top (example: Hokkaido, Tokyo, Daimyo etc).

[2] *wajin:* Term that refers to the people of pre-modern Japan. The Ainu and Okinawans are not included in this category. However, since the Ainu and Okinawans are also Japanese citizens in modern-day Japan, I decided to use the term *wajin* instead of "Japanese" to refer to non-Ainu people.

[3] Tokugawa period: 1600-1868. During this period, the Tokugawa Shogunate ruled Japan from Edo, the seat of power. All foreign trade and diplomacy were approved in Edo in the guise of maritime prohibitions. Within Japan, the Shogunate exerted its power and influence over the various Daimyo, who each controlled a Han, or feudal domain. There were approximately 266 Han in Tokugawa Japan.

[4] Names of Japanese people are written in Japanese order, with family name first.

[5] Doshin Hokkaido Newspaper November 17 2009 [Online] available from: www:hokkaido-np.co.jp/news/politics/200495.html (accessed 30 November 2009)

[6] Sasaki Toshikazu, ("Uimam to Shikki" ["Uimam and Lacquerware Bowls"]) in: Honda Yoko, ed., (Ainu no koeki-sekai [Trade World of the Ainu]) (Sapporo: Yogen-gaisha Karin-sha, 2008) pp. 77-78

[7] Ibid., p. 77

[8] Richard Siddle, Race, Resistance and the Ainu of Japan (London: Routledge, 1996) pp. 32-33

[9] Brett L. Walker, The Conquest of Ainu Lands: Ecology and Culture in Japanese Expansion, 1590-1800 (Los Angeles: University of California Press, 2006) pp. 88-99

[10] Siddle, p. 33

[11] Robert F. Flershem and Yoshiko N. Flershem, (Ezo-chi Basho-ukeoinin: Yamada Bun'emon-ke no katsuyaku to sono rekishiteki haikei [The Merchants in Charge of Trading Posts in Ezochi: The Activities and Historical Background of the Yamada Bun'emon Family]) (Sapporo: Hokkaido Shuppan Kikaku Sento, 1994) p. 12

[12] Kikuchi Isao, ("Ezo-ga-shima to Hoppo-sekai" ["The Island of Ezo and the Northern World"]) in: Kikuchi Isao, ed., (Ezo-ga-shima to Hoppo-sekai [The Island of Ezo and the Northern World]) (Tokyo: Yoshikawa Kobunkan, 2003) p. 72

[13] Ezochi, as opposed to Wajinchi, was territory in Ezo that was not under direct control of the Matsumae domain.

[14] Walker, p. 90

[15] Flershem, pp. 16-17

[16] Walker, p. 91 and p. 97

[17] Ibid., p. 68

[18] In the first half of the Tokugawa period, the Ainu saw themselves as 'middlemen' between Japanese and Russian traders. Powerful Ainu communities in Nokkamappu, Kiitappu, and Akkeshi and on Kunashir and Iturup islands forged commercial relations that stretched all the way from Ezo to the Kamchatka Peninsula. With the introduction of the Russian-sponsored tribute system (the *yasak* system), these commercial networks extended all the way to the markets of Russia (Walker, p. 156). In the southern Kurils region, the language used in trade between the Ainu and Russians was Ainu (Walker, p. 169).

[19] Walker, p. 171

[20] In the late 18th century, shogunal policies cut Ainu from their traditional trade sphere and forced them to look inward to Japan for their livelihood. This changed the position of the Ainu people within the political sphere of Japan. Whereas previously they had been inhabitants of an island (Ezo) that was located outside the Tokugawa polity, by being prohibited from trading freely with the Russians, the Ainu were being incorporated into the Japanese state. The rules which prohibited contact with foreigners that were applied to Japanese subjects were being applied to the Ainu. This implies how the Shogunate was attempting to "Japanize" the Ainu people. First, shogunal policies tried to change the external appearance of the Ainu and make them more "Japanese". This policy did not succeed, however, due to the firm resistance of the Ainu people. Shogunate officials such as Kondo Jozo took charge of implementing forceful methods of "Japanizing" Ainu living on Iturup, an island that lay on the borderline between Japan and Russia (Kikuchi, p. 80). This was one large step in which the Ainu lost their independence to the Japanese state.

[21] Walker, p. 156, p. 159, and pp. 160-161

[22] Ibid., pp. 158-159

[23] Ibid., pp. 159-160

[24] Toshikazu Sasaki, et al., (Ainu no-michi [The Ainu Road]) (Tokyo: Yoshikawa Kobunkan, 2005) pp. 180-181

[25] Shigeru Kayano, Our Land was a Forest: An Ainu Memoir (Boulder: Westview Press, 1994) translated by Kyoko Selden and Lili Selden, p. 36

[26] Sasaki, et al., p. 181

[27] The Saru River flows through south-central Hokkaido.

[28] Kayano, p. 28

[29] Sasaki, et al., p. 181

[30] Kikuchi, pp. 76-77

[31] Walker, pp. 112-115

[32] According to Ainu beliefs, all natural phenomena, such as nature (including animals, plants, and fish), epidemics, fire, water, wind, earthquakes, tsunami, lightning and geographical features (such as mountains, lakes, oceans, and swamps) are possessed of a *kamuy* (Shigeki Akino, et al., (Ainu bunka no kiso-chishiki [Basic Knowledge about Ainu Culture]) (Tokyo: Sofokan, 2007) pp. 138-140 and p. 143). *Kamuy* is the term for 'god' or 'spirit'.

[33] Walker, p. 93 and p. 109

[34] Ibid., p. 97

[35] Fred C.C. Peng, and Peter Geiser, The Ainu: The Past in the Present (Hiroshima: Bunka Hyoron Publishing Company, 1977) p. 260

[36] Walker, pp. 205-206

[37] It was therefore the animal that willingly came before the most righteous hunter and purposely got killed.

[38] Walker, pp. 123-124

[39] Siddle, p. 34

[40] Walker, p. 123

[41] Shakushain led an uprising against the *wajin* in 1669. He was chief of the Shibuchari Ainu. Onishibi was chief of the Hae Ainu. Disputes often arose between these two Ainu communities, allegedly, because Hae Ainu often crossed into Shibuchari territory and pillaged their natural resources. (Walker, pp. 54-55)

[42] Ibid., p. 124

[43] Ibid., p. 127

[44] Ibid., pp. 205-206

[45] Ibid., p. 89

[46] Ibid., pp. 89-90

[47] The first period of shogunal rule in Ezo began in the late 18th century.

Bibliography

English Sources

Kayano, Shigeru, <u>Our Land was a Forest: An Ainu Memoir</u>
Boulder: Westview Press, 1994, translated by Kyoko Selden and
Lili Selden
    This source was useful because it was written from an
Ainu's point of view. The writer, Mr. Kayano Shigeru, is of Ainu
descent, andt he knows many things about Ainu folklore and
customs. The book provided the reader with an idea of how the
Ainu felt about losing their unique way of life to the new life
imposed on them by the *wajin*. On the other hand, it was a little
biased because it sympathized solely with the Ainu's standpoint.
The writer's emotions also made the source subjective.

Peng, Fred C.C., and Peter Geiser, <u>The Ainu: The Past in
the Present</u> Hiroshima: Bunka Hyoron Publishing Company,
1977
    This source approached the history of the Ainu from an
anthropological perspective. It was useful for this research
because it investigated the role of leadership in Ainu
communities.

Siddle, Richard, <u>Race, Resistance and the Ainu of Japan</u>
London: Routledge, 1996
    This source offered precise explanations about the
changing nature of the relationship between the Ainu and the
wajin.

Walker, Brett L., <u>The Conquest of Ainu Lands: Ecology
and Culture in Japanese Expansion, 1590-1800</u> Los Angeles:
University of California Press, 2006
    This source was immensely valuable for this research.
Walker's study of the Ainu was insightful and analytical. It was a
great piece of scholarship, a work which explored many fields
of history, such as culture, diplomacy, epidemics, and medicine.
This source portrayed the dynamic relationship between the
Ainu and the *wajin* from 1590 to 1800, frequently relating it to
events taking place in the larger framework of the Tokugawa
polity.

Japanese Sources

Akino, Shigeki, et al., (Ainu bunka no kiso-chishiki [Basic Knowledge about Ainu Culture]) Tokyo: Sofokan, 2007
This source contained detailed information about the Ainu's spiritual beliefs. It provided a clear explanation about the different types of *kamuy* and their significance in the Ainu's worldview.

Flershem, Robert G., and Yoshiko N. Flershem, (Ezo-chi Basho-ukeoinin: Yamada Bun'emon-ke no katsuyaku to sono rekishiteki haikei [The Merchants in Charge of Trading Posts in Ezochi: The Activities and Historical Background of the Yamada Bun'emon Family]) Sapporo: Hokkaido Shuppan Kikaku Sento, 1994
This source was helpful because it investigated the economic relationship between the *chigyonushi* and the merchants from mainland Japan. On the other hand, it was too detailed. It lacked conciseness and clarity, which meant that the reader often lost the thread of the argument amidst the jumble of specialized words.

Kikuchi, Isao, ("Ezo-ga-shima to Hoppo-sekai" ["The Island of Ezo and the Northern World"]) in: Kikuchi Isao (ed.) (Ezo-ga-shima to Hoppo-sekai [The Island of Ezo and the Northern World]) Tokyo: Yoshikawa Kobunkan, 2003
This source was very valuable for this research. It illustrated the relationship between the Ainu and the *wajin* using reliable evidence. The book did not antagonize the *wajin* merchants, and it did not portray the Ainu as being the objects of mere compassion. The book sought to define the reality of the Ainu's way of life in Ezo, not create a generalized overview of their history as a conquered people.

Sasaki, Toshikazu, et al., (Ainu no michi [The Ainu Road]) Tokyo: Yoshikawa Kobunkan, 2005
This source provided summaries about the Ainu's history. It was useful because it explained how the burgeoning economy of the Tokugawa polity, with its constant demand for fertilizer, instigated merchants at *wajin*-controlled fisheries in Ezo to force the Ainu to work long hours with little pay. The herring caught by the Ainu labourers were shipped off to mainland Japan to be used as fertilizer.

Sasaki, Toshikazu, ("Uimam to Shikki" ["Uimam and Lacquerware Bowls"]) in: Honda Yoko (ed.) (Ainu no koeki-sekai [Trade World of the Ainu]) Sapporo:Yogen-gaisha Karin-sha, 2008

This source explained about the trade between the Ainu and the *wajin* that took place at the beginning of the Tokugawa period. It showed what items were being exchanged between the Ainu and the *wajin* and how each side benefitted from the other during *uimam* ceremonies.

Internet Sources:

Doshin Hokkaido Newspaper November 17 2009 [Online] Available from: www.hokkaido-np.co.jp/news/politics/200495. html, Accessed 30 November 2009.

This source explained about the Ainu's political status in modern-day Japan.

Other Sources

Interview with Mr. Kayano Shiro at the Kayano Shigeru Ainu Museum in Nibutani on 7 July 2009, 2 hours.

The interview with Mr. Kayano Shiro was incalculably valuable for this research. Mr. Kayano Shiro explained many things about the Ainu political situation in mainstream Japanese politics. He also recounted his father's (Mr. Kayano Shigeru, the eminent Ainu writer and political activist) contribution to boosting the Ainu community's prestige in Japanese politics. Mr. Kayano Shiro demonstrated the difficulties encountered in campaigning for Ainu people's rights, such as: a) difference of opinion between Ainu communities located in different parts of Japan b) reluctance of Ainu people to admit to their Ainu identity and c) the indifference of the majority of the Ainu community to the efforts made by a few select Ainu elites to gain political rights for the Ainu. Mr. Kayano Shiro kindly took his time to speak with me about many Ainu-related topics. The issues that we discussed were highly thought-provoking. Although the subject matters that we discussed during our interview were not directly used in this investigation, my paper definitely benefitted from his expertise.

VARSITY ACADEMICS®

Since 1987, *The Concord Review* has published 1,022 history research papers, averaging 6,000 words, on a wide variety of historical topics by high school students in thirty-seven countries. We have sent these essays to our subscribers in thirty-two countries. This quarterly, the only one in the world for the academic work of secondary students, is tax-exempt and non-profit, and relies on subscriptions to support itself.

The cost of a yearly subscription is $40 [foreign subscriptions $45, foreign air mail $50]. **Orders for 26 or more [class sets] will receive a 40% discount.** Schools in California, Connecticut, Georgia, Massachusetts, New Hampshire, New York, Singapore, Thailand, Vermont, and Virginia now have class sets, and we hope you will consider ordering one. We are listed with the major subscription services, and you can also place your order through them.

Please send your pre-paid orders,
with your name and address, to:

TCR Subscriptions
730 Boston Post Road, Suite 24
Sudbury, MA 01776 U.S.A.

[visit our website/blog at http://www.tcr.org/blog]

We are a 501(c)(3) tax-exempt Massachusetts corporation.

David Hackett Fischer
Historians' Fallacies: Toward a Logic of Historical Thought
New York: Harper Perennial, 1970, p. 14

...But there are many historical problems of primary
importance to all inquirers, whatever their opinions may be, which are
clearly not metaphysical. "How many people voted in the election of
1840?" "How did the price of cotton change in the 1850s?" "What did
the Halfway Covenant mean to the men who made it?" "Was Franklin
Roosevelt more interventionist than a majority of the American
people in 1940, or less so?" Non-metaphysical questions can be
exceedingly complex and sophisticated. "How and when did habits
of authority develop and decline in English and American politics?"
"How did the personality patterns of Negro slaves change during the
period of their enslavement?"

These are urgent questions, and they are empirical questions,
which can be put to the test. The reader will note that not one of
them is a "why" question. In my opinion—and I may be a minority
of one—that favorite adverb of historians should be consigned to
the semantical rubbish heap. A "why" question tends to become a
metaphysical question. It is also an imprecise question, for the adverb
"why" is slippery and difficult to define. Sometimes it seeks a cause,
sometimes a motive, sometimes a reason, sometimes a description,
sometimes a process, sometimes a purpose, sometimes a justification.
A "why" question lacks direction and clarity; it dissipates a historian's
energies and interests. "Why did the [U.S.] Civil War happen?" "Why
was Lincoln shot?" A working historian receives no clear signals
from these wooly interrogatories as to which way to proceed, how to
begin, what kinds of evidence will answer the problem, and indeed
what kind of problem is raised. There are many more practicable
adverbs—who, when, where, what, how—which are more specific and
more satisfactory. Questions of that sort can be resolved empirically,
and from them a skilled historian can construct a project with much
greater sophistication, relevance, accuracy, precision, and utility,
instead of wasting his time with metaphysical dilemmas raised by his
profound "why" questions, which have often been turned out to be
about as deep as the River Platte.

It is improbable that this will happen, among historians, in
the foreseeable future. "Why" questions are rooted in the literature
and institutionalized in the graduate schools, and for most of my
colleagues a historical discipline without them is as strange as a system
of non-Euclidean geometry...

Ralph Waldo Emerson Prize 2012

REASSESSING THE NEEDHAM QUESTION: WHAT FORCES
IMPEDED THE DEVELOPMENT OF MODERN SCIENCE
IN CHINA AFTER THE 15TH CENTURY?

Jonathan Lu

Abstract

Why did modern science not develop in China, despite the fact that up until the 15th century, ancient China led the West for over a millennium in scientific discovery and technological advancement? This is the so-called "Needham Question," named after Joseph Needham (1900-1995), a brilliant Cambridge Sinologist, biochemist and historian of science who first posed the question in the 1940s. This essay will analyze Needham's own answer to this question, as well as the main theories that offer historical, philosophical, political, economic and cultural perspectives on the paradox. It will also assess the relevance of The Needham Question to the study of the history of science and technology, particularly in the context of China's astonishing re-emergence as a global economic and political power.

The author is a Freshman at Stanford. He was a Senior at Chinese International School in Hong Kong, where he wrote this IB History (Higher Level) paper for Mr. David Walker in the 2010/2011 academic year.

Introduction

Writing in 1620, the English philosopher Francis Bacon proclaimed the three greatest interventions in world history to be printing, gunpowder and the compass. According to Bacon:

> These three have changed the whole face and state of things through-out the world; the first in literature, the second in warfare, the third in navigation; whence have followed innumerable changes, in so much that no empire, no sect, no star seems to have exerted greater power and influence in human affairs than these mechanical discoveries.[1]

Not surprisingly for a man of his era, Bacon presumed that these inventions had originated in Europe. It was not until the end of World War II, however, that a relatively obscure English scientist from Cambridge University revealed that all three inventions identified by Bacon, and indeed, hundreds of other scientific, mathematical and technological discoveries had emanated from China. The scientist was Joseph Needham (1900-1995), a tall, bril-liantly erudite and eccentric biochemist obsessed with the history, language, science, and civilization of China.

Needham's revelations were nothing short of stunning. At the time, many in the West looked down upon modern China as a backward, impoverished and illiterate nation. The Jesuits, who first entered China in the late 16th century, opened the West to many of the marvels of Chinese civilization. However, these were largely confined to the fine silk and ceramic products produced by Ming Dynasty artisans, and the rich texts of the Confucian canon.[2] Scientific prowess was not something Westerners com-monly attributed to the Chinese people.

Not until the appearance of the British scholar did the world begin to comprehend the breadth and significance of China's contributions. In the remaining five decades of his life, Needham would co-author the largest, most definitive compendium of the history of Chinese science and technology ever produced. *Science and Civilization in China,* first published in 1954, comprises

24 volumes and documents the origins of over a thousand agricultural, astronomical, chemical, engineering, mathematical,
medical, metallurgical, and military discoveries and inventions.
Described by fellow Cambridge scientist and Sinologist Laurence
Picken as "perhaps the greatest single act of historical synthesis
and intercultural communication ever attempted by one man,"
Science and Civilization in China is an astonishing encyclopedia of
creativity and genius, and opened not only the Western world to
ancient China's brilliant scientific history, but also Chinese eyes
to the glory of over two millennia of invention.[3]

Over the course of his remarkable discoveries, Needham
continued to be perplexed by one question: Why, given the
magnificent inventions of its long and ancient past, did scientific
development in China come to an abrupt halt around 1500? Why
did the scientific revolution of the 16th century and the industrial
revolution of the late 18th century occur in Europe and Britain,
but not in China? China had for over a millennium been far more
advanced in science, engineering, and medicine than the West;
but sometime around 1500, this innovation suddenly stopped,
seemingly without reason. Needham became so obsessed with
this question and its many possible answers that he devoted much
of the second half of his life to addressing it. It became known
as "The Needham Question," and scientists and historians of science from around the world have put forth a variety of possible
answers to help understand what happened in China, particularly
in comparison with the western world.

Needham's Introduction to China

Following Great Britain's entry into World War II, China
desperately sought the British government's support for its academic institutions, scholars, and scientists, all under siege by Japanese occupation forces. The Nationalist Chinese were particularly
keen to salvage key documents and archives relating to strategic
scientific, medical and technological know-how. In response,

the British Commonwealth and Foreign Office established the Sino-British Scientific Cooperation Office and cast a net to find a qualified director.[4] Needham, a Sinophile fluent in Chinese, immediately applied for the position and in late 1942, found himself fulfilling a lifetime dream. He arrived in early 1943 in Kunming, in southwestern Yunnan Province, and proceeded onwards to the wartime capital city of Chongqing, where he remained stationed until 1946.

Over this three-year period, Needham travelled across non-occupied China, conducting 11 expeditions and collecting a cornucopia of scientific data. Through observation, investigation and meticulous research, he uncovered proof of the origins of more than 1,000 inventions, devices, processes, and compounds, many of which had until then been attributed to western science. In 1945, Needham published his main findings, including the origins of the printing press, gunpowder and magnetic compass, in his book, *Chinese Science.*[5]

Science and Civilization in China (SCC)

Returning to Cambridge in 1948, Needham soon submitted a proposal to Cambridge University Press to publish a definitive account of his findings in China. The original proposal, dated 15 May 1948, envisaged a one-volume treatise entitled "Science and Civilization in China."[6] Needham noted two objectives in his proposal: first, to present a complete history of science and technology in China; and second, to explain China's contribution to the history of world science and civilization.[7] Cambridge University Press immediately approved funding for the project, and just as quickly, Needham realized that the scope of his book could not possibly be contained within a single volume. The first volume appeared in 1954, and by the time of his death in 1995, *Science and Civilization in China* had grown to 15 volumes.

Even Needham's most discerning critics were astounded by *Science and Civilization in China.* Eminent British scientist Professor Mansel Davies wrote:

> [SCC] is perhaps the greatest work of scholarship achieved by one individual since Aristotle....Needham himself wrote more than 12 volumes....The first 10 volumes alone have 4,808 text pages, 1,202 illustrations, 1,285 bibliographies, and 549 index pages (in Chinese and Roman script). Whilst the size of the work is itself remarkable, it is the thoroughness, the depth, and the enlightenment found in these volumes which make them an unsurpassed historiographic treasure of the 20th century. Carefully detailed, systematic accounts and interpretations of Chinese achievements over 25 centuries in mathematics and astronomy, physics, chemistry, geology, zoology, botany, hydraulics, metallurgy, maritime science, textiles, hygiene, and medicine are presented.[8]

Needham passionately believed in the importance of framing his work in the context of world civilization. Dr. Gregory Blue, who was Needham's research assistant from 1977 to 1990, quotes Needham:

> One of the greatest needs of the world in our time is the growth and widespread dissemination of a true historical perspective, for without it whole peoples can make the gravest misjudgments about each other. Since science and its application dominate so much of our present world, since men of every race and culture take so great a pride in man's understanding and control over her, it matters vitally to know how modern science came into being. Was it purely a product of the genius of Europe, or did all civilizations bring their contributions to the common pool? A right historical perspective here is one of the most urgent necessities of our time.[9]

SCC currently comprises 24 volumes, with three additional volumes under preparation. Remarkably, it is still an active project at the Needham Research Institute at Cambridge, over six decades since its inception.

Scientific Development in Ancient China (circa. 400-1500)

It is important to understand the magnitude of scientific innovation in ancient China and compare it to the state of science and technology in Europe during similar periods. The Chinese have long appreciated the wonders of their storied past. The centerpiece of the magnificent opening ceremony of the 2008 Beijing Olympics was the depiction of the *si da fa ming* (the "Four Great Inventions of Ancient China"), namely the magnetic compass, gunpowder, papermaking, and printing. Showcasing scientific achievement was a metaphor not lost on the Chinese people, who embrace China's new-found pride and respect in the 21st century with excitement and confidence.

The scope of pre-modern Chinese scientific invention is breathtaking. In the fields of mathematics, physics, chemistry, biology, astronomy, medicine, metallurgy, and engineering (civil, mechanical, hydraulic, agricultural, and nautical), these discoveries ranged from transformational inventions such as the abacus, acupuncture, ball bearings, the blast furnace, calipers, cast iron, the mechanical clock, the horse collar harness, the iron plough, plant grafting, the propeller, to more prosaic—but no less ingenious—inventions such as matches, the toothbrush, folding umbrellas and perfumed toilet paper.[10] As Needham wrote, "the mere fact of seeing them listed brings home to one the astonishing inventiveness of the Chinese people."[11]

Needham's genius was to catalog, verify and document the origins of these achievements, large and small, in a manner that allowed Westerners and Chinese to recognize the brilliance of centuries of applied creativity. The table below shows a sample from *Science and Civilization of China*, reflecting a range of mechanical inventions and techniques that originated in China, with the approximate lag time (in centuries) in technology transfer to Europe. The results are startling:

Invention	China's Advancement over Europe (in centuries)
Rotary fan	14
Crossbow	13
Porcelain	11-13
Iron chain suspension bridge	10-13
Canal lock gates	12

Cast iron	10-12
Wagon mill	12
Magnetic compass	11
Paper	10
Wheelbarrow	9-10
Arched bridge	7
Gunpowder	5-6
Movable type printing	4

Source: *Science and Civilization in China*, Vol. 1, p. 242

Needham was able to identify several hundred examples of inventions from China that predated their first appearance in Europe. As Blue remarks, it is interesting to note that in contrast, the West was only able to contribute two mechanical elements to Chinese civilization at the time of the Jesuit missions in the 17th century, namely the Archimedean screw and the crankshaft.[12] Needham's work clearly demonstrates that from 400 to 1500, levels of science and technology in Chinese civilization far exceeded those of Europe.

Needham put his findings into perspective:

If...the Chinese were recording sunspot cycles a millennium and a half before Europeans noted the existence of such blemishes on the solar orb, if every component of the parhelic system received a technical name a thousand years before the Europeans began to study them, and if that key instrument of scientific revolution, the mechanical clock, began its career in early 8th century China rather than (as is usually supposed) in 14th century Europe, there must be something wrong with conventional ideas about the uniquely scientific genius of Western civilization.[13]

Needham's Response to the Question

As Needham began to uncover the ingenuity of ancient China's science and technology, the question which took on his name started to intrigue him. He addressed the question explicitly in his 1969 book, *The Grand Titration: Science and Society in East and West*.[14] He determined that there were two main reasons why Chinese science failed to modernize. The first had to do with the central influence of Confucianism and Taoism in Chinese culture, particularly informing attitudes toward nature and science amongst the educated elite. Confucianism, or more precisely the Neo-Confucian school which emerged dominant in the Song Dynasty (960-1279), was an ethical system emphasizing an inward-looking, mind-focused way of life. Social harmony, happiness and goodness arose from people developing a set of virtues that underlay everyday conduct. Such virtues included filial piety, veneration of ancestors, respect for elders, moderation and conformity of the individual to society.[15] Needham argued that this inward focus marginalized the importance of studying the natural world. In fact, it rendered science frivolous in the grander scheme of what mattered most in life.

Needham felt that Taoism also had a negative impact on the development of the scientific method in China. Taoism stresses love of and respect for nature. As a code of behavior, it teaches that man should leave nature alone—completely—and accept its way, whatever the consequences.[16] The external world is far too complex to be fathomed by analysis, observation or mathematical theories. Originating more than 2,000 years ago, Taoism received official status as a religion during the Tang Dynasty (618-907).[17] Needham believed that its *laissez-faire* attitude toward the natural world proved a cultural and intellectual inhibitor to scientific research and innovation:

It was not that there was no order in nature for the Chinese, but rather that it was not an order ordained by a rational personal being, and hence there was no conviction that rational personal beings would be able to spell out in their lesser earthly languages the divine code of laws which had been decreed aforetime. The Taoists, indeed, would have scorned such an idea as being too naïve for the subtlety and complexity of the universe as they intuited it.[18]

Secondly, Needham argued that modern science failed to develop in China because China lacked the kind of merchant-capitalist system that had been developing in Europe from the late Middle Ages to the Age of Discovery. Needham observed that China had started to lag in scientific innovation during this period.[19] He concluded that without a broad-based system of economic incentives, applied scientific research and development would be haphazard at best. Writing in *Science and Civilization in China*, Needham declared that:

> Interest in Nature was not enough, controlled experimentation was not enough, empirical induction was not enough, eclipse-prediction and calendar calculation were not enough—all of these the Chinese had. Apparently, only a mercantile culture alone was able to do what agrarian bureaucratic civilization could not—bring fusion-point to the formerly separated disciplines of mathematics and nature-knowledge.[20]

Since Needham first raised his question, there have been a multitude of theories attempting to resolve the puzzle. It is somewhat ironic that this question, which absorbed and perplexed Needham's great mind for decades, elicited even more elaborate and sophisticated answers from lesser scientists and historians of science than from the originator himself.

Philosophical Influences on Needham

The 20th century Chinese philosopher Yu-Lan Fung (*Feng Yulan*) had a great influence on Needham's thinking about Confucianism and Taoism.[21] In his seminal 1922 essay "Why China Has No Science," Fung argued that science, in the Anglo-Saxon sense of the term, had no place in China "because the Chinese concern themselves solely with the mind, whereas Europeans concern themselves with knowing and controlling matter."[22] He explained that since the Song Dynasty in the 10th century, the Chinese mind has been shaped by the forces of Confucianism, Taoism, and Buddhism. This so-called "Neo-Confucianism" continues to form the essence of Chinese philosophy today. Its basic tenet is that all conduct should be focused inward on the mind, and that happiness and meaning come from within. Fung wrote that the Chinese had no need for science *per se*: "They had no need or interest in analyzing the external world because it was their minds that they wished to conquer and nothing else."[23] Fung noted that in contrast, Descartes and Bacon, the two great philosophers of western science, had distinct notions of the purposes of science: "Descartes said that it is for certainty; Bacon said that it is for power."[24]

According to Fung, the Taoist belief that there is only one certainty, which is that nature holds all goodness and virtue, negated any need for scientific certainty. Confucians, in turn, had no need for scientific certainty since they sought to know only themselves within the context of self-reflection and discovery. They had no need for scientific power because there was no external force they wished or needed to conquer.[25] Moreover, Confucians could see no use in science if "intellectual certainty and the power to conquer the external world are not included in the idea of good."[26] This overview reveals the key differences between the Chinese and European philosophies of science, and their bearing on The Needham Question. Fung maintained that Europeans were focused on the external world, the world of atoms, the human body, structures, tools, and weapons. In contrast, the Neo-Confucians, heavily influenced by Taoist and Buddhist thinking (the latter even treats the "external world" as an illusion), believe that everything good is already within each person for eternity. So there is no use in searching externally for certainty, power, meaning, happiness, or logic.

In short, the Neo-Confucian beliefs that have dominated Chinese culture, politics and society for over 1,000 years hold that scientific methods and inventions designed to harness nature are fruitless exercises that detract from the pursuit of happiness and goodness. As literary critic Kenneth Rexroth noted in his review of *Science and Civilization in China*, Vol. 4:

Chinese science...is radically, fundamentally different, and demands a willed, sympathetic reorientation of perspective on the nature of nature....Chinese scientific thought has been far more organic than mechanical, permissive than authoritarian in its interpretation of Nature's ways.[27]

Needham himself wrote that Chinese science:

...derives from a world in which Nature works by "doing nothing" instead of by passing laws, in which the universe moves as a great web of interrelatedness of which man and his imperatives are only a part. That is basically a true picture of the Chinese universe. It is a universe of strange and wonderful things. It is a universe Western man is going to have to understand if we are going to survive happily together on a planet where, whether we like it or not, as Confucius said, 'all men are brothers.'[28]

The main problem with the arguments of Fung and Needham is that they cannot explain the stunning advances in science and technology which the Chinese produced from the Song Dynasty to end of the 15th century. In fact the Song period was one of the richest in terms of scientific discovery and inventiveness. By the end of the 11th century, China had coal-burning blast furnaces and produced twice as much pig iron as England did at the height of the Industrial Revolution.[29] The output of coal reached 150,000 tons and per capita income was estimated to be more than five times that of Europe.[30] China produced the most sophisticated textiles in the world at that time. Shen Kuo (1031-1095) and Su Song (1020-1101), two of the greatest scientists and inventors in Chinese history, lived during the Song period.

In the 13th century, a water-powered spinning machine similar to those used in Europe around 1700 was already producing linen thread.[31] China's sophisticated agriculture, industry and commerce astonished Marco Polo, whose native Venice was considered one of the most prosperous cities in Europe at the time. Following the Song era, key inventions included smallpox inoculation, the spindle wheel, bronze type printing, gunpowder, the trebuchet and bombs (12th century); lacquer and pasteurization of wine (13th century); sand clocks, rockets and rocket launchers (14th century), wallpaper and toilet paper (16th century) and the ginning machine (17th century).[32]

In reality, Neo-Confucianism's influence on impeding the development of science and technology in China lay not so much in its philosophical teachings *per se*, but in its enormous influence on the imperial civil service examination system.

The Imperial Civil Service Examination System

A number of scholars, most notably the economic historian Justin Yifu Lin, have argued that the root of The Needham Question lies in the nature and influence of the imperial civil service examination. This formidable system determined bureaucratic appointment and advancement from the 7th century to the beginning of the 20th century.[33] The examinations emphasized mastery of the Confucian canon and its attendant virtues to the near exclusion of mathematical and scientific study. Positions in the imperial bureaucracy conferred much sought-after power, social status and wealth; as a result, the civil service examinations had an enormous impact on the education of the elite. Lin's argument is that preparation for these examinations entailed at least two decades of intense study and "crowded out" any possible inquiry into non-essential subjects. The consequences of this focused academic endeavor were neglect (and official disdain) of the sciences.

In 221 BC, Emperor Qin united China and the country remained an absolute hereditary monarchy until the overthrow of the Qing Dynasty in 1911. Notwithstanding the replacement of dynastic rule first by a quasi-democratic republic and then by a Communist system, China has remained a unified country administered by a centralized bureaucracy for over 2,000 years.

One of the greatest reforms of the Qin Emperor was to establish a bureaucratic system of governance, which has remained largely intact over two millennia. An elaborate pyramidical structure comprising central, provincial, prefectural, county and township bureaus was formed to govern the newly united country.[34] Most importantly, Qin abolished the former hereditary-nepotistic system of appointing government officials and replaced it with a "recommendation system," in which government officials filled vacancies by referral.[35] The hope was that officials would recommend men they considered possessed of talent and virtue. The reality, however, was that the system became corrupted, with wealthy families often buying favor for their sons and relatives.

During the Sui Dynasty (580-618), the method of civil service appointment and promotion was again reformed. The recommendation system was replaced by a fair and impartial civil service examination.[36] Government officials began to be selected and promoted on the basis of merit, namely intellectual talent and virtue. By the time of the Song Dynasty (960-1279), all bureaucrats were selected by competitive examination.[37] This reform proved monumental in Chinese history, and made the imperial civil service unique for centuries in its emphasis on meritocratic selection and advancement. This system continued until it was abolished in 1904, in a vain attempt to reform the dying Qing regime.[38]

Initially, the civil service examination tested a wide range of subject areas, including mathematics, astronomy and the "laws of nature."[39] In 1313, however, mathematics and science-related subjects were eliminated, and by the time of the Ming Dynasty (1368-1644), the examination tested only the Confucian classics, i.e. the humanities.[40]

One of the greatest books on the state of science and technology in pre-modern China was *A Volume on the Creations of Nature and Man: Chinese Technology in the 17th century (T'ien Kung K'ai Wu)*, written by the famous Ming scientist Song Yingxing. His lament on his own book is a sad and poignant commentary on the times: "An ambitious scholar will undoubtedly toss this book onto his desk and give it no further thought; it is a work that is in no way concerned with the art of advancement in officialdom."[41]

Matteo Ricci, the great Jesuit scholar-priest who lived and travelled across China between 1583-1610, made a similar observation:

It is evident to everyone here that no one will labor to attain proficiency in mathematics or medicine who has any hope of becoming prominent in the field of philosophy. The result is that scarcely anyone devotes himself to these studies, unless he is deterred from the pursuit of what are considered to be higher studies, either by reason of family affairs or by mediocrity of talent. The study of mathematics and that of medicine are held in low esteem, because they are not fostered by honors as is the study of philosophy, to which students are attracted by the hope of the glory and the rewards attached to it.[42]

The core of the examination syllabus was the main Confucian canon, comprising *The Four Books* and *The Five Classics*.[43] These totaled over 430,000 characters and required six years of rigorous study.[44] To even quality to sit the final imperial examination, a scholar would have to pass an arduous progression of lower-level examinations. During the Ming and Qing era, these comprised preliminary, county, prefectural, academy, provincial and state examinations.[45] Competition was intense. The pass rate in the Ming era for the provincial examination was 4 percent; for the state level examination it was less than 10 percent.[46] The few who attained the vaunted status of *jinshi*, or top scholar, in the final imperial examination studied, on average, for over 25 years without pause. Only one in 3,000 examinees achieved this ranking.[47]

Historian Lin's response to The Needham Question is that for the ambitious educated classes, there was neither the time nor the incentive to study mathematics and science, or to perfect the techniques of scientific investigation, experimentation and hypothesis testing. By this reasoning, he argues that from the end of the first millennium to modern times, Chinese society never developed a scientific tradition.

It is worthwhile to consider more closely the examination's extreme emphasis on the Confucian classics. On the surface, this focus would be expected, given the dominance of Neo-Confucian thinking in society, and especially among the imperial elite. However, there was a less obvious and more ingenious rationale. According to Lin and China scholar C.K. Yang, the imperial bureaucracy for centuries remained small relative to the physical size of the country and its population because of the prevalent Confucian ethic. From the 16th century to the middle of the 17th century, the total number of Chinese government officials ranged from 10,000 to 14,000, while the population grew from 75 million to

100 million.[48] The ratio of bureaucrats to citizens in China was far lower than those in England (1:200) and France (1:280) at the time.[49] Even at the height of the Qing Dynasty in the mid 18th century, the total civil service did not exceed 40,000, within a total population of 200 million.[50]

China scholar Yang attributes the efficiency of pre-Qing government to the focus on Confucianism in the civil service examinations as well as the continuous assessment required for promotion. Imperial Chinese government placed great emphasis on the ethical virtues of its officials; magistrates and lower-level bureaucrats were expected to rule judiciously and create networks of similarly upright non-officials to provide leverage in local governance. Officials could be trusted to develop wide-ranging ties with merchants, village elders, artisan chiefs and other useful citizens to "get things done."[51] In contrast, the European civil services tended to emphasize specialization and technical skills. The Chinese civil service embodied the Confucian principles of honesty, moderation, piety, obedience, conformity, fairness and harmony. By selecting its officials on the basis of virtues rather than technical skills it was able to rule successfully with a relatively small corps of highly educated people. The continuous 2,000-year history of the Chinese bureaucracy serves as testimony to the power of this system.

Critiques of the Civil Service Examination Theory

One substantial criticism of the civil service examination theory comes from Nathan Sivin, a noted historian of Chinese science and medicine. He argues that China was not unique in creating a "scholar-bureaucrat class immersed in books, faced toward the past, and oriented toward human institutions rather than toward nature."[52] He observes:

In Europe at the onset of the Scientific Revolution, the intellectual world was filled with scholars and dons immersed in books, steeped in the classical Greco-Roman Judeo-Christian classics, and oriented towards the study of the humanities rather than on nature. This, however, did not prevent the great changes in scientific thinking and invention which would sweep across Europe.[53]

Sinologist and historian Derk Bodde concurred with this point, citing the state of academia in England during the early 17th century:

> Of course the Chinese situation was by no means unique in 1600. As a Western parallel, let us consider the early 17th century curriculum at Cambridge. The leading studies at the time were classics, rhetoric, and divinity; mathematics was slighted and the various sciences practically ignored. During William Harvey's years at Cambridge (1594-1602), the so-called medical course was principally devoted to logic and divinity, rather than "physick." And even as late as about 1630, the university statutes threatened Bachelors and Masters of Arts who failed to follow Aristotle faithfully with a fine of five shillings for every point of divergence from the *Organon*.[54]

However, Bodde noted that a remarkable sea change soon occurred at Cambridge in the mid-1600s, in which the study of mathematics, natural sciences and natural history began to be embraced, paving the way for the Newtonian revolution and ultimately, the Industrial Revolution.

Economic Factors

Needham strongly believed that the lack of economic incentives for merchants and the general failure of medieval era Chinese to establish a healthy capitalist system were key factors that impeded scientific and technological development in modern China.[55]

The economic history of China has largely been shaped by the continuous struggle to feed a large population, while maintaining social order. This goal was the main objective of virtually all its emperors, and remains a primary concern of today's Communist rulers. As more than 70 percent of the country's land mass is either mountainous or arid, China's agricultural policies have long focused on intensive farming of the arable land around the Yellow and Yangzi Rivers, and the high precipitation regions in the south. [56] Social scientists Kang Chao and Anthony Tang argue that China's large population created a long-term labor surplus, resulting in relatively little need for labor-saving technological innovation given persistent low real wages and sufficient farming productivity.[57] Moreover, excess labor in low-paying agriculture meant that there was little in the way of economic savings to finance capital investment. Without this stimulus, there were few commercial incentives for technological or mechanical innovation.[58] Historian Mark Elvin describes this situation as a "high level equilibrium trap" and suggests that it can answer The Needham Question.[59]

Comprehensive historical evidence, however, demonstrates that the labor argument is flawed. During prolonged periods of labor surplus, such as the 5th to 15th centuries, scientific and technological innovation flourished across China. Moreover, between the 14th and 19th centuries, per capita output of grains more than doubled, while the population quadrupled from 72 million in 1368 to 300 million in 1800.[60] The greatest weakness of the equilibrium trap theory is that it presumes scientific innovation to be the domain of the masses. While peasants in ancient China did produce much notable agricultural innovation, it was the educated classes who should have driven scientific advancement. The equilibrium trap theory is silent on why modern science did not take hold in any demographic.

Needham highlighted the longstanding hostility of the imperial bureaucracy toward the merchant classes as an explanation for his question. From the Han (206BC-220AD) to the Tang (618-907) periods, the state took an almost adversarial view of the merchant class:

> The prime objective of state policy was a settled, stable and contented peasant population, carefully registered and controlled, which would provide regular and ample taxation in kind, and be readily available for labor service or military service when required. In such a society, the merchant was conceived of as a disturbing factor.... Not only was he the advocate of a materialistic attitude...repugnant to the ethical precepts of Confucianism.... He also provided the population with a model of a possible means of social advancement based purely on the acquisition of wealth.... Moreover, he was an unstable element in society.[61]

During this period, the government tightly restricted the activities of *shang ren* (merchant businessmen). Commercial activity in large cities was confined to walled marketplaces, where trading hours, the types of goods exchangeable, dealings with foreign parties, transportation, distribution and freedom of travel were tightly controlled by local authorities.[62] Most importantly, under the Tang Dynasty, merchants and artisans were excluded from participation in civil service examinations, sending the clear signal that they were not worthy of government service.[63] This ban was not lifted until the Ming period.

However, Needham's anti-merchant argument also has flaws. According to Lin:

> Discrimination against merchants and artisans in ancient China was probably not as serious as Needham makes out...Historical data reveals that successful merchants, money lenders and industrialists of the Han period (206BC to AD8) were treated almost as social equals by vassals, kings and marquises. By the medieval period, big business and financial organizations had already appeared and were flourishing in China, most of them owned by gentry families. Therefore, young men who were not interested in books and learning but who had an adventurous personality could find socially approved outlets in commerce. Furthermore, during the Ming period, the discriminatory laws forbidding merchants to take civil service examinations were formally removed. After 1451, the channel for purchasing offices and even academic degrees was opened. Thus money could be directly translated into position and become one of the determinants of social status.[64]

In Needham's defense, Lin's argument neglects to mention that pre-modern China was not an actively trading society. In external trade, the Ming and early Qing governments virtually closed their doors to foreigners. China's isolationist foreign and economic policies mirrored its Neo-Confucian values. In contrast, western civilization arose around the Mediterranean, which became a natural channel for foreign trade and cultural exchange. The Greek, Roman, Byzantine, Portuguese, Spanish and French empires were all naval powers whose foreign policies were driven by mercantilism and colonization. Great Britain would follow suit from the 16th century onwards. These powers went to war to secure vital trades routes. Continuous war and economic competition served as vital catalysts to scientific and technological advancement across the European states. Such forces were a non-issue in China, and this fact profoundly impacted its technological evolution.

Politics and Bureaucracy in Pre-Modern China

China's long history differs most distinctly from that of Europe in that the former has, since 221BC, been one unified nation state under centralized bureaucratic rule with a common social philosophy and an essentially homogenous ethnic citizenry. The imperial bureaucracy was central to pre-modern Chinese politics. Some historians argue that this institution played a critical role in undermining the advancement of science and technology. Sinologist Karl Wittfogel, for example, wrote of "hydraulic despotism," hypothesizing that since the Eastern Zhou Dynasty (770BC-221BC), most of the country's economic and planning resources were committed to elaborate hydrological programs. These programs aimed to control the annual flooding of the Yellow and Yangzi rivers.[65] This investment, and the massive bureaucracy built to manage it, effectively crowded out resources that could potentially have been deployed in developing alternative scientific and industrial inventions.[66] Despite having some merit, Wittfogel's theory is far too narrow to explain why modern science did not develop in China despite centuries of such innovation during ancient times.

Soon after consolidating power in 221BC, the Qin Emperor ordered the burning of all books relating to history and the "laws of nature."[67] His motive was to rewrite history and propagate his own political philosophy of "legalism," which was devised to unify the country under an orderly system of laws and regulations.[68] In the ensuing centuries, other rulers conducted similar intellectual purges, especially in the sciences. As Bodde noted, the earliest complete surviving Chinese law code of 653 forbids the private possession of "all instruments representing celestial bodies."[69] Violators were punishable by two years imprisonment. Bodde argued that government control of astronomy, which continued through the Qing Dynasty, was probably an important reason why science failed to progress beyond a certain point. In 1600, Matteo Ricci, who had been highly regarded by the Chinese literati and high government officials, had to surrender his entire library of European mathematical and astronomical treatises to the Qing court prior to entering the Forbidden City in 1600.[70] He observed that by that time, most Chinese scholars had already lost interest in mathematics and astronomy because of age-old government restrictions.[71]

While the latter theory has some merit, it does not fully address The Needham Question. It is important to compare Europe's own process of scientific advancement at the time to best understand the Chinese situation. From medieval times through the Renaissance, there were also significant impediments in Europe to scientific inquiry and discourse. The Catholic Church over centuries tried directly and indirectly to control the flow of ideas; the most notorious effort in this regard was the Spanish Inquisition. The clash between faith-based dogma and reason came to a head during the Reformation. European men of science such as Copernicus, Galileo and Kepler faced daunting religious, social and political obstacles to free expression and interchange. Despite these barriers to intellectual exploration, the scientific revolution took place in Europe and set the stage for the Enlightenment and Industrial Revolution to follow. Why the same did not occur in China is the key question and accounted for Needham's main intellectual struggle.

Cultural Impediments

Needham stressed Confucianism's role in impeding scientific progress. Confucianism teaches respect for elders and teachers, and admonishes criticism, especially from young to old. It stresses social conformity and does not encourage free thinking. Rote memorization and veneration of the classics are deeply ingrained in Chinese culture. Celebration of antiquity was traditionally preferred to the celebration of scientific advancement or discovery. Zheng He (1371-1433), the great Ming Dynasty admiral, led a fleet of over 200 ships on seven expeditions that reached India, the Arabian peninsula and eastern Africa.[72] His voyages of discovery, however, were hardly recorded in Ming annals.[73] Zheng He is in fact noteworthy for the reason that he remains a relatively obscure figure in Chinese and world history, unlike Columbus, da Gama, Magellan, Drake and Raleigh. As Bodde observed:

> Reluctance to pursue massive exploration, settlement, trade and exploration abroad also contributed to the lack of scientific development. The voyages of Zheng He to the Indian Ocean and Africa were criticized as wasteful and useless. This contrasts dramatically with the inexorable drive of Europeans, especially from the late 15th century, to explore, colonize and ruthlessly exploit.[74]

Moreover, Confucian philosophy is distinctly anti-violence and anti-war. Never in their history have the Chinese glorified war as a noble undertaking.[75] Therefore, the Chinese people historically felt no need to develop advanced weaponry or major transportation technology—that is, until the foreign incursions of the mid 19th century, when the Qing found themselves hopelessly outclassed in weaponry, logistics and naval strength by the British. Bodde noted that "Confucians had a conviction that a military class does not properly belong to a truly well-ordered state."[76] John King Fairbank wrote more emphatically:

> War is not easy to glorify in the Chinese tradition because ideally it should never have occurred. The moral absolute is all on the side of peace. No economic interest sufficed to glorify warfare; no wealthy neighbors enticed Chinese freebooters across the border or over the sea.... Generals had few triumphs; and they lost their heads as

often as anyone else. Chinese youth were given no youthful worship of heroism like that in the West...Likewise holy wars are not easy to find in the Chinese imperial records, just as an avenging God and the wrath of Jehovah are far to seek...The whole view of the world is less anthropomorphic and less bellicose than that of the Old Testament, or of Islam.[77]

These observations in particular support Needham's point: Confucian thought combined with anti-war and anti-mercantile philosophies discouraged serious interest in ambitious scientific and technological development. The Chinese government's restrictions on the merchant class during pre-modern times were in part a means of keeping businessmen's power in check; they were also a reflection of the Confucian ethic. Confucian Chinese society was hierarchical and comprised four major classes. In descending order, these where the *shi* (scholars), *nung* (farmers), *kung* (artisans), and *shang* (merchants).[78] In a society where the notion of face" and social status is paramount, the placing of the merchant class at the bottom strata of society is telling. The lowly status of the merchant in China also reinforced Needham's belief that disenfranchisement of this group was a major causal factor in China's failure to embrace scientific and technological innovation. Neither economic incentive nor social respect was accorded to entrepreneurship.

Another cultural response to The Needham Question suggests that imperial China, particularly in the Ming and Qing periods, was simply too arrogant to be curious about innovations and discoveries from the outside world. Lord Macartney, the British envoy who was sent in 1793 by King George III to visit the Qing emperor Qianlong in the hopes of opening up Sino-British trade, was summarily dismissed by the Qing court.[79] The Emperor's letter to the English monarch is revealing:

As your Ambassador can see for himself, we possess all things. I set no value on objects strange or ingenious, and have no use for your country's manufactures...It behooves you, O King, to respect my sentiments and to display an even greater devotion and loyalty in the future, so that, by perpetual submission to our Throne, you may secure peace and prosperity for your country thereafter.[80]

Since their first encounters with Spanish and Portuguese traders along the southern coast of China in the 15th and 16th centuries, the imperial Chinese looked down on all foreigners as "barbarians." This prejudice also applied to Western inventions and ideas. The Chinese conceived of themselves as the Middle Kingdom between Heaven and Earth; this hubris can explain why they were generally uninterested in embracing foreign science and innovation. However, this pride still cannot fully explain why indigenous modern science did not develop beyond the 15th century, given the preceding centuries of spectacular ingenuity.

Idiosyncrasies of the Chinese Language

Another answer to the Needham paradox suggests that the Chinese written language itself presented a major barrier to the development of modern science. Because Chinese is a pictographic language with no alphabet or universal building block system, it was very difficult to develop movable-type printing. Producing books, manuscripts, journals and any other form of mass printing was therefore time-consuming and expensive. This fact must have presented a great hurdle in the dissemination of scientific ideas, research and methodologies.

Movable-type was invented during the Northern Song Dynasty (1041-1048).[81] Characters were engraved on moistened clay blocks and placed under a categorization system within an iron frame. These clay typesets were later replaced with wood and then bronze. However, the complex nature of Chinese characters made large-scale printing cumbersome. In 1298, it took several months to print 100 copies of the 60,000-character book *Shengde Gazetteer*, entailing the production of 30,000 wooden block characters.[82] In 1319, it took half a year to print a few dozen copies of *The Extended Meaning of The Great Learning*, which utilized over 100,000 wooden block characters.[83] In 1773, the Qing government had 253,000 bronze moveable types made to print 64 sets of *The Collection of Rare Editions at the Hall of Military Eminence*.[84] In contrast, soon after movable-type printing became available in Europe in the middle of the 15th century, information exchange grew at an astonishing rate as printing presses became more widely available.

But the movable-type theory begs more questions than it resolves. Most obviously, how can it explain the fact that the scientific and industrial revolutions took place in Western Europe and Britain, whereas they did not do so in the Arab, Persian, Greco-Roman and Ottoman worlds, cultures whose languages were also alphabet-based? Moreover, it fails to explain why the Chinese language did not seem to inhibit the development of pre-modern science and technology in China over such a long period of time. Needham himself dismissed the theory:

> There is a commonly received idea that the ideographic language was a powerful inhibitory factor to the development of modern science in China. We believe, however, that this factor is generally grossly overrated. It has proved possible in the course of our work to draw up large glossaries of definable technical terms used in ancient and medieval times for all kinds of things and ideas in science and its applications...We are strongly inclined to believe that if social and economic factors in Chinese society had permitted or facilitated the rise of modern science there as well as in Europe, then already 300 years ago the language would have been made suitable for scientific expression.[85]

The Chinese language is not just a medium for communication and expression. It is, more importantly, the principal carrier of Chinese culture. Imbedded within almost every picture-based character is a legacy of history, customs, folklore and philosophical teachings; in essence each word is a story that conveys profound meaning. Much of this meaning is subtle and nuanced. In a way, the Chinese language can be considered an even more sophisticated means of knowledge transmission than any alphabetic or phonetically-based language. Indeed, the scientific wisdom of the ancients was spread around society through this very mechanism, and new characters were invented to convey new concepts, inventions and discoveries.

The Needham Question and the Industrial Revolution

An obvious corollary question to the Needham puzzle, and one which Needham himself pondered, is: Why did the Industrial Revolution originate in Britain, and not in China? This question would appear easier to address than The Needham Question itself. By the middle of the 18th century, the great universities of Britain and Europe had been heirs for over four centuries to the individual, free-thinking rationalism emanating from the Age of Reason, the Renaissance, the Reformation and the Age of Discovery. Britain was in the throes of the Enlightenment. Science was blossoming at universities and academies, and free exchange between scholars and scientists in Britain and the continent was more the norm than the exception.

In addition, the British Patent System of 1624 laid the grounds for the Industrial Revolution in Britain in two ways, according to economic historian and Nobel laureate Douglass North.[86] Firstly, it gave clear incentives to inventors by protecting their intellectual property rights for a defined period of time. Secondly, by making public the key technical processes of each patent, the system provided a legitimate mechanism for technology and knowledge transfer—and its attendant benefits to other would-be inventors within society.

Ultimately, the furthering of economic, commercial and military interests pursuant to Britain's mercantilist and colonization policies of the 16th to 19th centuries were the fundamental drivers of British scientific and technological innovation. These factors were wholly absent in pre-modern China. The Chinese considered such policies repugnant and irrelevant. China simply had no force driving it to an industrial revolution.

Conclusion

Based on the weight of historical evidence, the most persuasive answers to The Needham Question are the influence of Neo-Confucianism and the lack of clear economic incentives for systematic innovation. Neo-Confucianism inhibited the advancement of science in two ways: firstly, in its philosophical teachings; and secondly, in its impact on the imperial civil service examination system. The examination system itself effectively crowded out scientific study and development. By the time China realized the need to develop strategic technologies, the Qing Empire was already crumbling under incursions from more advanced European nations. Gunboat diplomacy, the Opium Wars, their resulting "unequal treaties," humiliating defeats in the Sino-Japanese War and the Boxer Rebellion, and invasion by Japan on the eve of World War II were the consequences of failing to embrace modern science and technology over so many centuries. When finally forced into war and the world marketplace, China suffered for its years of self-sufficient isolation.

How significant was The Needham Question during Needham's lifetime, and how relevant is it today?

The Needham Question attracted keen intellectual interest from academia in the West. Writing at the age of 93, Needham summarized the intellectual importance that he attached to the question:

If you wish to explain why Europeans were able to do what the Chinese and Indians were not, then you are driven back upon an inescapable dilemma. One of the horns is called pure chance, the other is racialism however disguised. To attribute the origin of modern science entirely to chance is to declare the bankruptcy of history as a form of enlightenment of the human mind. Racialism, in the political sense, has nothing in common with science. Racialism is neither intellectually respectable nor internationally acceptable. Humankind requires a great revival of interest in the relations of science and society, as well as a study ever more intense of the social structures of all the civilizations, and the delineation of how they differed in glory from one another.[87]

In essence, Needham believed that science and civilization are inextricably linked. In his mind, Ming and Qing society did not consider the advancement of science necessary or important. He felt that value judgments which equated scientific prowess with cultural superiority were spurious to the Chinese. To many westerners, Needham seemed an apologist for China's failure to develop and adopt modern science and technology. Perhaps he was; however, his observations were informed by a deep and nuanced appreciation of Chinese thinking and morality.

At the conclusion of his final volume of *SCC*, Needham highlighted the moral importance of his quest: "If a single word was to be sought to describe the guiding thread which has run through all the volumes, I would be inclined to use the word 'justice.' When I started writing, justice was not being done in the West to the other great civilizations."[88]

The Needham paradox also underpins "The Great Divergence" theory put forth by Samuel Huntington in *The Clash of Civilizations and the Remaking of World Order* (1996) and Kenneth Pomeranz in *The Great Divergence: China, Europe, and the Making of the Modern World Economy* (2000). The Great Divergence theory analyzes the reasons why economic growth took off in Europe and the New World in the period following 1600, while by comparison the economies of Qing China, Mughal India and Tokugawa Japan stagnated. Pomeranz argues that the main cause, not surprisingly, was the Industrial Revolution and the fact that modern science and technology were neither encouraged nor embraced by Asian societies during this period. The fact that the Age of Reason, the Renaissance, the Age of Discovery, the Reformation and the Enlightenment took place in Europe also weighs in the calculus. The various theoretical answers to The Needham Question are important contributing factors in this discussion.

It is evident, however, that the conditions present when The Needham Question was first conceived no longer apply in today's China. The influence of Confucianism has been on the wane since 1949. As noted, the Chinese Communist Party (CCP) discouraged adherence to Confucianism in an attempt to replace it with Communist ideology, mainly to maintain their control over society. Perhaps more detrimental to Confucianism has been the post-Mao era focus on economic growth and consumerism. Deng Xiaoping proclaimed in 1992 that "to get rich is glorious," and pushed the country into economic overdrive. Consumerism, materialism and a form of extreme capitalism have replaced Confucianism, Taoism and Buddhism as the ethos of many in China—especially the urban, upwardly mobile younger generation.

"Capitalism with a Chinese face" has taken sway over the country. Since the Deng market reforms of the late 1970s , GDP growth has been the key performance metric for the country's leadership. Entrepreneurship has been embraced, along with technological innovation. Successful businessmen, unlike the merchants of pre-modern China, are the new heroes of the aspiring middle classes. In 2002, the CCP took the unprecedented step of inviting leading capitalists into the party's membership.[89] In today's China, the Confucian social order has been turned upside down. In one of history's great ironies, *shang ren*, the merchant class, now sit close to the apex of society, right alongside the ruling Communist party elite.

Politically, the CCP and central government control society and most of the economy. The Chinese bureaucracy is still large; however, it is no longer defined by meritocratic civil service examinations. Party loyalty is now the main arbiter of appointment and advancement. Moreover, government is generally business friendly, given the emphasis on economic growth. The most important difference between modern and imperial Chinese government is that the civil service today is no longer the principal conduit to social status and wealth. Power still resides in the CCP, but more and more Chinese prefer to find success in the private sector.

As noted, post-Deng Chinese culture has changed radically from that of ancient and imperial China. In fact, it is changing more rapidly than any culture in the history of mankind. While Confucian values appear to remain strong within the family unit, an almost extreme materialism is consuming much of contemporary Chinese society. Needham's observation that there were no economic incentives encouraging merchants to invest in scientific invention is now quite the opposite. Venture capital, stock markets and fierce domestic and global competition provide tangible incentives for scientific and technological innovation. Entrepreneurs and scientists are responding, and there are a growing number of technology-related success stories coming from China.

Most importantly, the leadership of the CCP and the state are now the domain of scientists and engineers. A remarkable 70 percent of Politburo and State Council members have advanced degrees, of which 62 percent are in natural sciences, applied sciences or engineering.[90] This statistic reflects decades of Soviet-style central planning. The enormous investment in physical infrastructure (highways, bridges, airports, railways, telecommunications and energy—including the massive Three Gorges Project) is a testimony to an industrial engineering-based economic model. Government funding for scientific research and development has grown at a compound annual rate of 17 percent over the past decade, and in 2009 was RMB548 billion (or US$88 billion), representing 1.6 percent of GDP.[91] The government is targeting to spend 2.5 percent of GDP on scientific R&D by 2020, implying an annual spending of well over US$250 billion within a decade.[92] The number of students enrolled in higher education has grown from four million in 1999 to more than 19 million today.[93] The most popular university majors are engineering (61 percent) followed by business, finance and accounting (24 percent).[94] The Confucian legacy has indeed been turned upside down.

Given these circumstances, it would appear that China is ripe for scientific discovery and technological innovation. Needham biographer Simon Winchester echoes many contemporary observers of the Chinese economy in his bullish assessment. He argues that China's former scientific stagnation

...may be seen in due course as more of a hiatus, more of a hiccup in China's long history, than a permanent condition. Today's China.. has become so rich, energetic, freewheeling, awesome, and spectacular—that the situation which so engaged Joseph Needham and the small army of Sinologists who followed in his footsteps may itself well have come to a natural end.[95]

A closer examination of modern China, however, indicates that we should be cautious about making overly optimistic predictions concerning Chinese scientific innovation. Beneath the veneer of stunning growth and heavy research and development lie several impediments to sustainable technological discovery. Education in China is a politically sensitive area and is tightly controlled by the CCP. The Chinese pre-tertiary education system is still heavily examination and rote learning based. Free, creative and critical thinking are impossible in a culture that emphasizes recitation and regurgitation, often of irrelevant and largely useless information. Many secondary schools and universities have poorly equipped science laboratories, and textbooks are often outdated. Teaching quality is erratic, and observers comment that teaching is poorest in higher education. Confucian values of social conformity and refraining from criticizing teachers and elders remain firmly engrained. There is evidence of widespread plagiarism and academic dishonesty, in part reflecting the lack of intellectual property rights protection.[96] Since 2002, nearly one third of college students have not been able to find satisfactory employment upon graduation, a testimony to the perceived poor quality of higher education.[97] There are restrictions on freedom of speech and expression, which impact freedom of thought and creativity. Moreover, the obsession with money making, consumerism and material success has made Chinese, young and old, more short-term in their thinking. Many businesses act short-term, often preferring speculative gains and "copycatting" to actual long-term investment in human resources and genuine innovation.

These factors are very different from those Needham and other investigators identified with The Needham Question. Nevertheless, they represent similar impediments to scientific and technological advancement in modern China. It may thus be premature to dismiss the Needham paradox as irrelevant.

Of greater importance than the relevance of The Needham Question, however, is the significance of Joseph Needham's life and work itself. On a multitude of levels, his intellectual accomplishments were monumental. At six feet five inches in height, he was literally a towering figure. His long life spanned all ten decades of the tumultuous 20th century. He mastered eight languages, three of them ancient. Even his name was epic; he was christened Noel Joseph Terence Montgomery Needham. He is the only person to have concurrently been appointed Fellow of the Royal Society, Fellow of the British Academy and Companion of Honour, three of the greatest accolades bestowed by the British establishment. It is telling that the man who now occupies his former study in Caius College, Cambridge is the renowned physicist Stephen Hawking.

F.W. Sanderson, Needham's headmaster at Oundle School, inspired his students to "always think in a spacious way, think on a grand scale."[98] Needham did not fail his mentor. Professor Mansel Davies wrote in Needham's obituary:

> Intellectually a bridge builder between science, religion and Marxist socialism, and supremely so between East and West, he has been called the Erasmus of the 20th century. A sober assessment suggests that, with the passage of time, he will be recognized as a greater figure than the scholar from Rotterdam.[99]

Kenneth Rexroth, one of Needham's most eloquent critics, wrote of *Science and Civilization in China*:

> Needham's book has the same stunning relevance as Gibbon's *Decline and Fall of the Roman Empire*....In sheer interest and lucidity, it is the superior of any history of science and related subjects since Heath's great work on Greek mathematics....There is no work on Chinese civilization in any language that will remotely compare with it, and there are few works which show our own culture at its best, or which raise those best qualities to new heights. Those new heights are reached by forcing us to discard all the baggage of our own conceit.[100]

Philosopher and literary critic George Steiner compared Needham with Proust, and hailed him not only as a remarkable scientist and historian, but also as a gifted artist:

> He is literally recreating, recomposing an ancient China, a China forgotten in some degree by Chinese scholars themselves and all but forgotten by the west. The alchemists and metal workers, the surveyors and court astronomers, the mystics and military engineers of a lost world come to life, through an intensity of recapture, of empathic insight which is the attribute of a great historian, but even more of a great artist.[101]

Needham's former research assistant, Dr. Gregory Blue, comments that "serious and widespread comparative study of the history of science would have been almost impracticable before the appearance of his [Needham's] work, but it is now inevitable."[102] Quoting Sivin, Blue brings attention to the more profound ethical impact of Needham's work: "In the course of broadening and deepening our integral understanding of traditional Chinese culture, practically every paragraph that Needham has written has been designed to be world history, and to urge upon readers a more humane perception of the future."[103]

Perhaps Needham's greatest contribution to humanity was his insistence on studying the history of science in the context of civilization. He saw the two as inextricably linked. He was trained as a scientist, but he lived, thought and wrote as a humanist. Indeed, the title of his magnum opus was purposefully constructed to link science with civilization. More importantly, Needham did not view subject areas as isolated silos, as areas for specialization *per se*. While he meticulously organized *Science and Civilization in China* using conventional taxonomy (mathematics, astronomy, medicine, metallurgy, alchemy, the main engineering disciplines), his genius was to frame these in the cultural context in which ideas, innovations and inventions evolved. His works make us realize that science cannot be fully understood or appreciated through mathematical logic, induction, hypothesis testing and other analytical methods. Needham insisted that science must be learned in the context of culture, language, history, religion, philosophy, and the economic environment—in short, the entire civilization of a people. In fact, he believed that science and technology form an integral part not just of a country's civilization, but also the entire human civilization.

If Needham were alive today, he would no doubt be delighted, and almost certainly not surprised, by China's astonishing economic resurgence. He would have considered the scientific stagnation of the last five centuries as a momentary pause in the timeline of history. However, he would likely be dismayed by the relentless pace of modernization, and its toll on Confucian-

Taoist values and the physical environment. Like many traditional Chinese who are ambivalent about China's race into modernity, Needham would surely hope that the Chinese people, led by an enlightened set of rulers, will somehow find their way back to the Neo-Confucian principles which guided ancient China for over a millennium. Given the perils of climate change, natural resource depletion, rampant pollution, and nuclear and biochemical weaponry, a firm re-rooting in Confucianism and Taoism would be welcomed not only in China, but by all humankind. Respect for nature, and focusing inward on the mind rather than on materialism, is an ethos that kept Chinese civilization stable, unified and harmonious for over 2,000 years. Needham, above all the humanist, offers modern China and the world precious lessons in the responsibilities of science to civilization.

Afterword

     I became interested in The Needham Question after reading Simon Winchester's biography of Needham entitled, *The Man Who Loved China* (New York: HarperCollins, 2008). The man's life, times and astonishing intellect were every bit as fascinating as the grand question he posed.

     Joseph Needham was born in 1900 in London, the son of an affluent doctor. He graduated from Cambridge with a degree in biochemistry in 1921 and received his Ph.D. in 1925. That year, he married Dorothy Moyle, herself a talented Cambridge scientist. He joined Gonville and Caius College, Cambridge as a biochemistry researcher, and became an authority in embryology and morphogenesis. In 1931, he published the three volume text *Chemical Embryology*, a seminal work documenting the history of embryology from ancient Egypt to the early 19th century.[104] He was elected a Fellow of the Royal Society a decade later, an immense achievement for such a young scientist.

     In 1937, he met and fell in love with Lu Gwei-djen, a research associate who had come to Cambridge from Nanjing, China. The two would have a lifelong affair lasting until her death in 1991. Interestingly, Needham's romantic relationship with Lu was sanctioned by Dorothy Needham, and the three enjoyed an unusually open and cordial friendship. It was Lu who introduced Needham to Chinese culture, civilization and language. She tutored him in classical Chinese and within two years, Needham could read and write at a high level of proficiency. Thus began his lifelong love of China, ancient and modern, scientific and humanistic.

Needham's intellectual and personal life was remarkably colorful, and his energies almost boundless. Besides teaching, researching and writing, he was an avid Morris dancer, a devoted Anglican lay preacher and an avowed nudist. His mastery of Chinese language, history and culture was exceptional for a man who started studying them in his late 30s. He was as eccentric as he was brilliant, and Needham lore abounds. An encounter in Fujian at the height of the Second Sino-Japanese war sheds light on the man's fascinating persona:

> Needham and his party were travelling on horseback with guides through a remote, forested region. Suddenly, they came up against another horseback party on the trail, led by a notorious local bandit, their terrified guides whispered. Needham dismounted, stepping in front of the party, up to the bandit leader's horse, and with his customary vigor executed an English folk dance. The bandit watched with interest. When Needham had finished, the bandit dismounted, stepped forward, and performed one of his own ethnic dances. The ice thus broken, everyone laughed and shook hands, and the two parties proceeded on their respective ways.[105]

At the same time, this Morris-dancing nudist could leave most readers breathless with his titanic intellect and erudition. Below is a not atypical entry from *Science and Civilization in China*:

> The philosophy of history was brilliantly studied in the T'ang period with "The Generalities of History of Liu Chih-Chi" in AD710—the first treatise on historiographical method in any language, quite worthy of comparison with the work of the European pioneers Bodin and de la Popolinire, eight and half centuries later. At that later time, China was also to have her Giambattisto Vico in the person of Chang-Hsueh-Cheng. But it was Liu-Chih-Chi's son Liu Chih (fl. C732) and another T'ang scholar, Ta Yu, who invented a new form of encyclopaedic

institutional history, the former with his "Governmental Institutes," the latter with the famous "Comprehensive Institutes—a Reservoir of Source Material on Political and Social History," issued in AD801. But the climax to this sort of work was not reached until the Yuan period, when in 1322, "The Comprehensive Study of the History of Civilization" by Ma Tuan-Lin saw the light. His lucid and outstanding treatise in 348 chapters was essentially a general history of institutions...it paralleled the sociological history initiated by Ma's near contemporary, the great Ibn Khaldun, and the history of institutions later to be achieved by Pasquier, Giannone and de Montesquieu.[106]

Also adding color to Needham's profile was his sympathy toward Communism. As early as the Bolshevik Revolution, when Needham was still a teenager, he exhibited an emotional (as opposed to intellectual) attachment to Marxist socialism.[107] At Cambridge, he was an active member of several socialist groups. He supported the Republicans against the Fascists during the Spanish Civil War, and later became enamored with the Communist party movement in wartime China.[108] He was welcomed by Mao Zedong and China's premier Zhou Enlai during the Chinese Civil War and in the decades thereafter.[109]

Equally fascinating was his involvement with UNESCO. Needham lobbied hard to have "science" added as a pillar division to what was originally going to be the United Nations Education and Cultural Organization.[110] In 1946, he was invited by long-time Cambridge friend Julian Huxley, the founding Director-General of UNESCO, to assume the directorship of its sciences division. Needham served happily in Paris for UNESCO until 1948. He had not planned to leave his comfortable and stimulating position in Paris so quickly. He was forced out by pressure from the CIA, who had discovered Needham's history as a longtime Communist sympathizer.

He returned to Cambridge in 1948, where he lived until his death in 1995. He served as Master of Caius College from 1966-1976, and spent the remainder of his working life supervising the colossal *Science and Civilization in China* series.

[1] Francis Bacon, Novum Organum Book I, Aphorism 129 (London, 1620) http://en.wikisource.org/wiki/Novum_ Organum/Book_I_(Wood) (accessed 3 October 2010)

[2] Immanuel C.Y. Hsu, The Rise of Modern China (New York: Oxford University Press, 2000) p. 106

[3] Eric Hobsbawm, "Era of Wonders," London Review of Books Vol. 31, No. 4 (26 February 2009) p. 19

[4] Simon Winchester, The Man Who Loved China (New York: HarperCollins, 2008) p. 54

[5] Robert K.G. Temple, The Genius of China: 3,000 Years of Science, Discovery and Invention (New York: Simon & Schuster, 1986) p. 3

[6] Winchester, p. 170

[7] Ibid., p. 172

[8] Mansel Davies, "Obituary: Joseph Needham," The Independent (27 March 1995) http://www.independent. co.uk/opinion/obituaryjoseph-needham-1612984.html (accessed 3 October 2010)

[9] Joseph Needham, "The Historian of Science as Ecumenical Man: A Meditation in the Shingon Temple of Kongsosammai-in on Koyasan," Chinese Science: Explorations of an Ancient Tradition (Cambridge, Massachusetts: MIT Press, 1973) p. 18

[10] Winchester, pp. 267-277

[11] Joseph Needham, Science and Civilization in China Vol. 7, Part II (Cambridge University Press, 2004) p. 215

[12] Gregory Blue, "Joseph Needham's Contribution to the History of Science and Technology in China," Science and Technology in the Transformation of the World eds. Anour Abdel-Malek, Gregory and Miroslav Pecujlic (Tokyo: The United Nations University Press, 1982) Sec. 5, p. 3

[13] Joseph Needham, "The Roles of Europe and China in the Evolution of Oecumenical Science," Advancement of Science (September, 1967) p. 83

[14] Joseph Needham, The Grand Titration: Science and Society in East and West (London: Allen & Unwin, 1969) pp. 16-41; 118-122)

[15] H.K. Chang et al., eds., China: Five Thousand Years of History and Civilization (Hong Kong: City University of Hong Kong Press, 2007) p. 230

[16] Colin A. Ronan, The Shorter Science and Civilization in China: 1 (Cambridge: Cambridge University Press, 1978) pp. 94-98

[17] Chang, et al., p. 378

[18] Joseph Needham, Science and Civilization in China Vol. 1 (Cambridge University Press, 1954) p. 581

[19] Needham, The Grand Titration, pp. 184-187

[20] Joseph Needham, Science and Civilization in China Vol. 3 (Cambridge University Press, 1959) p. 168

[21] Needham, The Grand Titration, pp. 115-116

[22] Yu-Lan Fung, "Why China Has No Science—An Interpretation of the History and Consequences of Chinese Philosophy," The International Journal of Ethics (April 1922) p. 258, http://www.jstor.org/pss/2377487 (accessed 9 October 2010)

[23] Ibid., p. 261

[24] Ibid., p. 259

[25] Ibid., p. 261

[26] Ibid., p. 261

[27] Kenneth Rexroth, "Science and Civilization in China," The Nation 10 November 1956

[28] Needham, The Grand Titration, p. 28

[29] Chang, et al., p. 79

[30] Eric L. Jones, The European Miracle: Environments, Economies, and Geopolitics in the History of Europe and Asia (New York: Cambridge University Press, 2003) p. 202

[31] Ibid., p. 202

[32] Winchester, pp. 267-277

[33] Justin Yifu Lin, "Needham Puzzle, Weber Question and China's Miracle: Long Term Performance since the Sung Dynasty," paper prepared for the *World Economic Performance: Past, Present and Future—Long Term Performance and Prospects of Australia and Major Asian Economies* seminar 5-6 December 2006 at the School of Economics, University of Queensland, Australia, pp. 12-13 http://www.uq.edu.au/economics/cepa/docs/seminar/papers~nov2006/Lin-Paper.pdf (accessed 3 October 2010)

[34] Ibid., p. 13

[35] Ibid., p. 13

[36] Ping-Ti Ho, The Ladder of Success in Imperial China: Aspects of Social Mobility, 1369-1911 (New York: Columbia University Press, 1962) p. 32

[37] Lin, p. 14

[38] Ho, p. 32

[39] Ibid.,. p. 12

[40] Lin, p. 14

[41] Ibid., p. 16

[42] Louis J. Gallagher, <u>China in the Sixteenth Century:</u> <u>The Journals of Matteo Ricci, 1593-1610</u> (New York: Random House, 1953) p. 32

[43] Chang, et al., pp. 552-553

[44] Lin, p. 14

[45] Ibid., pp. 14-15

[46] Ibid., p. 15

[47] Ibid., p. 15

[48] Ho, p. 259

[49] John Halligan, <u>Civil Service Systems in Anglo-American Countries</u> (Cheltenham: Edward Elgar Publishing Ltd., 2003) p. 41

[50] C.K. Yang, "Some Characteristics of Chinese Bureaucratic Behavior," <u>Confucianism in Action</u> David S. Nivison and Arthur F. Wright, eds. (Stanford, California: Stanford University Press, 1959) pp. 161-163

[51] Ibid., p. 164

[52] Nathan Sivin, <u>Science in Ancient China: Researches and Reflections</u> (Aldershot, England: Variorum, 1995) p. 57

[53] Ibid., pp. 57-58

[54] Derk Bodde, <u>Chinese Thought, Society and Science</u> (Honolulu: University of Hawaii Press, 1991) p. 215

[55] Needham, <u>The Grand Titration</u>, p. 211

[56] Anthony Tang, "China's Agricultural Legacy," <u>Economic Development and Cultural Change</u> Vol. 28 (October 1979) p. 3

[57] Kang Chao, <u>Man and Land in Chinese History: An Economic Analysis</u> (Stanford, California: Stanford University Press, 1986) p. 227

[58] Tang, p. 7

[59] Mark Elvin, <u>The Pattern of the Chinese Past</u> (Stanford, California: Stanford University Press, 1973) p. 95

[60] Dwight H. Perkins, <u>Agricultural Development in China, 1368-1968</u> (Chicago: Aldine Publishing Group, 1969) pp. 13-17

[61] Denis C. Twitchett, "Merchant, Trade and Government in Late T'ang," in <u>Asia Major</u> New Series 14, Vol. 1 (1968) p. 65

[62] Ibid., pp. 66-74

[63] Ibid., p. 71

[64] Lin, p. 12

[65] Karl A. Wittfogel, <u>Oriental Despotism: A Comparative Study of Total Power</u> (New Haven: Yale University Press, 1957) p. 24

[66] Ibid., p. 24

[67] Jonathan D. Spence, The Search for Modern China (New York: W.W. Norton & Company, 1990) p. 636

[68] Ibid., p. 636

[69] Bodde, p. 191

[70] Hsu, p. 99

[71] Bodde, p. 191

[72] Edward L. Dreyer, Zheng He: China and the Oceans in the Early Ming, 1405-1433 (Old Tappan, New Jersey: Pearson Longman, 2006) p. 86

[73] Ibid., p. 122

[74] Bodde, p. 251

[75] Ibid., p. 248

[76] Ibid., 203

[77] John King Fairbank, "Introduction: Varieties of the Chinese Military Experience," Chinese Ways in Warfare eds. Frank A. Kierman and John King Fairbank (Cambridge, Massachusetts: Harvard University Press, 1974) p. 7

[78] Bodde, p. 203

[79] Hsu, p. 156

[80] Ibid., p. 161

[81] Chang, p. 573

[82] Ibid., p. 574

[83] Ibid., p. 574

[84] Ibid., p. 574

[85] Needham, The Great Titration, p. 38

[86] James Bessen and Michael J. Meurer, Patent Failure: How Judges, Bureaucrats and Lawyers Put Innovations at Risk (Princeton, New Jersey: Princeton University Press, 2008) p. 77

[87] Needham, Science and Civilization (2004) p. 23

[88] Ibid., p. 206

[89] Joseph Kahn, "China's Communist Party, 'to Survive,' Opens its Doors to Capitalists," The New York Times (4 November 2002) http://query.nytimes.com/gst/fullpage.htm l?res=9F01E1D9153EF937A35752C1A9649C8B63 (accessed 30 October 2010)

[90] Cheng Li, "China's Midterm Jockeying: Gearing Up for 2012," http://www.hoover.org/publictions/china-leadership-monitor/3601 (accessed 30 October 2010)

[91] Evan Thorpe, "Bringing R&D to China," in The China Business Review (March 2010) p. 19

[92] Ibid., p. 19

[93] Yao Li, John Walley, Shunming Zhang and Xiliang Zhao, "The Higher Educational Transformation of China and

its Global Implications," Working Paper No. 13849, <u>National Bureau of Economic Research</u> (March 2009) p. 6

[94] Ibid., p. 6

[95] Winchester, p. 262

[96] Xinwen Yuan, "Why Upgrade Academic Misconduct?" <u>The People's Daily</u> (11 August 2009)

[97] Li, et al., p. 9

[98] Winchester, p. 16

[99] Davies (27 March 1995)

[100] Rexroth, p. 5

[101] Winchester, p. 240

[102] Blue, p. 3

[103] Shigeru Nakayama and Nathan Sivin, eds., <u>Chinese Science: Explorations of an Ancient Tradition</u> (Cambridge, Massachusetts: MIT Press, 1973) p. xxxi

[104] Winchester, p. 28

[105] John Derbyshire, "In Search of Chinese Science," <u>The New Atlantis</u> (Spring 2009) p. 2, http://www.johnderbyshire.com/Reviews/China/needham/html (accessed 2 October 2010)

[106] Davies (27 March 1995)

[107] Sarah Lyall, "Joseph Needham, China Scholar From Britain, Dies at 94," <u>The New York Times</u> (27 March 1995) http//www.nytimes.com/1995/03/27/obituaries/joseph-needham-china-scholar-from-britain-dies-at-94.html (accessed 3 October 2010)

[108] Winchester, p. 94

[109] Ibid., p. 94, 96, 23-237

[110] Ibid., p. 165

Bibliography

Primary Sources

Bacon, Francis, <u>Novum Organum</u> Book I, Aphorism 129, London, 1620 http://en.wikisource.org/wiki/Novum_Organum/Book_I_(Wood) (accessed 3 October 2010)

Cheng, Li, "China's Midterm Jockeying: Gearing Up for 2012," http://www.hoover.org/publictions/china-leadership-monitor/3601, 11 May 2010 (accessed 30 October 2010)

Davies, Professor Mansel, "Obituary: Joseph Needham," The Independent 27 March 1995, http://www.independent.co.uk/opinion/obituaryjoseph-needham-1612984.html (accessed 3 October 2010)

Kahn, Joseph, "China's Communist Party, 'to Survive,' Opens its Doors to Capitalists," The New York Times 4 November 2002, http://query.nytimes.com/gst/fullpage.htm l?res=9F01E1D9153EF937A35752C1A9649C8B63 (accessed 30 October 2010)

Lyall, Sarah, "Joseph Needham, China Scholar From Britain, Dies at 94," The New York Times 27 March 1995, http//www.nytimes.com/1995/03/27/obituaries/joseph-needham-china-scholar-from-britain-dies-at-94.html (accessed 3 October 2010)

Needham, Joseph, and Dorothy Needham, eds., Science Outpost: Papers of the Sino-British Science Co-operation Office (British Council Scientific Office in China) 1942-1946 London: Pilot Press, 1948

Thorpe, Evan, "Bringing R&D to China," The China Business Review March 2010

Yuan, Xinwen, "Why Upgrade Academic Misconduct?" The People's Daily 11 August 2009

Interviews

Dr. Gregory Blue, Professor of History, University of Victoria, Canada and personal assistant to Joseph Needham, 1977-1990
I interviewed Dr. Blue via email exchanges during November and December 2010.

Dr. Peter L. Lee, Honorary Secretary, East Asian History of Science Foundation, Hong Kong
Dr. Lee was a research fellow at Gonville and Caius College Cambridge, 1976-1977, and worked under Joseph Needham. I interviewed Dr. Lee in Hong Kong on 9 December 2010 (on the anniversary of Needham's 110th birthday).

Secondary Sources

Ashton, T.S., The Industrial Revolution 1760-1830 Oxford: Oxford University Press, 1997

Bessen, James, and Michael J. Meurer, Patent Failure: How Judges, Bureaucrats and Lawyers Put Innovations at Risk Princeton, New Jersey: Princeton University Press, 2008

Blue, Gregory, "Joseph Needham's Contribution to the History of Science and Technology in China," in Abdel-Malek, Anour, Gregory Blue and Miroslav Pecujlic, eds., Science and Technology in the Transformation of the World Tokyo: The United Nations University Press, 1982

Bodde, Derk, "Evidence for 'Laws of Nature' in Chinese Thought," Harvard Journal of Asiatic Studies Vol. 20, 1957

Bodde, Derk, Chinese Thought, Society and Science Honolulu: University of Hawaii Press, 1991

Chang, H.K., et al., eds., China: Five Thousand Years of History and Civilization Hong Kong: City University of Hong Kong Press, 2007

Chao, Kang, Man and Land in Chinese History: An Economic Analysis Stanford, California: Stanford University Press, 1986

Dawson, Raymond, The Legacy of China New York: Oxford University Press, 1964

Derbyshire, John, "In Search of Chinese Science," The New Atlantis Spring 2009, http://www.johnderbyshire.com/Reviews/China/needham/html (accessed 2 October 2010)

Dhruv, Rania, and S. Irfan Habib, Situating the History of Science: Dialogues with Joseph Needham New Delhi: Oxford University Press, 1999

Dreyer, Edward L., Zheng He: China and the Oceans in the Early Ming, 1405-1433 (Old Tappan, New Jersey: Pearson Longman, 2006

Elman, Benjamin A., <u>On Their Own Terms: Science in China, 1550-1900</u> Cambridge, Massachusetts: Harvard University Press, 2005

Elvin, Mark, <u>The Pattern of the Chinese Past</u> Palo Alto, California: Stanford University Press, 1973

Fairbank, John King, "Introduction: Varieties of the Chinese Military Experience," in <u>Chinese Ways in Warfare</u> Frank A. Kierman and John King Fairbank, eds., Cambridge, Massachusetts: Harvard University Press, 1974

Fairbank, John King, <u>Chinabound: A Fifty-Year Memoir</u> New York: Harper & Row, 1982

Fung, Yu-Lan, "Why China Has No Science: An Interpretation of the History and Consequences of Chinese Philosophy," <u>The International Journal of Ethics</u> Vol. 32, April 1922, http://www.jstor.org/pss/2377487 (accessed 9 October 2010)

Gallagher, Louis J., <u>China in the Sixteenth Century: The Journals of Matteo Ricci, 1593-1610</u> New York: Random House, 1953

Halligan, John, <u>Civil Service Systems in Anglo-American Countries</u> Cheltenham: Edward Elgar Publishing Ltd., 2003

Hart, Roger, "On the Problem of Chinese Science," <u>The Science Studies Reader</u> ed. by Mario Biagioli, New York: Routledge, 1999

Ho, Ping-Ti, <u>The Ladder of Success in Imperial China: Aspects of Social Mobility, 1369-1911</u> New York: Columbia University Press, 1962

Hobsbawm, Eric, "Era of Wonders," <u>London Review of Books</u> Vol. 31, No. 4, 26 February 2009

Hsu, Immanuel C.Y., <u>The Rise of Modern China</u> New York: Oxford University Press, 2000

Huff, Toby E., The Rise of Early Modern Science: Islam, China and the West Cambridge: Cambridge University Press, 1993

Jones, Eric L., The European Miracle: Environments, Economies, and Geopolitics in the History of Europe and Asia New York: Cambridge University Press, 2003

Li, Yao, John Walley, Shunming Zhang, and Xiliang Zhao, "The Higher Educational Transformation of China and its Global Implications," Working Paper No. 13849, National Bureau of Economic Research March 2009

Lin, Justin Yifu, "Needham Puzzle: Why the Industrial Revolution Did Not Originate in China," in Economic Development and Cultural Change Vol. 43, No. 2, Chicago: University of Chicago Press, January 1995

Lin, Justin Yifu, "The Needham Puzzle, Weber Question and China's Miracle: Long Term Performance Since the Sung Dynasty," paper prepared for the "World Economic Performance: Past, Present and Future—Long Term Performance and Prospects of Australia and Major Asian Economies," seminar held at the School of Economics, University of Queensland, Australia, http://www.uq.edu.au/economics/cepa/docs/seminar/papers~nov2006/Lin-Paper.pdf (accessed 3 October 2010)

Miyazaki, Ichisada, China's Examination Hell: The Civil Service Examinations of Imperial China New Haven, Connecticut: Yale University Press, 1976

Nakayama, Shigeru, Joseph Needham, and Nathan Sivin, eds., Chinese Science: Explorations of an Ancient Tradition Cambridge, Massachusetts: MIT Press, 1973

Needham, Joseph, Science and Civilization in China Vols. 1, 3, 4, 7, Cambridge University Press, 1954-2004

Needham, Joseph, "The Roles of Europe and China in the Evolution of Oecumenical Science," Advancement of Science September, 1967

Needham, Joseph, <u>The Grand Titration: Science and Society in East and West</u> London: George Allen & Unwin, 1969

Needham, Joseph, <u>Science in Traditional China: A Comparative Perspective</u> Cambridge, Massachusetts: Harvard University Press, 1981

Perkins, Dwight H., <u>Agricultural Development in China, 1368-1968</u> Chicago: Aldine Publishing Group, 1969

Rexroth, Kenneth, "Science and Civilization in China," <u>The Nation</u> 10 November 1956

Ronan, Colin A., <u>The Shorter Science and Civilization in China: 1</u> Cambridge: Cambridge University Press, 1978

Sivin, Nathan, <u>Science and Technology in East Asia</u> New York: Science History Publications, 1977

Sivin, Nathan, <u>Science in Ancient China: Researches and Reflections</u> Aldershot, England: Variorum, 1995

Spence, Jonathan D., <u>To Change China: Western Advisors in China, 1620-1960</u> Boston: Little, Brown, 1969

Spence, Jonathan D., <u>The Search for Modern China</u> New York: W.W. Norton & Company, 1990

Sung, Ying-hsing, <u>T'ien-kung K'ai-wu: Chinese Technology in the Seventeenth Century</u> College Station, Pennsylvania: Pennsylvania State University Press, 1966

Tang, Anthony, "China's Agricultural Legacy," in <u>Economic Development and Cultural Change</u> Vol. 28, Chicago: University of Chicago Press, October 1979

Temple, Robert K.G., <u>The Genius of China: 3,000 Years of Science, Discovery and Invention</u> New York: Simon & Schuster, 1986

Twitchett, Denis C., "Merchant, Trade and Government in Late T'ang," in <u>Asia Major</u> New Series 14, Vol. 1, London, 1968

Winchester, Simon, <u>The Man Who Loved China</u> New York: HarperCollins, 2008

Wittfogel, Karl A., <u>Oriental Despotism: A Comparative Study of Total Power</u> New Haven: Yale University Press, 1957

Yang, C.K., "Some Characteristics of Chinese Bureaucratic Behavior," in David S. Nivison and Arthur F. Wright, eds., <u>Confucianism in Action</u> Stanford, California: Stanford University Press, 1959

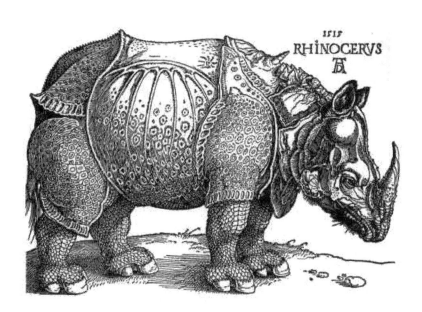

Ralph Waldo Emerson Prize 1996

A DRAMATIC REVIVAL:
THE FIRST GREAT AWAKENING IN CONNECTICUT

Sarah Bahn Valkenburgh

The Great Awakening of 1735-1745 was a reaction to a decline in piety and a laxity of morals within the Congregational Churches of New England. Itinerant evangelizing generated renewed enthusiasm and spread the message of revival throughout the churches of Connecticut. Although the Great Awakening stimulated dramatic conversions and an increase in church membership, it also provoked conflicts and divisions within the established church. As the movement became more radical and emotions less restrained, the subsequent factions which emerged from a difference in opinions concerning the Awakening led to the decline of the revival in Connecticut. The Great Awakening subsided around 1745 because proponents could not sustain enthusiasm, while the government of the colony began regulating itinerant preaching and persecuting New Light supporters of the Awakening. This striking revival of religious piety and its emphasis on salvation ultimately transformed the religious order of Connecticut.

The author graduated *summa cum laude* from Dartmouth and is a graduate of Harvard Medical School. She wrote this paper as a Junior at Greens Farms Academy in Greens Farms, Connecticut for Scott Reisinger's AP United States History course during the 1993/1994 academic year.

The decline in piety among the second generation of Puritans, which stemmed from economic changes, political transformations, and Enlightenment rationalism, was the primary cause of the Great Awakening. During the eighteenth century, political uncertainty and economic instability characterized colonial life and diverted devout Puritans from religious obligations. The first Census in 1790 showed 1 million blacks and 4 million whites in the United States, and there had been a strong development of manufacturing and intercolonial trade. Although this transformation promoted an increase in the standard of living for many merchants and manufacturers in the growing towns and villages, fluctuations in overseas demand and European wars caused inconsistencies within the colonial market. The English government, moreover, was contending with the death of Queen Anne (1714) and the Jacobite effort to usurp King George I (1715 and 1745), and thus the political life of the colonists was also inherently unstable. Not only did economic and political change detract from religious life and the image John Winthrop outlined in 1630 of "a city upon a hill," but the rationalism of the Enlightenment also challenged Orthodox Calvinism. Denouncing the idea of the "inherent depravity" of human nature, the Enlightenment emphasized the accumulation of knowledge through logic and reason. This trend promoted the introduction of math, science, law, and medicine into the college curriculums, which had been primarily focused upon theology and ancient languages during the 1720s.[1] Emphasis upon economic success, political developments, and rational thought pre-empted concerns for the soul and instilled a confidence in salvation despite a laxity of morals. Individual morals declined as Puritans within the community turned increasingly to Arminianism, the belief that preparation for heaven was easily managed and therefore less important, to justify their participation in secular affairs. The supporters of the Awakening pointed to the apparent degeneration of Puritan values to explain the need for revival.

In addition to secular causes of decline, compromise within the Congregational Church contributed to the weakening of religious commitment. To compensate for the decline in piety, which began as early as the middle of the seventeenth century, and to insure a steady, growing congregation, the Congregational Churches of Connecticut and Massachusetts adopted the Halfway Covenant in 1662, which ultimately led to further degeneration of Puritan influence. Prior to 1662, membership in the church required 'regeneration' and credible testimony of a specific conversion experience. The church baptized the second generation of Puritans as infants with the assumption that they would be converted later in life. As politics and economics superseded religion, however, the second generation of Puritans failed to experience an outward conversion. To sustain the population of the congregation, the church adopted the Halfway Covenant, which allowed the children of unregenerate Puritans to be baptized but forbade them to partake of the Lord's Supper and denied them suffrage. Isolating the third generation of Puritans from the traditional means of receiving God's grace, this Covenant furthered the degeneration of the church. In 1690, Solomon Stoddard, pastor of the church in Northampton, Massachusetts from 1669 to 1729, eliminated the Halfway Covenant and allowed the non-confederates, the "halfway members" of the church, to receive Communion. When Stoddard was ordained on September 11, 1672, he had already earned two degrees at Harvard, served as the college's first librarian, and preached for some time in Barbados. An educated and experienced leader within the community and among the clergy throughout New England, Stoddard believed in extending full Communion to all to assure the continued existence of the church.[2] Although the churches of the Connecticut Valley soon followed his example, the second and third generations of Puritans failed to demonstrate the same devotion and discipline that the original Puritans had practiced.[3] John Whiting of Hartford expressed this sentiment and the need for revival in an election sermon of 1686, saying:

> Is there not too visible and general a declension; are we not turned (and that quickly too) out of the way wherein our fathers walked?...A rain of righteousness and soaking showers of converting, sanctifying grace sent from heaven will do the business for us, and indeed, nothing else.[4]

Many devout church members believed the Great Awakening of 1735-1745 was necessary to combat secular influences in the lives of the Puritans and reinstitute the authority of the Congregational Church.

To restore discipline to the churches of Connecticut, a group of ministers and laymen, selected by the General Court, drafted the Saybrook Platform, fifteen "Articles for the Administration of Church Discipline."[5] Approved by minister and Governor Gurdon Saltonstall in 1708, the document was printed and distributed at the cost of the colony. The Saybrook Platform established control over the churches, calling for consociations in each county to oversee major ecclesiastical decisions such as ordinations, installations, and dismissals of Congregational ministers. The Platform also created an association of ministers to assist with consultations, the licensing of candidates, and the recommendation of supplies and pastors. The elimination of local power and the establishment of a hierarchy within the church contradicted the Puritan belief in the autonomy of the congregation, a belief which had stimulated both their rejection of the Anglican Church in the early 1600s and the Great Puritan Exodus. Attempting to unify the churches and establish moral discipline among the unregenerate, the Saybrook Platform created bitter controversies and caused divisions throughout the colony. New London County renounced the proposed articles, and New Haven County interpreted it minimally. In Fairfield County, however, because of a severe decline in piety and discipline, the consociation became a full-fledged court and thus helped to restore order to a degenerated society.[6] Although the Platform did not succeed in every county, it heightened Puritan belief in man's inherent depravity and pointed to the need for revival.

Itinerant evangelists, primarily George Whitefield and James Davenport, spread the revival to churches in Connecticut, alarming conservatives and awakening spiritual concern. In the fall of 1740, George Whitefield, a twenty-six-year-old evangelist who had stirred emotions throughout England, toured the seaboard of the Connecticut Valley and amplified the spirit of the Awakening.

In his sermons, many of which were printed by his good friend Benjamin Franklin, he emphasized the irresistibility of grace and advocated justification by faith. In response to Whitefield's success in arousing sinners and instilling a concern for salvation, the Eastern Consociation of the County of Fairfield met on October 7, 1740 and voted to invite Whitefield to preach in several towns within the district. Acknowledging that "...the Life and Power of Godliness in [these] Parts is generally sunk to a Degree very lamentable," the Consociation requested that Whitefield share his ministry provided he did not denounce unconverted ministers or demand contributions for his orphan house in Georgia.[7] In response to this invitation, Whitefield preached in New Haven on October 26 and Fairfield on October 28. In his journal Whitefield quoted the Governor as saying, with tears streaming down his aged face, "I am glad to see you and heartily glad to hear you." In Fairfield he "preached, in the morning, to a considerable congregation, and in the prayer after the sermon, [he] scarcely knew how to leave off."[8] In a letter to Eleazar Wheelock on November 24, 1740, William Gaylord of Norwalk wrote,

> I realy desired his Coming and was heartily glad to See him, because I believe he excells in that which we (especially in these Parts) want most, I mean Zeal for God and compassion for immortal sins.

Yet in the same letter, Gaylord also declared that Whitefield:

> lays vastly too much Weight upon the Affection, Tears and Meltings etc. that appear in the Face of the Assembly, as an Argument of his success.[9]

Eleazar Wheelock, a New Light preacher from Lebanon and one of Connecticut's greatest proponents of the Awakening, served as the "chief intelligencer of revival news." Because he was the established minister of the North Society of Lebanon, Wheelock received only moderate criticism for his enthusiasm and his itinerant evangelizing. In 1741 he campaigned boldly throughout the colony, and that same year, he wrote 465 sermons to promote the revival.[10] In his letter to Wheelock, Gaylord emphasized Whitefield's powerful oratory and his ability to arouse emotion and enthusiasm among the unconverted members of the church. In hopes of experiencing a conversion, thousands of people travelled across the colony to hear Whitefield's sermons. Nathaniel Cole of Middletown, Connecticut described the riverbanks where Whitefield was preaching as "black with people and horses."[11] Clearly many churches eagerly anticipated Whitefield's sermons and earnestly desired conversion by the Holy Spirit. Although many conservatives opposed Whitefield's enthusiasm and emphasis on emotion, he succeeded in spreading the message of revival throughout the colony.

A second, more radical New Light itinerant, James Davenport, followed Whitefield's example and travelled to congregations throughout Connecticut. He, too, believed in sudden, conscious conversion and employed five specific tactics to garner support and convey his message. Davenport attacked the unconverted ministry, declaring that unregenerate ministers were as damaging to spirits as "swallowing ratsbane or bowls of poison to their bodies."[12] Moreover, Davenport "exploited anticlericalism for evangelical purposes" and preached in locations subversive to the established order, places such as fields, orchards, or barns.[13] Anticlericalism, the opposition to the influence of church and clergy in public affairs, emphasized the need for purity and revival within the church, a church untainted by the secular affairs of the colony. Davenport also employed loud music, often marching through the streets late at night, disturbing the peace, and attracting unfavorable attention. Davenport's final and most important tactic was his theatrical, encouraging oratory and his powerful, extemporaneous sermons. One incident that occurred in New London, Connecticut, clearly exemplified Davenport's radical tactics. On March 6, 1743, he convinced his followers that to be saved, they must burn their idols. Singing psalms and hymns, the participants in this outburst burned their books on the street. Captured by Davenport's rhetoric, the enthusiasts built a second bonfire comprised of petticoats, silk gowns, short cloaks, cambick caps, red-heeled shoes, fans, necklaces, and Davenport's breeches.[14] Although a moderate convinced them not to burn the pile, the threat of the fire illustrated the extent of Davenport's radicalism, a radicalism which characterized the stimulating effects of the Great Awakening on the unconverted. The bizarre events instigated by

James Davenport shocked "Old Lights" and established clergy, disrupting the conservative order of the Congregational Church and the conventional system of Puritan values.

Itinerant preachers succeeded in converting hundreds of unregenerate Puritans and increasing church membership throughout the colony. The Great Awakening witnessed a revival of outward conversions which occurred in three stages: the recognition of sin accompanied by fear, distress, or anxiety, a further dependence upon God's mercy, and, finally, a relief from distress characterized by euphoric emotion.[15] On July 8, 1741, Jonathan Edwards of Northampton, Massachusetts illustrated the second stage of conversion in his famous sermon delivered in Enfield, Connecticut, "Sinners in the Hands of an Angry God," in which he equated mankind with a spider held over a fire. Born into a family of Puritan ministers, Jonathan Edwards rejected the ideas of both his father and his grandfather, Solomon Stoddard. At age five, he read Latin and Greek, engaged in philosophical discussions, and read the theories of John Locke and John Calvin. In 1734 Edwards turned to Locke's theories that sensation was directly connected to learning and that words could be linked to sensory images. One of the first proponents of the Awakening, he employed vivid, passionate language to arouse compassion among his congregants and spread the revival message throughout the Connecticut Valley. To a shrieking, groaning congregation in Enfield, Edwards declared that "...there is no other reason to be given, why you have not dropped into hell since you arose in the morning, but that God's hand has held you up."[16] Davenport, too, elevated emotions and inspired a dramatic number of conversions within the congregations of Connecticut. On July 23, 1741, one thousand listeners travelled to Groton to hear him preach, and the following day one hundred people from the town of Stonington claimed to have experienced an outward conversion.[17] Moreover, in the outburst of enthusiasm in March of 1741 that followed the seven sermons of Gilbert Tennent, a prominent evangelist from New Jersey, eighty-one people joined the Congregational Church of New London. The son of a Presbyterian minister, Tennent preached on the importance of a conversion experience, delivered sermons with powerful emotion, and inspired several important itinerant evangelists, including George Whitefield. Tennent travelled to Connecticut in 1741 because the conservative Philadelphia synod thwarted the spread of the Awakening in New Jersey.[18] The itinerants stimulated emotional outpourings which ultimately led to an unprecedented number of conversions and a dramatic rise in church membership.

These New Light preachers heightened the Puritans' awareness of the depravity of human nature and inspired conversion experiences among Puritans throughout the colony. The events at the church in Lyme, Connecticut in 1735 illustrate the awakened sense of danger and concern for salvation among the unregenerate. The steep climb in church membership began in 1732, when fifty-two people joined the church within ten months. Although he had heard about the revival in Massachusetts, Reverend Jonathan Parsons did not believe or understand the Awakening until on March 29, 1735 he observed that "…a deep and general Concern upon the minds of the Assembly discovered itself at that Time in plentiful Weeping, Signs and Sobs."[19] Yielding to the supplications of the congregation, Parsons began writing three sermons per week and preaching from old lectures. Sick of "vain Mirth and foolish Amusements" by April 1735, the inhabitants of Lyme, Connecticut formed religious societies within the existing church, studied the Bible, and conversed about religion. In lieu of the traditional feasting, dancing, music, and games of Election Day, May 14 (1735), the Congregationalists requested a lecture.[20] Parson's audience reacted with deep anguish, lamentations, and outcries: women were thrown into hysterics and several stout men fell "as though a cannon had been discharged, and a ball made its way through their hearts."[21] After both George Whitefield and Gilbert Tennent preached at the church in Lyme, the congregation continued to grow through the 1740s. Between June 1741 and February 1742 there were 150 conversions, primarily among the youth; however, three or four people were fifty-year-olds, two were nearly seventy, and one convert was ninety-three.[22] Thus the Great Awakening touched the congregation at Lyme, terrifying some and comforting others through itinerant evangelizing and increased devotion to the church.

Despite the success of the New Light clergy and laymen, the radicalism and emotional excesses of the Awakening alienated conservatives, steady Christians, and settled ministers and split the colony into three factions soon after Whitefield's first visit in 1740. The "Old Lights," predominantly in New Haven County, opposed the Awakening and the reactions it produced while the "New Lights," located primarily in the eastern half of the colony, favored its stimulating effects on the churches. As the emotional excesses of the Awakening became more pronounced, however, the New Light faction split into two groups, the moderates and the radicals. Reverend Ebenezer Wight of Stamford declared to the Fairfield West Association that his church "had for a considerable time been sadly broken and divided."[23] The Old Lights sought rationalism in theology and substituted morality for religion. Solomon Stoddard, for example, preached that anyone with respectable morals who performed charitable tasks within the community could be baptized into the church. Although moderate New Lights saw a need for the revival but opposed its excessiveness, radical New Lights favored all aspects of the revival and went so far as to establish thirty or more separate churches in southeastern Connecticut.[24] The movement divided not only the laymen, but also the clergy of the Congregational Churches in the 1740s. Of the four hundred ministers in New England, 130 supported the revival and viewed conversion as necessary, and thirty of these ministers were considered violent by the Old Lights. When the conflict peaked in 1743, the Old Lights claimed that there had been no revival. The New Light clergy, on the other hand, supported the veracity of the Awakening and the effusion of the Holy Spirit, but cautioned radicals against enthusiasm and Arminianism, belief in justification through works.[25] The inherent radicalism of the Great Awakening, therefore, divided both the congregations and the established clergy into two distinct factions.

The antirevivalists who viewed the movement as insincere found the errors of the Awakening to be many: enthusiasm, justification by faith, itinerant evangelizing, lay exhortations, ordinations, separation from the established churches, judgment of the unconverted, and emotional extravagance. Old Lights denounced enthusiasm, and the emphasis on emotional experiences, arguing that man was an innately rational being. They rejected the revivalist notion of salvation through faith and an understanding of "spiritual knowledge," a knowledge which comes from self-examination and what Jonathan Edwards called a "sense of the heart." Antirevivalists believed in justification through works and said that men could attain salvation through "time, exercise, observation, instruction" and the development of their talents. Although they de-emphasized the role of predestination and justification through faith, the Old Lights did not adhere to Arminianism, a sect based on justification through works which eventually gave rise to deism and rationalism. Old Lights continued to believe in the inherent depravity of human nature and the need for conversion by the Holy Spirit as a sign of salvation. They concluded, furthermore, that itinerant evangelizing, lay exhortations, ordinations of enthusiasts, and the creation of separate churches, were subversive to church order. Primarily conservative church members and established clergy, the antirevivalists felt threatened by the increase in lay participation and the competing churches. Accusations against the unconverted ministry further enraged both the accused and their loyal congregants, who argued that revivalists were discrediting the ideal of a "more perfect union" of God's people in the colonies. The ordinations of new ministers challenged the roles of established clergy, many of whom feared they would lose their congregation to the younger, enthusiastic New Lights. Most importantly, however, the antirevivalists decried emotional extravagances and viewed conversion experiences as an abuse of human nature. Influenced by Enlightenment Rationalism, critics of the revival argued for a rational interpretation of the Bible.[26] One of the underlying issues of the Awakening was whether or not conversions were indeed a manifestation of the Holy Spirit upon God's chosen people or whether the emotional outbursts were merely expressions of deep human sentiment. Because they did not believe in the veracity of the revival or the conversion experiences, Old Lights disparaged

New Light activity in order to maintain authority and preserve order within the established church communities.

Because the Congregational Church dominated all aspects of colonial life during the seventeenth and eighteenth centuries, the formation of separate churches posed a tremendous threat to the established order of the colony. Ministers were the leaders of the community, usually serving for life. The average tenure of the New London County ministers, for example, was 43.4 years, and seventy-four percent of these ministers served for the duration of their lives, dying in office. The meeting house was both the church and the political center of the town, the location for society meetings. Regardless of whether or not they attended the Congregational Church, colonists paid mandatory property taxes to the Congregational Church to fund both the minister's salary and the construction of the meetinghouse. Until the Great Awakening sparked divisions within the churches, the Congregational Church of Connecticut monopolized the religious life of the colonists.[27] When New Lights began challenging the traditional establishment, however, separate churches destroyed the harmony of the religious order of Connecticut and stimulated religious intolerance.

Separatists, those who wanted to establish a pure communion comprised solely of converts of the revival, emerged from the New Lights faction and established churches throughout the colony. In Windham County, separatists Elisha and Solomon Paine, who were influenced by the revival in 1721, aspired to establish a school for lay exhorters during the climax of the Awakening in 1740-1741. By 1745, however, Elisha Paine's enthusiasm offended both Old Lights and New Lights, and the ministers of Windham County wrote a letter criticizing Paine's life and the excesses of the movement. Subsequently, Paine was sentenced to prison for his extravagances, and his vision of a separate, pure church and school was never realized.[28] The attempts to create a separate church in New Haven were more successful, however. Inspired by Davenport's attack on pastor Joseph Noyes in 1741, several people issued fourteen articles of complaint and prompted a meeting of the consociation on January 25, 1742. The County Court granted

the dissenters, sixty persons led by James Pierpont, Jr., permission
to establish a separate church, which became known to Old Lights
as the "Tolerated Church" of White Haven.[29] Finally, one of the
earliest and most significant separations occurred in New London
after the preaching of Gilbert Tennent and James Davenport in
1741. On November 29, 1741, five prominent members of the
established church, John Curtis, John Hempstead, Peter Harris,
and Christopher and John Christophers, absented themselves
from church and began meeting in the home of John Curtis.
One hundred and fifteen individuals of diverse geographic and
occupational backgrounds eventually formed the New London
Separate Church. The separatists, however, were notably younger
than the congregationalists; the average age of the male separatist was 25.3 as compared to 45.3, and, similarly, the average age
of the female separatist was 29.8 as compared to 41.8.[30] Most of
the separatists, moreover, were of a lower social and economic
standing than the established church members, and most had
no strong connections to the Congregational Church. Previously
rejected by the Old Light ministerial association, Timothy Allen
formed the nucleus for the Separatist Church by establishing the
Shepherd's Tent, an organization which prepared students for
itinerant careers and rejected traditional colleges. In May, 1742,
however, when the Connecticut Assembly outlawed itinerancy, Allen was sentenced to prison, and the New Lights of New London
became isolated from the established community.[31] Although the
Separatist Churches enjoyed only limited success as a result of
government persecution, they underscored the divisions inspired
by the Great Awakening and the radicalism of the New Light faction.

In addition to the divisions caused by the establishment of
separate churches, the emotional extravagance of the itinerants
ultimately led to increased opposition to the revival. The tactics of
James Davenport, for example, alienated not only members of the
established church but also his friends and colleagues. Although
lower classes continued to believe in him and God's salvation,
Davenport's fanaticism heightened class conflict and disrupted
congregations throughout Massachusetts and Connecticut. In his

rebellion against the ministry, Davenport attacked conventional education and even denounced reading the Bible. Therefore, on July 20, 1742, the grand jury of Suffolk County indicted him for committing heresy and serving as an instrument of Satan and then exiled him from Massachusetts on the grounds of insanity.[32] Davenport returned to Connecticut where he continued to preach until the crisis which occurred at Christopher's Wharf, New London on March 6, 1743, the infamous bonfire. This incident furthered the decline of the separatist movement and embarrassed New Lights, who claimed that anarchy did not have to result from the revival. Influenced by Reverend Eleazar Wheelock, Davenport ultimately recanted his principles and admitted to his emotional enthusiasm.[33] Other itinerants such as George Whitefield and Gilbert Tennent also contributed to a rising opposition and the decline of the New Light influence. Whitefield charged that ministers had "in a great measure lost the old spirit of preaching" and claimed that universities were places of darkness. In these accusations and other radical teachings, Whitefield alienated the upper classes and the ministers of established congregations. Similarly, Gilbert Tennent opposed learned ministers and thus insulted and threatened the tradition of an educated ministry.[34] In denouncing conventional education and the established ministry, the itinerants not only inspired divisions between Old Lights and New Lights, but they also increased conflicts between social classes. The Awakening, moreover, became a struggle of power between the established clergy and the itinerants, who ultimately disrupted unity within the Congregational Churches of Connecticut. The conflicts and divisions which emerged from the radicalism and excesses of the Great Awakening led to its inevitable decline in the early 1740s.

To preserve their role as leaders of the church and to re-establish organization and unity within the congregation, several ministers began attacking New Light radicals. The Great Awakening challenged the tradition of deference within the colony of Connecticut. The attacks on the prominent members of society and the rise of the lower classes in challenging the hierarchical order weakened the social order of the colony and promoted both social mobility and democracy. In the winter of 1742-1743, as people were questioning the verity of the Awakening, Reverend Charles Chauncy attacked the extravagances of the revival. A liberal from Boston and a former advocate of the Great Awakening, Chauncy wrote *The Late Religious Commotions in New England* (March 1743) in which he denounced the excesses of the revival as sacrilegious. Later that year, in *Seasonable Thoughts on the State of Religion in New England,* Chauncy stated that true religion was not "shriekings and screamings, convulsion-like tremblings and agitations, strugglings and tumblings." True joy, Chauncy claimed, came instead from sober and obedient Christian living.[35] Reflecting on the enthusiasm in New England, Chauncy observed that "the plain Truth is, an enlightened Mind, not raised Affections, ought always to be the Guide of those who call themselves Men."[36] Moreover, the Associated Ministers of the County of Windham addressed the errors of the revival in a letter written to the people of several societies in Windham in 1745. Religious revivals, they claimed, were works of God manifested in signs of the Holy Ghost, signs such as frights, terrors, recognition of sin, joy, and comfort. They wrote, however, that many people had been deceived by these outward experiences, becoming instruments of Satan. In the letter, the ministers denounced five principal beliefs to which New Lights adhered, and they stated that it was not the will of God to separate the converted from the unconverted. They denied the opinion that saints knew one another and could recognize "true ministers" by inward feelings. In an effort to protect their own role within the community, the ministers denounced the beliefs that one need only to be a Christian to preach the Gospel and that there was a greater presence of God at meetings led by lay-preachers. Finally, the ministers said that God had not disowned the ministry and their churches or their ordinances in the years of the Great Awakening.[37] Chauncy and the ministers of Windham articulated the opinion of ministers throughout the colony, and the success of his work and that of others helped to further the weakening of the revivalist movement.

As the radicals encountered opposition from Old Lights, New Lights, and the established ministry, the colonial government began to regulate New Light activity and persecute dissenters. In 1743 the Connecticut Assembly revoked the Toleration Acts of 1708 and 1727, which had increased the privileges of dissenters and granted New Lights the rights to worship as they pleased. The Assembly further prohibited formation of new churches without express approval from the Connecticut legislature and thus thwarted establishment of Separatist churches within the colony.[38] In "An Act for Regulating Abuses and correcting Disorders in Ecclesiastical Affairs," the government claimed that itinerant preaching had caused divisions which destroyed the ecclesiastical constitution established by the laws of the colony and prevented the growth of piety. This piece of legislation prohibited itinerant evangelizing, lay preaching, and the licensing of ministers without permission from the Saybrook Platform. It also stated that ministers who preached outside of their own congregation could not collect a salary and that any foreigner who preached the Gospel would be exiled from the colony.[39] This Act and the revocation of the Tolerance Act led to excommunications from the church, arrests, and the imprisonment of church members for attending Separatist Churches or failing to pay taxes to the established churches. Several revivalists were expelled from Yale for participating in New Light activities and still others were removed from official positions.[40] Clearly, the restrictions against New Light activity, especially the elimination of itinerant evangelizing, an influential aspect of the movement, and the persecutions of dissenters helped to suppress the Great Awakening less than ten years after it had begun.

Although the Great Awakening only lasted from 1735-1745, it not only increased church membership but also stimulated education and promoted a separation of church and state. As itinerants inspired New Lights to study the Bible, converts focused increasingly on education in lieu of games, music, and other forms of entertainment. The Great Awakening influenced the founding of prestigious universities, including Princeton, Dartmouth, Brown, Rutgers, Washington and Lee, and Hampden-Sydney.[41] Because tolerance, one of the results of the Awakening, was associated with atheism, the Standing Order ended the Holy Commonwealth, or church-state.[42] Thus, the Great Awakening affected not only affairs within the church, but it also transformed the colonial government and had a profound impact on secondary education.

The Great Awakening, furthermore, effected significant social leveling and led to increased religious tolerance within the colony of Connecticut. The Awakening underscored the inherent depravity of the human soul, teaching that all were sinners in the eyes of God, regardless of class. Common emotional experiences united the rich and the poor under a common self-consciousness, and lay participation increased dramatically.[43] James Davenport claimed that the right to speak out was a gift from the Holy Spirit, and a new, informal language of worship emerged as the congregation gained a voice in religious affairs. Because the revivalists taught that joy and salvation were available to all laymen, regardless of class, there was an infusion of democracy into the churches which ultimately led to an increase in democracy and social mobility within the community.[44] Moreover, the divisions inspired by the Great Awakening and the subsequent decline of the Congregational monopoly, presented other denominations with the opportunity to establish new churches. Ironically, the Great Awakening promoted religious tolerance as the Congregational Church split into Old Light and New Light factions and new denominations, such as the Baptist Church, attracted new members. The Awakening also established voluntarism, asserting that religious affiliation was not an obligation but a right that men and women could freely exploit. Ultimately, the persecuting acts such as itinerant regulation and the Saybrook Platform were eliminated from revised government legislation. With the challenges to the social order and the monopoly of the Congregational Church, new Tolerance Acts were passed in 1777 and 1784.[45] The consequences of the Great Awakening, therefore, were not limited to the religious life of the colony, but rather influenced the lives of colonists throughout Connecticut.

The first Great Awakening in Connecticut, which occurred nearly two hundred and fifty years ago, dramatically affected the lives of the colonists and the religious life in Connecticut. A reaction to a laxity in morals within the church, the Great Awakening spread through the words of itinerant evangelists and stimulated theatrical conversions and a powerful commitment to the church. Although the movement ultimately subsided as excesses alienated established members of the church, its repercussions extended beyond colonial borders and the year 1745. All religions depend on revivals to awaken piety and perpetuate a steady, devout populace. The Great Awakening of 1735, though all-encompassing and dramatic, was one in a number of recorded revivals throughout church history. In the western and southern frontiers, Americans experienced the Second Great Awakening from 1800-1840, a revival which also emphasized emotion as opposed to reason, and stressed salvation as opposed to predestination.[46] Even today, Billy Graham's "Youth for Christ Crusade" and his evangelistic campaigns throughout the United States echo the religious movements which occurred more than two centuries ago. Religious history is not a linear progression of events, but a circle of recurring incidents, a cycle of peace and disorder, of silence and awakening. A common core of beliefs, beliefs in democracy, manifest destiny, or salvation, form the foundation for a dynamic American society. According to religious historian William G. McLoughlin, awakenings and ideological crises redefine this core of beliefs, enabling Christians to emerge as revitalized, confident citizens. Each new manifestation of the Holy Spirit empowers the rising generations to understand the nature of redemption.[47] The Great Awakening not only influenced the lives of those converted, but also affects the lives of Americans today.

[1] Mary Beth Norton, <u>A People and a Nation</u> (Boston: Houghton Mifflin Co., 1990) pp. 76-79, 94-98

[2] Patricia J. Tracy, <u>Jonathan Edwards, Pastor</u> (New York: Hill and Wang, 1979) p. 22

[3] C.C. Goen, <u>Revivalism and Separatism in New England, 1740-1800</u> (New Haven: Yale University Press, 1962) pp. 3-5

[4] M.H. Mitchell, <u>The Great Awakening and Other Religious Revivals in Connecticut</u> (New Haven: published for the Tercentenary Commission of Connecticut by the Yale University Press, 1934) p. 2

[5] Alan Heimert, <u>The Great Awakening: Documents Illustrating the Crisis and Its Consequences</u> (New York: The Bobbs-Merrill Company, 1972) p. xxxi

[6] Goen, p. 2

[7] Invitation to George Whitefield from the Eastern Consociation of Fairfield County, October 7, 1740 as quoted in Richard L. Bushman, <u>The Great Awakening: Documents on the Revival of Religion, 1740-1745</u> (Williamsburg: Kingsport Press, 1969) pp. 23-24

[8] <u>George Whitefield's Journals</u> (Edinburgh: The Banner of Truth Trust, 1960) pp. 480-481

[9] William Gaylord, letter to Eleazar Wheelock, 24 November 1740 as quoted in Bushman, pp. 39-40

[10] Edwin Scott Gaustad, <u>The Great Awakening in New England</u> (New York: Harper and Brothers, 1957) p. 45

[11] Diary of Nathaniel Cole, 23 October 1740 as quoted in Heimert, p. 44

[12] James Davenport, as quoted in Monroe Stearns, <u>The Great Awakening, 1720-1760</u> (New York: Franklin Watts, Inc., 1970) p. 44

[13] Harry S. Stout and Peter Onuf, "James Davenport and the Great Awakening in New London," <u>Journal of American History</u> 71 (1983) p. 566

[14] David S. Lovejoy, <u>Religious Enthusiasm and the Great Awakening</u> (Englewood Cliffs: Prentice-Hall, 1969) p. 68

[15] Goen, p. 12

[16] Jonathan Edwards, "Sinners in the Hands of an Angry God" as quoted in Monroe Stearns, <u>The Great Awakening, 1720-1760</u> (New York: Franklin Watts, Inc., 1970) pp. 34, 38

[17] Goen, p. 20

[18] Stearns, p. 10

[19] Jonathan Parsons as quoted in Heimert, p. 190

[20] Jonathan Parson's Journal, April 1735, as quoted in Heimert, p. 196

[21] Jonathan Parson's Journal, July 1741, as quoted in Stearns, p. 38

[22] Joseph Tracy, The Great Awakening (New York: Arno Press, 1969) p. 145

[23] Reverend Ebenezer Wight as quoted in Estelle S. Feinstein, Stamford from Puritan to Patriot (Stamford: Stamford Bicentennial Corporation, 1976) p. 155

[24] Mitchell, p. 15

[25] Goen, p. 31

[26] Alan Heimert and Perry Miller, "The Great Awakening: Jonathan Edwards," Intellectual History in America: Contemporary Essays on Puritanism, the Enlightenment, and Romanticism ed. Cushing Strout (New York: Harper and Row, Publishers, 1968) pp. 37-39, 45

[27] Bruce C. Daniels, The Connecticut Town: Growth and Development: 1635-1790 (Middletown: Wesleyan University Press, 1979) pp. 111-115

[28] Heimert, pp. 399, 410

[29] Goen, p. 86

[30] Stout and Onuf, p. 562

[31] Goen, pp. 570-572

[32] Stearns, p. 44

[33] Stout and Onuf, pp. 556-578

[34] Stearns, p. 43

[35] Ibid., p. 46

[36] Heimert and Miller, p. 38

[37] The Associated Ministers of the County of Windham, letter to the People of Several Societies of Windham, 1745, as quoted in Heimert, pp. 400-406

[38] Daniels, p. 101

[39] "An Act for Regulating Abuses and correcting Disorders in Ecclesiastical Affairs" published by Charles J. Hoadly, ed., The Public Records of the Colony of Connecticut, VIII (Hartford, 1874) pp. 454-457, and reprinted in Bushman, p. 58

[40] Mitchell, p. 17

[41] Stearns, p. 55

[42] Mitchell, p. 20

[43] Goen, p. 28

[44] Stout and Onuf, p. 570

[45] Mitchell, p. 18

[46] Norton, p. 206

[47] William G. McLoughlin, <u>Revivals, Awakenings, and Reform</u> (Chicago: The University of Chicago Press, 1978) pp. xii-xv

Bibliography

Bushman, Richard L., <u>The Great Awakening: Documents on the Revival of Religion, 1740-1745</u> Williamsburg, VA: Kingsport Press, 1969

Cherry, Conrad, <u>The Theology of Jonathan Edwards: A Reappraisal</u> Garden City: Anchor Books, 1966

Clarke, Elizabeth W., <u>The First Three Hundred Years</u> Greenwich: The First Congregational Church of Greenwich, 1967

Daniels, Bruce C., <u>The Connecticut Town: Growth and Development 1635-1790</u> Middletown: Wesleyan University Press, 1979

Feinstein, Estelle S., <u>Stamford From Puritan to Patriot</u> Stamford: Stamford Bicentennial Corporation, 1976

<u>George Whitefield's Journals</u> Edinburgh: The Banner of Truth Trust, 1960

Goen, C.C., <u>Revivalism and Separatism in New England, 1740-1800</u> New Haven Press, 1962

Gaustad, Edwin Scott, <u>The Great Awakening in New England</u> New York: Harper and Brothers, 1957

Heimert, Alan and Perry Miller, "The Great Awakening," in <u>Intellectual History in America: Contemporary Essays on Puritanism, the Enlightenment, and Romanticism</u> Cushing Strout, ed., New York: Harper and Row, Publishers, 1968,   pp. 21-34

Heimert, Alan, <u>Religion and the American Mind, From the Great Awakening to the Revolution</u> Cambridge: Harvard University Press, 1966

Lambert, Frank, "Subscribing For Profits and Piety: The Friendship of Benjamin Franklin and George Whitefield," The William and Mary Quarterly 3rd series, Vol. L, No. 3, July 1993

Lovejoy, David S., Religious Enthusiasm and the Great Awakening Englewood Cliffs, NJ: Prentice-Hall, 1969

McLoughlin, William G., Revivals, Awakenings, and Reform Chicago: The Chicago University Press, 1978

Mitchell, M.H., The Great Awakening and Other Religious Revivals in Connecticut New Haven: Yale University Press, 1934 (a publication for the Tercentenary Commission of Connecticut)

Morgan, Edmund S., "The Halfway Covenant," in Intellectual History in America: Contemporary Essays on Puritanism, the Enlightenment, and Romanticism Cushing Strout, ed., New York: Harper and Row, Publishers, 1968, pp. 35-46

Remer, Rosalind, "Old Lights and New Money: A Note on Religion, Economics and the Social Order in 1740 Boston," The William and Mary Quarterly XLVII (1990) pp. 566-573

Stout, Harry S. and Peter Onuf, "James Davenport and the Great Awakening in New London," Journal of American History 71 (December, 1983) pp. 556-578

Stearns, Monroe, The Great Awakening, 1720-1760 New York: Franklin Watts, Inc., 1970

Tracy, Joseph, The Great Awakening New York: Arno Press, 1969

Tracy, Patricia J., Jonathan Edwards, Pastor New York: Hill and Wang, 1979

Chris Bellamy
Absolute War
New York, Vintage Books, 2007, pp. 488-489

On 17 October [1944] all the women selected to make up Aviation Group 122 boarded a train in Moscow for a secret location. Once the train was moving, there were told it was Engels, on the other side of the Volga. They spent nine days on the train, and food was scarce. At one station there were piles of fresh cabbage, and they ate it there and then 'just like rabbits.' From then on, for the rest of the war, they called each other 'brother rabbit.' The combat record of all three 'rabbit' units, who also referred to themselves as 'Raskova's Regiments,' was outstanding. The 46th Guards, as the 588th Regiment became in February 1943, became the most famous, in part, because it was the worst equipped. The Po-2 (U-2) biplane was a flimsy wood-and-canvas contraption. Flying it at night must have been a terrifying experience. The regiment got the name 'the night witches,' apparently because that was what the Germans called them. One reason may be that in order to hit targets by surprise, bearing in mind that the Po-2 biplanes were tinderboxes and carried no defensive armament, the pilots would sometimes cut the engine and then glide in to deliver their bombs before restarting it. This was a standard tactic used by all Soviet light bombers at night. It 'increased the unexpectedness of the attack and reduced losses.' The result, in the Po-2's case, was a whooshing sound, like a witch's broomstick in the night, and then explosions. Soldiers were superstitious people.

The most famous woman pilot actually served with three others in an otherwise all-male squadron. Lidiya Litvak had been a flying instructor and joined Raskova's group, but was later assigned to the 437th Fighter Regiment, one of four women in an otherwise all-male unit. The male pilots did not trust them to be their 'wingmen' so they formed their own flight, fighting at Stalingrad. Litvak achieved twelve personal and four shared kills, plus a reconnaissance balloon. She was reported missing on 1 August 1943. The most effective woman sniper was Lyudmilla Pavlichenko ["Because women breathe better than men, they make better shots—and because they are more patient, and resistant to cold, they are particularly suitable as snipers." p. 487], who killed a total of 309 Axis troops before finding herself in Sevastopol in June 1942. She was one of those considered valuable enough to be evacuated by submarine, just before the fortress fell. Snipers often worked in pairs. Between them, Mariya Polivanova and Natalya Kovshova scored more than 300 kills before German troops surrounded them in fighting near Novgorod, south of Leningrad, on 14 August 1942. They fired until they ran out of ammunition, and then waited for the Germans to come forward. Then they blew themselves up with hand grenades, taking some of the enemy with them. They became two of the total of ninety-two Soviet women who were made Heroes of the Soviet Union during the war or later.

Ralph Waldo Emerson Prize 2003

AN ANALYSIS OF ALEXANDER KERENSKY'S HANDLING OF GENERAL LAVR KORNILOV

Michael Korzinstone

The revolution that broke out in Petrograd, the capital of Russia, in February of 1917, would be the first of two revolutions that would characterize that year in Russian history. The fall of the Tsar, Nicholas II, effectively ended the Romanov dynasty. Out of this revolution emerged the 'Dual Authority', an unofficial and uneasy partnership between the "Petrograd Soviet of Soldiers', Sailors' and Workers' Deputies," and a Provisional Government headed by Prince Lvov. The Provisional Government was to govern, and the Soviet was to act as a watchdog, making sure that the government considered the interests of workers and soldiers.[1] By the summer of 1917, due to the crushing burden of maintaining the increasingly unpopular war effort, the mandate of the government seemed to be breaking down. The spread of local Soviet bodies throughout Russia, the growth of trade unions, and worker control of the factories were all evidence of dissatisfaction with the Provisional Government.[2] This sentiment reached an apex in early July when the Bolsheviks staged an unsuccessful putsch against the government. Two days after the suppression of the uprising, Alexander Fedorovich Kerensky took charge of the Provisional

The author is a graduate of the Wharton School. He wrote this IB Extended Essay for Dr. Stephen Johnson at Upper Canada College in Toronto, Ontario, during the 2002/2003 academic year.

Government and proceeded to arrest Bolshevik leaders such as Leon Trotsky and Lev Kamenev.[3] According to Michael Lynch, "a fortnight after the July Days, the Bolshevik Party stood on the verge of destruction."[4] One major issue facing Kerensky was the state of the military and its inability to wage an effective campaign against the Germans during the First World War.[5] Aleksei Brusilov, who of all the old Tsarist generals had made the greatest efforts to adjust to the new political and military of Russia, had not succeeded in elevating the battle worthiness of the army.[6] Kerensky turned to General Lavr Kornilov, the son of a Siberian Cossack, to take control of the army, restore its capacity to fight, and thus elevate the government's strength and authority. Kerensky's relationship with Kornilov, however, was not without complication, and on August 27, 1917, a final break occurred. The events that transpired between the two men have since been referred to as the 'Kornilov Affair.' How then, did Kerensky's handling of General Kornilov affect the position of the Provisional Government? An investigation of a variety of primary and secondary sources suggests that Kerensky's decision to pursue a campaign against an alleged counterrevolutionary plot headed by his Commander-In-Chief, General Lavr Kornilov, fatally weakened the position of the Provisional Government and enabled the Bolsheviks to recover from their July debacle and seize power in Russia in October 1917.

One can gain insight into the significance of Kerensky's handling of General Kornilov through an evaluation of the historiography surrounding it. According to Jorgen Munck, most historians have been in "complete agreement that the Kornilov revolt was one of the turning points of the Revolution."[7] Munck, however, suggests that there is "considerable difference" with respect to many details and interpretations. George Katkov and William Chamberlin confirm Munck's interpretation of the historiography, as they both believe that the Kornilov Affair was of prime importance in contributing to the fall of Kerensky's Provisional Government.[8] Katkov and Chamberlin, characterized by Michael Lynch as representing the 'optimist' and 'pro-Bolshevik western' schools of thought, respectively, also confirm Munck's suggestion that differences in opinion exist over some of the details and gen-

eral interpretations of the affair.[9] Such a divergence in opinion can
be observed in Katkov's belief that there was no Kornilov plot to
stage a coup, but that it was the "confusion created by Kerensky"
which resulted in the "denunciation and dismissal of Kornilov as
a counterrevolutionary."[10] As a result of this, according to Katkov,
there was "disorganization" and "disorientation" in the Russian
political system and military, which culminated in the fall of the
Provisional Government.[11] Chamberlin disagrees, and believes
that it was Kornilov's "mission...to head the unsuccessful counterrevolutionary movement against the Provisional Government."[12]
Edward H. Carr, another member of the 'pro-Bolshevik western'
school of thought, believes, like Chamberlin, that in 1917 Russia
experienced an attempted "military coup from the Right—the
Kornilov insurrection."[13] Orlando Figes, however, sides with Katkov,
suggesting that Kornilov was "far from plotting the overthrow of the
Provisional Government," and that the notion of a Kornilov coup
is merely an "enduring myth of the Russian Revolution."[14] When
examining Soviet historiography, the matter is clearly defined; a
counterrevolutionary conspiracy was under way which included
Kerensky acting as a puppet of the capitalists.[15] Finally, Richard
Pipes suggests that the Kornilov Affair resulted from Kerensky's
"sense that...the army was likely to breed a counterrevolutionary
Napoleon," and his ensuing decision to engineer a plot to topple
the General.[16] Pipes, an American member of the 'non-determinist'
school of thought, argues against the notion that the Bolshevik
seizure of power was inevitable, but instead, that it was Kerensky's
scheming that "enabled the Bolsheviks to recover from their July
debacle."[17] Clearly, one can find a consensus amongst historians
that the Kornilov Affair played a significant role in altering the
course of events in Russia in 1917. There is, however, discrepancy
when addressing the issue of whether it was Kerensky's responsibility or not.

Kerensky's decision to placate the left rather than to keep
his promises for military reform is the factor that can be attributed
with initiating tensions between Kornilov and Kerensky. Kornilov
indicated that he would accept the appointment as Commander-
In-Chief and "bring the people to victory and to a just and hon-

ourable peace," only once a commitment was made by the Prime Minister to accept certain reforms.[18] In Kornilov's opinion, it was imperative that Soviet Order No. 1 be abolished, and that measures be taken to ensure that commanders be afforded the respect and disciplinary authority that was required to wage effective warfare against the German enemy.[19] Kerensky's acceptance of these proposals was sent by telegraph to the Stavka, Russian military headquarters, on July 29, 1917. According to Richard Pipes, Kerensky "neither could nor would" keep his promises. Kerensky could not deliver on his pledges for reform because he was not a free agent, but the "executor of the will" of the Soviet, which viewed Kornilov's suggested reforms as counterrevolutionary and unacceptable.[20] According to Orlando Figes, Kerensky's political strategy relied on the premise of "straddling right and left," allowing him to maintain his position as the central figure in his coalition Provisional Government.[21] For this reason, Allan Wildman believes that "Kerensky deftly avoided committing himself," fearing alienating socialist supporters.[22] Pipes suggests that the issue of military reform "became the main source of conflict" between Kornilov and Kerensky.[23] By deciding to placate the left rather than to adhere to his promises, one can clearly see how Kerensky initiated tensions with Kornilov.

The divisiveness observed at the Moscow State Conference of August 12-15, between the political left and right over the reform issue, was what implanted the illusion of a counterrevolution in Kerensky's mind. Kornilov, frustrated with the government's lack of resolve in implementing his reforms, said to his colleague, General Lukomsky, "Mr. Kerensky evidently does not wish me to be present at the State Conference in Moscow, but I shall certainly go there, and will insist on my requests being accepted and fulfilled at last."[24] Many historians, including Ronald Kowalski, have come to view the Moscow State Conference as the critical turning point in the relations between Kornilov and Kerensky.[25] When Kornilov arrived at the Bolshoi theatre, the site of the conference, he was greeted by crowds of right-wing Kadets and non-socialists who cheered him. Kerensky interpreted Kornilov's popularity as a direct threat, later saying that "after the Moscow Conference, it was clear to me that the next attempt at a blow would come from the right, and not from the left."[26] Richard Pipes developed the theory that once this conviction lodged in Kerensky's mind, it became an "idee fixe" and everything that happened subsequently "only served to reinforce it."[27] Regarding his controversial speech to the conference, Kornilov later wrote in his deposition, "I thought it essential to make known to the country the real state of affairs in its armed forces, and to point out how necessary it was to raise their battle worthiness."[28] Conservative newspapers such as *Novoevremia* openly criticized Kerensky following Kornilov's speech, and made claims that "at the helm of the ship of state are people who oppose the idea of defending the state."[29] No evidence exists to suggest that Kornilov formulated this political campaign, but Pipes suggests that Kornilov, "as its beneficiary...came under suspicion."[30] General Lukomsky noted in his account of the Kornilov Affair, that Kornilov confided in him and said, "I have no personal ambition. I only wish to save Russia, and will gladly submit to a strong Provisional Government."[31] Kornilov was not planning a coup; however, after the Moscow State Conference, Kerensky was convinced that a counterrevolution was brewing on the right.

Kerensky's fear of a counterrevolution and his subsequent scheming, rather than Kornilov's alleged desire to lead a coup, was the factor that forced the break between the two men. In mid-August, Savinkov, Kerensky's deputy, received information from French intelligence sources indicating that the Bolsheviks were planning another putsch for the beginning of September. Kerensky realized the potential to use this piece of intelligence to hurt Kornilov. Kerensky asked Kornilov to send the Third Cavalry Corps to Petrograd in order to suppress the expected Bolshevik putsch; Kornilov complied without hesitation.[32] Later, however, after the eventual August 27 break between the two men, Kerensky would claim in a message to Russian soldiers, that "General Kornilov...has now by his deeds demonstrated his treachery. He has withdrawn regiments from the front, weakening its resistance to the pitiless enemy, the German, and he sent all these regiments against Petrograd."[33] Harold Williams, a New Zealand-born correspondent of the *Daily Chronicle*, recognized in 1917, that Kerensky had betrayed

Kornilov. Williams made this observation when Kerensky reneged on his agreement to deploy troops to Petrograd and "suddenly raised a cry of panic against Kornilov."[34] Kerensky's handling of the Vladimir Lvov incident further confirms his intent to destroy Kornilov.[35] In order to obtain proof of a Kornilov conspiracy, Kerensky initiated a telegraph conversation with Kornilov, in which he impersonated Lvov. Richard Pipes suggests, however, that "this brief dialogue was a comedy of errors with the most tragic consequences."[36] Nowhere does Kerensky explicitly ask Kornilov about his alleged demand for dictatorial powers, but rather makes assumptions based on vague remarks.[37] Orlando Figes believes that Kerensky came to realize that "as long as things were kept vague," he might succeed in exposing Kornilov as a traitor. According to Figes, Kerensky believed that this would result in the revival of his own political fortunes, as the revolution would rally behind him to defeat his traitor.[38] On the basis of such weak evidence, Kerensky planned an open break with Kornilov, ignoring Savinkov's suggestion that he communicate with Kornilov once more, in order to clear up what Savinkov thought to be an obvious misunderstanding. While these events took place, Kornilov proceeded with preparations to quell the anticipated Bolshevik uprising, as had been reported by French intelligence. On August the 27th, at 2:40 a.m., Kornilov cabled Savinkov to tell him that the "corps is assembling in the environs of Petrograd toward evening August 28."[39] If Kornilov's intentions were to use the troops against the Provisional Government rather than the Bolsheviks, as Kerensky insisted, he would not have forewarned it by telegraph. Kerensky's scheming reached its pinnacle, when on August 27, he sent a radio-telegram addressed to the whole nation accusing Kornilov of treason. Only once he was accused of rebelling, did Kornilov call for the overthrow of the Provisional Government. Kornilov's eventual revolt was reactionary, not pre-meditated.[40] The preceding evidence systematically demonstrates that the final break between Kornilov and Kerensky was not the product of an ambitious general, but rather that of a desperate politician.

One of the most significant by-products of the rift between Kornilov and Kerensky would be the rejuvenation of the Bolsheviks. According to Michael Lynch, "certainly it was the Bolsheviks who gained most" from the Kornilov Affair because "they had been able to present themselves as defenders of Petrograd and the Revolution, thus wiping out the memories of the debacle of the July Days."[41] In an attempt to suppress Kornilov's phantom putsch, Kerensky requested help from the Soviet. On August 27, after deliberating, the Soviet approved, on a Menshevik motion, the creation of a "Committee to Fight the Counterrevolution." Since, however, the Bolsheviks were the only group in the Soviet with a military entity, this action essentially placed the Bolsheviks in charged of the Soviet military contribution.[42] With respect to this development, Donald Treadgold wrote that "the only ones to profit from the imbroglio were the Bolsheviks, who wrenched from the Soviet an official authorization to form a Red Guard."[43] As Trotsky put it, "the army that rose against Kornilov was the army-to-be of the October revolution."[44] The actions taken by Kerensky's government, according to Moisei Uritskii, "rehabilitated" the Bolsheviks.[45] Such a rehabilitation was also evident in the government's decision to release all of the Bolsheviks in custody except for the few that had already been caught up in legal proceedings for their involvement in the Bolshevik uprising in July.[46] In Figes' opinion, "without the Kornilov movement, they [the Bolsheviks] might never have come to power at all."[47]

Despite the Prime Minister's immediate success in suppressing General Kornilov's "revolt," the political outcome of the affair was one that was not favourable for Kerensky, leaving him unable to govern and Russia in a state of political instability. Boris Kolonitskii suggests that "Kerensky's victory over Kornilov was his own political defeat, in that his political base, the coalition of 'living forces', was undermined, and his personal authority plummeted."[48] William Chamberlin agrees with Kolonitskii, and suggests that "although Kornilov's coup collapsed without firing a shot, its political consequences were momentous... it knocked the feeble underpinning of confidence completely from under the Provisional Government."[49] Following the Kornilov Affair,

Kerensky took measures to satisfy his desire to continue his old policy of trying to balance himself between the conservative and radical forces in the country.[50] He made concessions to the left by summoning the "Democratic Conference" in Petrograd on September 14, from which delegates of the propertied classes would be excluded. In addition, Kerensky appeased the left by appointing the anti-Kornilov, General Verkhovsky, as War Minister, and by appointing Admiral Verderevsky, who was popular with moderate socialists, to the post of Naval Minister. Kerensky, however, simultaneously tried to form a new coalition government in which the Kadets of the political right would be included. The developing political polarization of Russia, however, surfaced at Kerensky's conference where the events were ultimately a microcosm for the situation throughout Russia.[51] One can look to the September 20th edition of *Den'*, a Russian newspaper, for an effective summary of the developing crisis of political polarization. Regarding the conference, the article stated that "the struggle of opposite political aspirations did not allow it [the conference] to tell the exhausted nation anything else but the story of the deep and dangerous crisis which was undermining it."[52] The political fallout from the Kornilov Affair clearly hurt Kerensky; however it also gave way to a great increase in Bolshevik political fortunes. According to Chamberlin, up to the Kornilov Affair, the Provisional Government owed whatever stability it had to the fact that the majority of the Soviets offered it formal support due to their moderate socialist majorities.[53] After the Kornilov Affair, however, the center-left Mensheviks and Socialist Revolutionaries lost many supporters who were gravitating to the Bolsheviks on the extreme left.[54] This polarization also helped elevate Kadet fortunes, as non-socialists moved from the centre to the right. Kerensky's wife clearly summarized the situation when she said that "the prestige of Kerensky and the Provisional Government was completely destroyed by the Kornilov Affair; and he was left almost without supporters."[55] Clearly, the political outcome of Kerensky's break with Kornilov was not one that was favourable for Kerensky, as it left the Provisional Government without many supporters and stimulated the growth of the Bolshevik movement.

One can determine that as a result of Kerensky's campaign to 'save the revolution', he lost complete control of the Russian army, a fact that would later contribute to his demise. Kerensky and Kornilov's mutual counter-accusations of treachery were, according to George Katkov, "particularly confusing and demoralizing to the troops." According to Katkov, these accusations also helped fuel Bolshevik claims that a counterrevolution was "rearing its ugly head."[56] The culprits, according to the Bolsheviks, were the officers, landowners and capitalists posing as sympathizers of the revolution but really supporters of Kornilov, with a hidden agenda to return to Petrograd as the ruling class of Russia.[57] The susceptibility of the soldiers to such propaganda translated into behavior of an anarchical nature, including the arbitrary lynching of officers.[58] According to Jorgen Munck, the Kornilov Affair left the Supreme Command with a greatly diminished authority that suffered "irreparable damage."[59] Kerensky's loss of control over the Russian army would eventually lead to his demise. In October, when the prospect of a potential Bolshevik insurrection took a more prominent position in Kerensky's mind, he went to the headquarters of the Petrograd Garrison to personally assume control of operations there. Upon his arrival, however, he learned that the Garrison was completely disaffected and would not, therefore, offer resistance to a Bolshevik putsch.[60] As a result of Kerensky's break with Kornilov, Kerensky would lose complete control of the Russian army, and would not be afforded its protection when the Bolsheviks staged their coup in late October.

Like the demoralization and insubordination of the soldiers in the military, the state of affairs in town and country were also good indicators of the weakness of Kerensky's Provisional Government after the suppression of the Kornilov revolt. Many peasants believed that members of the property-owning and educated classes, like the officers, were counterrevolutionaries who supported Kornilov's pseudo-mutiny.[61] Under the influence of deserting troops who traveled through the countryside, peasants were encouraged to engage in their own social warfare against the privileged. A state of near-anarchy ensued.[62] The October 1st edition of *Russkiia vedomosti* read, "the wave of pogroms grows and expands to overflowing throughout Russia...the unbridled mob, with darkest animal instincts unleashed, loots and pillages everything that it finds at hand."[63] The government's inability to control this havoc is demonstrated by a pair of documents, both addressed to provincial, regional, and municipal commissars. The first document is a letter that was written by the Minister of War, Major General Verkhovskii, which informed the commissars of his recently issued Order No. 51 of October 11. In the letter, Verkhovskii outlines the nature of this order, an order largely formulated to restore order throughout Russia. After explaining the methodology that was selected to accomplish this grave task, the Minister concluded by saying, "the goal is set, the means are furnished."[64] The inability of the government to control the unruly behavior in the countryside can be determined by examining the second document, a telegram dated on October 21st from the Minister of the Interior, Boris Nikitin. It should be noted that Nikitin acknowledges in his telegram that there is an "incessant growth of anarchy, which threatens the internal situation of the country."[65] Considering that ten days earlier, Nikitin's colleague, the Minister of War, said "the goal is set, the means furnished," one is made aware of the government's inability to control the havoc throughout Russia. From the preceding evidence it is clear that following the Kornilov Affair, Kerensky's Provisional Government lost not only the ability to control the military, but the ability to control domestic affairs as well.

Lenin's writings to the Bolshevik Central Committee in the autumn of 1917 are good indicators of how Lenin believed that the Kornilov Affair provided the Bolsheviks with the necessary pre-requisites for a successful coup.[66] To illustrate why he believed that Russia was ripe for the plucking, Lenin wrote on September 14th, that during the July days, "we did not yet have a majority among the workers and soldiers of the capitals. Now we have majorities in both Soviets." Lenin wrote that this change in fortunes was "created only by the history of July and August...by the experience of the Kornilov Affair." Lenin also wrote that during the July Days, "there was no general revolutionary upsurge of the people. Now there is, after the Kornilov Affair. This is proven by the situation in the provinces." A third significant factor that Lenin believed would allow the Bolsheviks to wage a successful putsch compared to July, was that "at that time there were no vacillations on a serious, general, political scale among our enemies." Lenin also communicated to the committee, that in July, the Bolsheviks "could not have retained power...before the Kornilov Affair, the army and the provinces could and would have marched against Petrograd." In Lenin's mind, however, after the Kornilov Affair, "the picture is entirely different." The preceding statements made by Lenin in his letter to the Bolshevik Central Committee clearly demonstrates how Lenin believed that the Kornilov Affair was crucial in establishing the essential pre-requisites for a successful insurrection.

Upon taking the reigns of the Provisional Government in July of 1917, Kerensky sought to restore the military's ability to fight. One measure taken by Kerensky to help improve Russia's position in their bloody conflict with the Germans, was to promote General Lavr Kornilov to the post of Commander-In-Chief of the armed forces. Kornilov, however, was hesitant to unconditionally accept this post, fearing that without the implementation of various military reforms, his efforts would be fruitless. Thus, Kornilov communicated to Kerensky that he would only accept the position if Kerensky promised to implement his proposed reforms. On July 19, 1917, Kerensky agreed. How then, did Kerensky's handling of General Kornilov affect the position of his own government? Kerensky had hoped that his appointment of the General to the position of Commander-In-Chief would help revitalize the military, and thus strengthen his government's authority. This, however, was not the case. Upon the completion of an investigation of a broad collection of primary and secondary sources, evidence was found to suggest that Kerensky came to view Kornilov as a dangerous rival, and as a result, an illusion developed in his mind of a counterrevolution brewing on the right. The investigation has also shed light on Kerensky's pre-emptive actions to subdue this phantom counterrevolution, and its ensuing effects. Kerensky's decision to force a break between himself and Kornilov resulted in a polarized political arena, a dysfunctional military, provinces in a state of anarchy, and a revitalized Bolshevik party. When considering this point, one can ponder whether if Kerensky had handled the situation differently and instituted Kornilov's reforms instead of placating the left, would the Bolsheviks have ever been able to recover from their July experience and take control of Russia? If so, would Russia have made a successful transition to democracy through their planned Constituent Assembly, as advocated by Kerensky? While such a suggestion is conceivable, one must realize that the government had other challenges which placed pressure on its sustainability. These challenges included the Provisional Government's desire to continue the greatly unpopular war effort, its difficult task of facilitating a peaceful and orderly transition to a Constituent Assembly, and finally, its challenge of achieving a solution to the Land Question through the aforementioned assembly. Nevertheless, when considering Kerensky's actions, it is found that Kerensky's decision to pursue a campaign against a phantom counterrevolutionary plot allegedly headed by his Commander-In-Chief, General Lavr Kornilov, left the Provisional Government in a desperate state, void of supporters, and enabled the Bolsheviks to recover from their July debacle and seize power of Russia in October of 1917.

[1] In accordance with Marxist theory, many socialists in the Soviet believed that the bourgeoisie had to govern before their inevitable demise, and the ensuing rise of the proletariat. Thus, they believed that a necessary waiting period was required, and the Provisional Government would be allowed to govern until its aforementioned abdication of power. Michael Lynch, Reaction and Revolutions: Russia 1881-1924 (London: Hodder & Stoughton, 1992) p. 42

[2] Ibid., p. 87

[3] Richard Pipes, A Concise History of the Russian Revolution (New York: Alfred A. Knopf, 1995) p. 127

[4] Lynch, p. 88

[5] General Knox, a British military observer attached to the Russian army, commented to the British ambassador on returning from a visit to the Northern front, that the Russian army was in a 'deplorable state of affairs' and that 'units have been turned into political debating societies.' William Chamberlin, The Russian Revolution: 1917-1918 (Princeton: Princeton University Press, 1935) p. 227

[6] Ibid., p. 193

[7] Jorgen Munck, The Kornilov Revolt (Aarhus: Aarhus University Press, 1987) p. 8

[8] Chamberlin, p. 221; George Katkov, Russia 1917: The Kornilov Affair (New York: Longman, Inc., 1980) p. xii

[9] Lynch, p. 3

[10] Katkov, p. 161

[11] Ibid., p. 161

[12] Chamberlin, p. 192

[13] Edward Hallett Carr, The Bolshevik Revolution: 1917-1923 (Baltimore: Penguin Books, 1950) p. 103

[14] Orlando Figes, A People's Tragedy: The Russian Revolution 1891-1924 (London: Jonathan Cape, 1996) p. 445

[15] This sentiment can be appreciated by examining cartoons drawn by the famous Soviet political satirist and poster artist, Viktor Deni. One of his cartoons in particular, drawn in 1935, depicts Kerensky as a counterrevolutionary puppet in a military uniform, being manipulated by the strings of a capitalist. Ronald Kowalski, The Russian Revolution: 1917-1921 (London: Routledge, 1997) pp. 78-79

[16] Pipes, A Concise History, p. 129

[17] Richard Pipes, The Russian Revolution (New York: Alfred A. Knopf, 1990) p. 439

[18] Chamberlin, p. 195

[19] Order No. l, issued by the Petrograd Soviet in March 1917, made all military orders dependent upon its consent and placed discipline at a regimental level under the discretion of soldiers' councils rather than in the hands of officers. Pipes, Russian Revolution, p. 441

[20] Ibid, p. 442

[21] Figes, p. 447

[22] Alan Wildman, "The Breakdown of the Imperial Army in 1917," in Critical Companion to the Russian Revolution ed. E. Acton, V.I. Cherniaev and W. G. Rosenberg (Bloomington: Indiana University Press, 1997) p. 25

[23] Pipes, Russian Revolution, p. 442

[24] "General Lukomsky's account of the Kornilov Affair," in The Russian Provisional Government 1917: Documents Vol. 3, eds. Robert Paul Browder and Alexander Kerensky (Stanford: Stanford University Press, 1961) Doc. 1263

[25] Kowalski, p. 73

[26] Kerensky "not only saw but needed to see" Kornilov as a counterrevolutionary force. The reason for this, according to Pipes, was that Kerensky believed that to become leader of democratic Russia, he had to represent the democratic left, and to do so, had to share in its fear of a counterrevolution. During the summer of 1917, various reports of counterrevolutionary conspiracies surfaced in newspapers such as the Menshevik Novaia zhizn. Kerensky depended on Menshevik support in the Soviet, and therefore needed to address their concerns. Pipes, Russian Revolution, pp. 445, 447-448

[27] Ibid., pp. 445, 447-448

[28] Katkov, p. 56; One can achieve an understanding of the divisive effect that Kornilov's ideas had on the delegates by reading an article printed in the August 17th issue of the newspaper, Rech', just days following the conference. According to the article, the Moscow State Conference "shifted the line of demarcation between the representatives of the population into two camps" and by doing so, has "opened the question of the present composition of the government." "Article printed in Rech' on August 17, 1917," in Browder and Kerensky, Doc 1255

[29] This claim was made in the August 13 issue of Novoe vremia. Pipes, Russian Revolution, p. 447

[30] Ibid., p. 47

[31] "General Lukomsky's account of the Kornilov Affair," Browder and Kerensky, Doc. 1263

[32] Pipes, Russian Revolution, p. 448

[33] Ibid., p. 461

[34] I. Zohrah, "The Socialist Revolutionary Party, Kerensky and the Kornilov Affair From the Unpublished Papers of Harold W. Williams," New Zealand Slavonic Journal (1991): 153-154

[35] Chamberlin, p. 209; Vladimir Nikolaevich Lvov (not to be confused with Prince George Lvov, the former Prime Minister), a self-appointed "savior" of the country, was Procurator of the Holy Synod in the first Provisional Government. Lvov held this post until July 1917, when he was dismissed by Kerensky's second Provisional Government. After meeting once with General Kornilov and pretending to be a representative of Kerensky, Lvov subsequently met with Kerensky, pretending to be an ambassador of Kornilov. Lvov told Kerensky that the General demanded to be given full dictatorial rights, and that he expected Kerensky's resignation to be forthcoming. According to Richard Pipes, there is little doubt that this message delivered by Lvov to Kerensky had been concocted not by Kornilov, but by Lvov himself. Pipes, A Concise History, pp. 132-133

[36] Pipes, Russian Revolution, p. 456

[37] Figes, p. 450; When Maximilian Filonenko, a member of the Socialist Revolutionary party, saw the tapes from the Hughes Apparatus (a communications device), he observed that "Kerensky never stated what he was asking and Kornilov never knew to what he was responding." Kerensky, however, maintained to the end of his life, that Kornilov had "affirmed not only Lvov's authority to speak in Kornilov's name, but confirmed also the accuracy of the words which Lvov had attributed to him." Pipes, Russian Revolution, p. 456

[38] Figes, p. 450

[39] Pipes, Russian Revolution, p. 457

[40] Furthermore, Pipes makes an important observation, highlighting the fact that if counterrevolutionary plans had been in existence, then some of the generals would have followed Kornilov's ultimate appeal for a coup in Petrograd. They did not, however, and Kornilov was subsequently arrested. Pipes, Russian Revolution, p. 461

[41] Lynch, p. 92

[42] Chamberlin, p. 217

[43] Donald W. Treadgold, Twentieth Century Russia (Boulder: Westview Press, 1995) p. 104; It should also be

noted, that when ratifying their security plans, the Provisional Government also requested that the sailors of the cruiser Aurora, known for their Bolshevik sympathies, assume responsibility for the protection of among other things, the Winter Palace. Ironically, only two months later, the sailors of the Aurora would be the first ones to fire on the Winter Palace during the Bolshevik insurrection against the Provisional Government. In addition to this, Kerensky also distributed 40,000 guns to those "defending" the revolution, many of whom would assist the Bolsheviks in their October putsch. Figes, p. 455

[44] Ibid., p. 455

[45] Moisei Uritskii was a member of the Bolshevik Central Committee, a body responsible for determining the day-to-day direction of the party. Pipes, Russian Revolution, p. 466

[46] This amnesty was extended to Leon Trotsky, Vladimir Antonov-Ovseenko, and P.E. Dybenko, three men who would later play prominent roles in the Bolshevik coup of late October. By October 10, all but 27 Bolsheviks were free and preparing for their next putsch. Ibid, p. 467

[47] Figes, p. 455

[48] Kolonitskii's reference to a "political base," alludes to Kerensky's reliance on a coalition of support from the Socialist Revolutionaries and Mensheviks on the left, and from the Kadets on the right. Boris I. Kolonitskii, "Kerensky," in Acton, et al., p. 146

[49] Chamberlin, p. 277

[50] Ibid., p. 277

[51] At the conference, Kamenev, a Bolshevik representative, urged that no coalition government be established. Kamenev spoke eloquently, and was ultimately successful in persuading the representatives to adopt a firmer stance when dealing with the Kadets, thus signifying a widening in the bridge between left and right. Before Kamenev spoke, the conference passed a resolution in favour of a coalition government with the Kadets, but after the speech, that decision was rescinded in favour of a motion excluding the Kadets from a coalition government. Katkov, p. 125

[52] "Article printed in Den' on September 20, 1917," in Browder and Kerensky, Doc. 1361

[53] Chamberlin, p. 277

[54] Bolshevik gains from the political polarization that ensued after the Kornilov Affair can best be appreciated by

comparing the local election results for the Moscow Soviet from before the affair with the results after. It can be observed that the Socialist Revolutionaries and Mensheviks controlled 58.9% and 12.2% of seats in the Moscow Soviet before the affair, respectively. After the affair, that number dropped to 14.7% and 4.2%. The Bolsheviks, however, won an additional 37.8% of the seats in the Moscow Soviet, to control a total of 49.5% of the seats by September 1917. This polarization also occurred on the right, as Kadet control grew from 17.2% of all seats in June 1917 to 35.5% in September 1917. Pipes, <u>Russian Revolution</u>, p. 466

[55] Figes, p. 455

[56] Katkov, p. 122

[57] Ibid., p. 122

[58] One can achieve an appreciation of this behavior in the September 2nd edition of the Bolshevik paper, <u>Izvestiaa</u>, where accounts of violence in the region of Vyborg were documented. It was written that, "At first three generals and a colonel, who were arrested earlier... on charges of supporting Kornilov, were dragged out of the guardhouse by the crowd, thrown off the bridge, and killed in the water. This was immediately followed by lynchings in the regiments." "Article printed in <u>Izvestiaa</u> on September 2, 1917," in Browder and Kerensky, Doc 1309

[59] Munck, p. 121; One can best appreciate the lack of control that the government and commanding officers had over the military by considering two important documents. In a jointly signed order to the army and the fleet on September 3rd, Kerensky and General Alekseev (Chief of Staff) ordered that "all troop organizations function in a correct manner," and that they operate "free from any interference in the combat and operative work of commanding personnel." When examining the second document, a military intelligence report from the commander of the 6th Siberian Corps and 3rd Siberian Division, one is made aware of the lack of control that the government had over the military. Written nearly one month after the first document, this intelligence report claims that "the situation of the officer personnel has become very difficult; open hostility and animosity are manifest on the part of the soldiers; the most insignificant event may provoke unrest." Clearly, the previously issued order had not been effective in influencing the conduct of the troops. "Order to the Army and the Fleet of September 3, 1917," in Browder and Kerensky, Doc. 1307; "Military Intelligence Report from the Commander of the 6th Siberian

Corps and of the 3rd Siberian Division: September 20-October 1, 1917," in Browder and Kerensky, Doc. 1311

[60] Kerensky's loss of control over the military can also be observed in the reaction to his subsequent orders to all available Cossack troops stationed in Petrograd to take positions in the streets. The Cossacks replied with a claim that they were already saddling their horses in preparations to leave. Military intelligence, however, refuted this claim, indicating that the Cossacks were lying and did not wish to fight for the Provisional Government. Katkov, p. 128

[61] Katkov, p. 123

[62] Chamberlin, p. 242; This tension was heightened by Kerensky's unwillingness to settle the land question before a Constituent Assembly could meet. Land shortage was a chronic social problem in Russia since the emancipation of the serfs in 1861. The February revolution had led the peasantry to believe that they would benefit from a major land redistribution program, and were agitated by Kerensky's incessant postponement of the issue. Thus, peasants were more inclined to be receptive of calls for social disobedience. Lynch, p. 88

[63] "Article printed in Russkiia vedomosti on October 1, 1917," in Browder and Kerensky, Doc 1334

[64] "Letter to Provincial, Regional, and Municipal Commissars from the Minister of War, Major General Verkhovskii concerning his Order No. 51 of Oct. 11, 1917," in Browder and Kerensky, Doc. 1339

[65] "Letter to Provincial, Regional, and Municipal Commissars from the Minister of the Interior, Boris Nikitin of Oct. 21, 1917," in Browder and Kerensky, Doc. 1340

[66] In his writings, Lenin was more pragmatic about the opportunity presented by the Kornilov Affair, and less willing to wait for the historical determinism of Marxism to run its course. Vladimir I. Lenin, Polnoe sobranie sochinenii (Moscow: Gospolitizdat, 1858-1965) pp. 239-241

Bibliography

Article printed in <u>Den'</u> on September 20, 1917, Doc. 1361.
In Robert Paul Browder and Alexander Kerensky (Eds.), <u>The
Russian Provisional Government 1917: Documents Vol. 3</u>
Stanford: Stanford University Press, 1961

Article printed in <u>Izvestiaa</u> on September 2, 1917, Doc.
1309. In Robert Paul Browder and Alexander Kerensky (Eds.),
<u>The Russian Provisional Government 1917: Documents Vol. 3</u>
Stanford: Stanford University Press, 1961

Article printed in <u>Rech'</u> on August 17, 1917, Doc. 1255.
In Robert Paul Browder and Alexander Kerensky (Eds.), <u>The
Russian Provisional Government 1917: Documents Vol. 3</u>
Stanford: Stanford University Press, 1961

Article printed in <u>Russkiia vedomosti</u> on October 1, 1917,
Doc. 1334. In Robert Paul Browder and Alexander Kerensky
(Eds.), <u>The Russian Provisional Government 1917: Documents
Vol. 3</u> Stanford: Stanford University Press, 1961

Browder, Robert Paul and Kerensky, Alexander Fedorovich,
(Eds.), <u>The Russian Provisional Government 1917: Documents
Vol. 3</u> Stanford: Stanford University Press, 1961

Carr, Edward Hallett, <u>The Bolshevik Revolution: 1917-1923</u>
Baltimore: Penguin Books, 1950

Chamberlin, William Henry, <u>The Russian Revolution: 1917-
1918</u> Princeton: Princeton University Press, 1935

Figes, Orlando, <u>A People's Tragedy: The Russian Revolution
1891-1924</u> London: Jonathan Cape, 1996

General Lukomsky's account of the Kornilov Affair, Doc.
1263. In Robert Paul Browder and Alexander Kerensky (Eds.),
<u>The Russian Provisional Government 1917: Documents Vol. 3</u>
Stanford: Stanford University Press, 1961

Katkov, George, <u>Russia 1917: The Kornilov Affair</u> New York:
Longman, Inc., 1980

Kolonitskii, Boris I. Kerensky. In E. Acton, V.I. Cherniaev and W. G. Rosenberg (Eds.), <u>Critical Companion to the Russian Revolution: 1914-1921</u> Bloomington: Indiana University Press, 1997

Kowalski, Ronald, <u>The Russian Revolution: 1917-1921</u> London: Routledge, 1997

Lenin, V.I., <u>Polnoe sobranie sochinenii</u> Moscow: Gospolitizdat, 1858-1965

Letter to Provincial, Regional, and Municipal Commissars from the Minister of the Interior, Boris Nikitin of Oct. 21, 1917, Doc. 1340. In Robert Paul Browder and Alexander Kerensky (Eds.), <u>The Russian Provisional Government 1917: Documents Vol. 3</u> Stanford: Stanford University Press, 1961

Letter to Provincial, Regional, and Municipal Commissars from the Minister of War, Major General Verkhovskii concerning his Order No. 51 of Oct. 11, 1917, Doc. 1339. In Robert Paul Browder and Alexander Kerensky (Eds.), <u>The Russian Provisional Government 1917: Documents Vol. 3</u> Stanford: Stanford University Press, 1961

Military Intelligence Report from the Commander of the 6th Siberian Corps and of the 3rd Siberian Division: September 20-October 1, 1917, Doc. 1311. In Robert Paul Browder and Alexander Kerensky (Eds.), <u>The Russian Provisional Government 1917: Documents Vol. 3</u> Stanford: Stanford University Press, 1961

Lynch, Michael, <u>Reactions and Revolutions: Russia 1881-1924</u> London: Hodder & Stoughton, 1992

Munck, Jorgan Larson, <u>The Kornilov Revolt</u> Aarhus: Aarhus University Press, 1987

Order to the Army and the Fleet of September 3, 1917, Doc. 1307 in Robert Paul Browder and Alexander Kerensky (Eds.), <u>The Russian Provisional Government 1917: Documents Vol. 3</u> Stanford: Stanford University Press, 1961

Pipes, Richard, <u>A Concise History of the Russian Revolution</u> New York: Alfred A. Knopf, 1995

Pipes, Richard, <u>The Russian Revolution</u> New York: Alfred A. Knopf, 1990

Treadgold, Donald W., <u>Twentieth Century Russia</u> Boulder: Westview Press, 1995

Wildman, Allan, "The Breakdown of the Imperial Army in 1917." In E. Acton, V.I. Cherniaev and W. G. Rosenberg (Eds.), <u>Critical Companion to the Russian Revolution: 1914-1921</u> (69-80) Bloomington: Indiana University Press, 1997

Zohrah, I., "The Socialist Revolutionary Party, Kerensky and the Kornilov Affair: From the Unpublished Papers of Harold W. Williams," <u>New Zealand Slavonic Journal</u> (1991) p. 1534

Edmund Burke
Reflections on the Revolution in France 1790
Oxford World Classics, 1999, p. 96-97

To avoid therefore the evils of inconstancy and versatility, ten thousand times worse than those of obstinacy and the blindest prejudice, we have consecrated the state, that no man should approach to look into its defects or corruptions but with due caution; that he should never dream of of beginning its reformation by subversion; that he should approach the faults of the state as to the wounds of a father, with pious awe and trembling solicitude. By this wise prejudice we are taught to look with horror on those children of their country who are prompt rashly to hack that aged parent in pieces, and put him into the kettle of magicians, in hopes that by their poisonous weeds, and wild incantations, they may regenerate the paternal constitution, and renovate their father's life.

Society is indeed a contract. Subordinate contracts for objects of mere occasional interest may be dissolved at pleasure— but the state ought not to be considered as nothing better than a partnership agreement in a trade of pepper and coffee, callico or tobacco, or some other such low concern, to be taken up for a little temporary interest, and to be dissolved by the fancy of the partners. It is to be looked on with other reverence; because it is not a partnership in things subservient only to the gross animal existence of a temporal and perishable nature. It is a partnership in all science; a partnership in all art; a partnership in every virtue, and in all perfection. As the ends of such a partnership cannot be obtained in many generations, it becomes a partnership not only between those who are living, but between those who are living, those who are dead, and those who are to be born.

Each contract of each particular state is but a clause in the great primeval contract of eternal society, linking the lower with the higher natures, connecting the visible and invisible worlds, according to a fixed compact sanctioned by the inviolable oath which holds all physical and moral natures, each in their appointed place.

Ralph Waldo Emerson Prize 2005

GYPSY LEGISLATION IN SPAIN, 1499-1783

Amy Rachel Motomura

Gypsies, also known as Roma, are nomadic peoples who can be found throughout Europe. They arrived in the western part the continent in the early 1400s, when western European states were becoming more centralized. With this consolidation of power came the rapid spread of anti-Gypsy laws across western Europe. As Gypsies were expelled from one country after another, they shuffled between them, and many of the Gypsies eventually ended up in Spain.[1] Over the course of almost three hundred years, from the late fifteenth century to the late eighteenth century, Spanish rulers attempted to deal with the Gypsy population within their state. At first, the Gypsies were welcomed, but this did not last long. They began to be perceived as threats to the Spanish people, culture, and religion. Thus, Ferdinand and Isabella, in 1499, initiated a long stream of anti-Gypsy legislation that lasted until Charles III's reign in 1783. Anti-Gypsy legislation presented an interesting problem for Spanish rulers because they had no precedents to follow. The Gypsies were not perceived to be a problem in Spain until the late 1400s, and therefore, when Ferdinand and Isabella issued the first law against Gypsies, they could not look back at the past to determine the most effective approach for either integrating or excluding the Gypsies.

The author is a graduate of Duke University's Pratt School of Engineering. She wrote this paper for Anthony McGinnis' AP European History course at Boulder High School in Boulder, Colorado in the 2002/2003 year.

From Ferdinand and Isabella to Charles III, each ruler saw that his predecessor's laws had been ineffective,[2] so he tried a slightly different approach. In retrospect, their policies can be analyzed in terms of two major elements: goals and methods. The laws' apparent goals ranged from expulsion to assimilation, while the methods varied from coercion to persuasion. Although most of the rulers mixed both methods and goals, in general their legislation began as largely coercive and supported by penalties of exile, whipping, and galley service. Eventually, the laws progressed to be more persuasive and to focus more on assimilation of Gypsies into Spanish society. The transition was by no means smooth, however, and the legislation's apparent goals vacillated wildly between the extremes of assimilation and expulsion,[3] with rulers often resorting to using the Gypsies as a labor force when they found that they could neither rid Spain of them nor integrate them. Many of the rulers also failed to see that their laws, regardless of the approach, were not being effectively implemented. In short, the three hundred years of anti-Gypsy legislation reflect the rulers' uncertainty, lack of definite policy choices, and failure to adequately enforce the laws. Ultimately, however, Charles III was able to create a law that would have a lasting impact.[4]

Although their ethnic background has been debated, the general consensus is that Gypsies originated in northern India. This is confirmed by their blood groups, certain cultural similarities, and the close relationship between Sanskrit and Romany, the language spoken by the Gypsies. There are conflicting theories about what place Gypsies held in Indian society or how they lived, but most historians believe that they were a loose federation of nomadic tribes living outside of the Indian caste system.[5] There are three main types of Gypsies mostly named for the areas to which they migrated: Kalderash Gypsies, Munush Gypsies, and Gitános; the last is the group found in North Africa, the South of France, Portugal, and Spain.[6]

Gypsies seem to have first entered Spain in the fifteenth century, arriving in southern Spain from North Africa across the Straits of Gibraltar and in northeastern Spain from France over the Pyrenees Mountains. Actual initial dates of arrival are not known, but the first official record was made in Barcelona in 1447. Their presence, recorded in *Annales de Cataluña*,[7] is believed to have been part of a mass movement of thousands of Gypsies into Barcelona.[8] It seems, however, that there were some Gypsy movements into Spain through North Africa before the 1440s.[9]

The Gypsies were unlike the Spaniards surrounding them in many ways. They had darker skin, non-European features, different dress, and spoke another language, Romany. They generally belonged to nomadic, tribe-like groups, and had their own system of government. While traveling throughout the country, they carried on trades of metalworking, mule clipping, horse trading, fortune-telling, and performing song and dance.[10]

Although they were very different from Spaniards, when Gypsies first arrived in Spain the rulers and their subjects gave them warm welcomes. Many of the early Gypsies found themselves the recipients of king-granted privileges, letters of immunity from certain laws, alms, and guarantees of armed assistance if needed. Much of this elevated status stemmed from the fact that when the Gypsies initially arrived in Spain in the 1400s, they claimed to be royalty from a place they termed the Kingdom of Little Egypt.[11]

The Spanish attitude toward Gypsies rapidly altered, however. By the 1470s, new, larger waves of Gypsies were appearing in Spain, encouraged by the success of the earlier immigrants. The Gypsies now did not receive the same type of treatment, partially because they no longer claimed to be Little Egypt's royalty. Also, the Spanish commoners began to resent the required alms-giving. Supporting the Gypsies strained the lower class's resources, and the Gypsies seemed to be a threat to Spanish safety, religion, and culture. They engaged in open conflicts with Spanish Church officials, abused their privileges, and began to be seen by Spaniards as "irredeemably truant, clannishly astute, ignorant, superstitious, and given to the occult...."[12]

Subsequently, Gypsies developed a bad name for themselves. They were accused of being thieves, scam artists, propagators of witchcraft and sorcery, and a people who had no respect for

Christian religious observances. In 1613 Miguel de Cervantes, the great Spanish author, wrote *La gitanilla,* a book which reflected the popular sentiment at the time toward Gypsies as a threat to public safety.[13] In one part he wrote:

> It seems that the Gypsies came into this world to be thieves; they are born to thieving parents, they grow up with thieves, they study to be thieves, and in the end, they turn out to be nothing but thieves; and their desire to steal and stealing are inseparable qualities that only disappear with death.[14]

Anti-Gypsy sentiment also came from Catholic leaders in Spain, who saw Gypsies' superstition as a threat to Spain's devout Christianity.[15] In the 1630s, Father Pedro de Figueroa wrote:

> Their actions place the Faith in grave danger, because they live an impious life, they intend nothing but wickedness, and their life goal is the greater neglect of their soul. Their deceits are either pacts with the demon, or lies in order to steal...I was correct to call them vassals of the demon because a band of Gypsies is no other but an arm of Satan.[16]

Such perceptions of Gypsies were what ushered in a new era in Spanish Gypsy history, one that would last almost three hundred years. Between 1499 and 1783, each monarch issued or revised Gypsy legislation at least twelve times. But despite the plethora of anti-Gypsy legislation, hardly any of it had any real effect on the Gypsy population.[17]

Even if the rulers had known exactly how they wanted to deal with the Gypsies and had created perfect laws, they probably still would have failed because few of the laws were ever enforced. Much of the reason that the laws were never effectively enforced was because of rampant corruption in the Spanish justice system. Often, Gypsies were able to bribe officials assigned to the task of executing the laws. Despite the fact that the commoners began to resent the Gypsies in the 1470s, the nobility continued to help them, even in hard times. In return for the help, Gypsies would often steal horses and give them to their benefactors. The nobles often claimed that they could not resist helping the Gypsies because of the women's seductiveness.[18] George Borrow, author of *The Zincali,* one of the few books in English focusing on Spanish

Gypsies, believes that corruption is the only way to explain why Gypsies continued to flourish in the face of such a barrage of laws against them. He writes, "Spanish justice has invariably been a mockery, a thing to be bought and sold, terrible only to the feeble and innocent, and an instrument of cruelty and avarice."[19] Even when the rulers realized this problem, as Philip IV (1621-1665) did, the laws they passed to punish people who helped Gypsies were ineffective because enforcement was put in the hands of the very people who were breaking the laws.[20]

Gypsies could also avoid the laws passed against them because of their nomadic nature and Spain's topography. It was almost impossible to find all of the Gypsies because they were not a settled community. In addition, Gypsies could easily hide in the Spanish wilderness, whose terrain lent itself to such elusiveness.[21]

The very beginning of anti-Gypsy legislation in Spain came at the end of the fifteenth century under Spain's first united reign. Before 1479, Spain was not a united nation. In 1469, however, Ferdinand, son of the King of Aragon, one kingdom in what would become Spain, married Isabella. Isabella was the sister of King Enrique VI of Castile, another kingdom in Spain. When Enrique VI died in 1474, it led to a war of succession between Isabella and Doña Juana, his daughter, who both tried to claim the throne. The civil war lasted from 1475 to 1479, ending in victory for Isabella and Ferdinand. In 1479, they began their united reign of Spain. They set out to restore law and order after the civil war and to consolidate centralized power.[22]

At first, it did not seem as though Ferdinand and Isabella would issue anti-Gypsy legislation. For example, they did not immediately cancel the Gypsies' privileges. They even issued some letters of protection for a limited duration, although the emphasis was less on alms and more on the Gypsies' rights to have legal and honest trades for their livelihoods.[23]

In 1499, however, Ferdinand and Isabella began the legal persecution of Spanish Gypsies. Their law's approach was based on making the Gypsies either assimilate or leave Spain. On March 4, this *Pragmatic Sanction of Medina del Campo* declared that Gypsies had to settle down within sixty days or face life-long exile from Spain. The law specified that they had to reside in already established towns and adopt honest trades under a "master whom they might serve for their maintenance." Alternatively, the Gypsies could leave Spain within the same sixty days to avoid punishment.[24] In 1502, Ferdinand and Isabella issued another pragmática which made all Gypsies, and in fact all inhabitants of Spain, officially Roman Catholics. In response to these decrees, the Gypsies in Spain neither left nor changed their lifestyles; this juxtaposition of law versus reality would set the tone for the next three hundred years of legislation.[25]

After Ferdinand and Isabella's lack of success, the next Spanish ruler tried his luck. Charles I, also Emperor Charles V of the Holy Roman Empire,[26] maintained the law of 1499's coercive attitude but shifted the emphasis away from exile. Instead of continuing to try to expel the Gypsies, he attempted to use them as a labor force for the state's benefit. In 1538, he reissued the *Pragmatic Sanction of Medina del Campo*. It declared:

> Decree of their Highnesses given in the year 1499, and Law No. 104 in the Decrees, confirmed and ordered to be observed in the court in which it was celebrated in Toledo in the year 1525, Law No. 58, in spite of any clause which may have been given to the contrary.[27]

He also added his own modifications, stating:

> Gypsies are not to move about these kingdoms, and those that may be there, are to leave them, or take trades, or live with their overlords under penalty of a hundred lashes for the first time, and for the second time that their ears be cut off, and that they be chained for sixty days, and that for the third time that they remain captive forever to them who take them.[28]

By 1539, however, Charles I made it clear that the preferred sentence for Gypsies was time in the chusma, or rowing force of the galleys. At Toledo, he declared that all male Gypsies between the ages of twenty and fifty would be put in the royal galleys for six years if caught in Spain. At this time the Spanish government was in dire need of galley squadrons due to warfare with the Islamic Empire in the Mediterranean.[29] When the 1539 law did not round up enough men for the galleys, Charles I issued another law in

1552, extending time in the galleys to all vagabonds. He defined vagabonds to include, in addition to Gypsies, foreign tinkers and the healthy mendicant poor. They were given four years for the first offense, eight for the second, and life for the third. Like previous and subsequent laws, Charles I's policies met with little success, as it was almost impossible to round up Gypsies because of corruption and their nomadic lifestyle.[30]

By the 1550s, Spain had had anti-Gypsy legislation for half a century, yet the state had not been able to successfully control or remove them. The Castilian Cortes, or parliament, now took up the issue, continually complaining about the Gypsies and suggesting more action. Under the Cortes' pressure, the next ruler, Philip II, son of Charles I and widower of Mary Tudor of England, renewed and sharpened the previous anti-Gypsy legislation, as his predecessor had done.[31] Philip II continued to focus on using Gypsies to man the galleys, but made his laws even more coercive and restrictive.

In 1559, Philip II reissued all of the previous anti-Gypsy laws and extended them to any women who dressed in Gypsy fashion. In 1575, he modified Charles I's laws of 1539 and 1552, decreeing that all able-bodied Gypsy men serve in the galleys, regardless of their age or whether they were nomadic or settled. To avoid a failure similar to his father's, he called for a nationwide Gypsy-hunt. Although it was erratically conducted, many Gypsies were rounded up, including some who were non-nomadic. Gypsies with sedentary occupations were given a token salary, while the itinerant ones were forced into the chusma without pay.[32]

Despite his success in capturing Gypsies for the galleys, Philip II's laws were otherwise ineffective. He therefore tried again, keeping with the same general policies but adding new restrictions. In 1586, Philip II stated, as he had in 1559, that all old edicts should be observed. He also added that Gypsies could not continue their thievery and cheating, that Gypsies could not sell any goods without an approval bearing a notary public signature saying that they had a settled residence, and that without such forms, all goods they sold would be considered stolen property.[33]

As before, these measures met with limited success, and the Castilian Cortes was not satisfied. Two of its members wrote a report that condemned Gypsies and recommended further actions against them. They suggested that Gypsy men and women be separated and forced to marry non-Gypsy peasants, and that their children be raised in orphanages until the age of ten. After that, girls would provide domestic service, while boys became apprentices. This report was of great significance: not because Philip II implemented its suggestions—he had them shelved—but because they provided a basis for later laws that would emphasize forced assimilation through the breaking up of Gypsy families.[34]

The seventeenth century in Spain saw a dramatic increase in popular support for anti-Gypsy legislation. This was the result of a series of published works in the 1600s, mostly diatribes against Gypsies written by priests, legal luminaries, and theologians. These recounted all of the previous rumors and accusations, as well as ones that were significantly more sensationalized. Common complaints included child-stealing, heresy, licentiousness, theft, and treason. The works also contained numerous solutions for the Gypsy problem. The most common suggestion was strictly enforced expulsion of all Gypsies in Spain, a policy over which galley service had been preferred since Charles I in 1539.[35]

Philip II's successor, Philip III, and the Castilian Cortes did not adopt this policy of expulsion, however. They continued the effort to force Gypsies into the galleys, following the policies of Charles I and Philip II. In 1609, all adult males were ordered to serve for six years in the galleys, and this time not even settled Gypsies were offered pay for their service. The only exception to the required service was for men who were engaged in agriculture.[36] The continued use of the galleys to isolate the Gypsies represented the continued uncertainty about whether Gypsies should be forced to assimilate or be excluded from Spanish society.

Philip III's most notable anti-Gypsy legislation was enacted in 1619. In this law he did follow the diatribes' lead and modified his policy's coercive element to be the threat of expulsion, returning to the punishment in Ferdinand and Isabella's law enacted in

1499. Also like Ferdinand and Isabella, Philip III stressed Gypsies' assimilation into Spanish society, reversing the policy of separation through forced galley service. In adding more details about the assimilation, he attacked traditional Gypsy custom much more strongly than Ferdinand and Isabella had done. He said that Gypsies were a "collection of vicious people drawn from the dregs of Spanish society" and ordered that Gypsies conform to the rules put forth by his predecessors, settle in cities of over one thousand families, have nothing to do with cattle, and give up their Gypsy names, dress, and language. If the Gypsies conformed and abided by his rules, then they would be spared, but otherwise they would be expelled from Castile with the threat of death upon their return.[37]

The laws under Philip III reflected a stronger desire than ever to eliminate the Gypsy way of life from Spain. This legislation, said Philip III, was "in order that, forasmuch as they are not such by nations, this name and manner of life may be for evermore confounded and forgotten."[38] This quote suggests the next development in anti-Gypsy legislation: that Gypsies perhaps were not their own race or nation, thus making assimilation rather than exclusion the obvious goal. This new element appeared under the next Spanish ruler, Philip IV. His legislation originally treated Gypsies as Spaniards, not as a separate people, representing a significant change in the conceptual view of Gypsies. Although in a later law he rescinded this approach, it would be very influential under Charles III in the late 1700s.[39]

Philip IV, under pressure from the Cortes and his advisors, issued a pragmatic sanction on May 8, 1633. It continued the course set by Philip III of forced assimilation, but integrated the idea that Gypsies were "arrant" Spaniards.[40] This law was extremely coercive and the most brutal to date. It stated "that the laws hitherto adopted since the year 1499 have been inefficient to restrain their excesses...."[41] Philip IV said that "those who call themselves Gitános are not so by origin or by nature but have adopted this form of life for such deleterious purposes as are now experienced."[42] Thus, because Gypsies were supposed to be merely delinquent Spaniards, he declared that "Gitáno" was no longer a word. Gypsy dress and customs were to be abandoned and their colonies to be broken up: Gypsies could not participate in dances or performances, speak Romany, live in traditional Gypsy barrios (town districts in which Gypsies typically congregated), marry each other, or meet with other Gypsies. The punishments for these offenses were six years in the galleys for men and flogging and banishment for women, and in addition, anyone who caught a wandering Gypsy could make him or her his slave. Although these provisions were extremely severe, the laws were not successfully implemented, as before.[43]

Philip IV's law marked a change in another respect: he was the first to acknowledge the rampant corruption that hindered the execution of his predecessors' laws. He tried to curb this corruption in the justice system by imposing heavy fines for nobles who helped Gypsies, and sending commoners who aided them to the galleys. Yet, this law was just as ineffective as other laws related to the Gypsies. When he created this law, Philip IV placed it in the hands of the same officials who were the recipients of bribery and the dispensers of aid.[44]

Much of the motivation behind the gradual change in goals to assimilation can be attributed to the economic situation in the 1600s. Philip IV found himself king in a time of deep economic decline, in which huge areas of land went out of cultivation, villages disappeared, and laborers found themselves poverty-stricken. Large numbers of ethnically non-Gypsy farmers were leaving their land to live as Gypsies in an attempt to avoid the economic realities of the day. To combat this trend, Philip IV issued another pragmatica on May 8, 1633, stating that anyone who was not a Gypsy but acting as one would receive two hundred lashes and spend six years in the galleys.[45] Because Spain had suffered great depopulation due to economic hardships, Philip IV restricted the use of expulsion that had been theoretically revived under Philip III, deeming that Spain simply could not afford any more population losses, even if that population would be Gypsies.[46]

Instead of exile, Philip IV returned to the former policy of forced service in the galleys. To justify his new law, he no longer considered Gypsies Spaniards, returning to defining and alienating them as a separate race. In 1635, Philip IV issued a royal decree demanding that all unemployed Gypsy men between the ages of twenty and fifty years be sent to the galleys. In 1639, he modified this to state that all Gypsy men had to row in the galleys,[47] saying: "There is a great need for galleymen and rowers, and everywhere there is an excess of this odious race, who are all spies, thieves, and liars."[48] To round up the men, Madrid's alcaldes de casa y corte, a royal magistrate with jurisdiction over the capital city set up a special junta, or council. Philip IV was forced to give this order at least twice, however, because it was not heeded.[49]

Under Spain's next ruler, Carlos II, better known to the English-speaking world as Charles II, Gypsy policy became even more muddled than before. He took steps both to assimilate and exclude Gypsies, making his goals somewhat unclear. In November 1692, he said that Gypsies could not live in towns with under one thousand families, have any trade other than farming, wear traditional Gypsy dress, speak Romany, live in separate quarters of towns, have anything to do with cattle without a public notary, or possess firearms. It seemed, however, that Gypsies took no heed of this law.[50]

On June 12, 1695, Charles II passed another edict. It reiterated that Gypsies could not live any life other than one based on farming, in which women and children were required to participate, and stated that they were banned from any other trade, especially that of the blacksmith. They also could have no contact with horses, in or out of the house, under a penalty of two months in prison. This punishment also applied to anyone lending a horse to a Gypsy. For farm work, they were allowed only a mule or other such "lesser beast." Gypsies were allowed to leave their homes only for reasons related to agriculture and only then if they had written permission; if this was not obeyed they faced six years in the galleys. As they were not allowed to travel, Gypsies were also barred from attending or selling at fairs and markets.[51]

It remains ambiguous in this legislation whether Charles II wanted the Gypsies to be integrated into society or whether he wanted to marginalize them. He supported assimilation through his restriction of traditional Gypsy language and dress and his requirement that they live in larger established towns. Yet many of his policies tried to separate Gypsies from Spanish society, such as denying them the right to attend fairs or have any trade other than farming.

Despite Charles II's apparent uncertainty regarding Gypsy policy, he retained one important part of Philip IV's understanding of the situation: he kept the laws against aiding Gypsies. He declared that anyone helping Gypsies would be fined six thousand ducats if a noble and sent to the galleys for ten years if a plebian. Unfortunately, like his predecessors, he did not see the futility of this law.[52]

Charles II attempted to add one innovation to Gypsy legislation. He expressed interest, not seen before him, in determining the number of Gypsies and their status. He ordered a census to be taken of all Gypsies and their occupations, weapons, and livestock. It is uncertain, however, whether this census was actually taken because no record survives.[53]

When Charles II's reign ended, Spain found itself with a Gypsy population that had been there for over two hundred years, yet the state still did not have the upper hand. Spain had been ruled throughout this period by the Hapsburgs, but after the War of Spanish Succession ended in 1713, Philip V, grandson of Louis XIV of France and a Bourbon, came to power. After seeing the ineffectiveness of the Hapsburgs' policies toward the Gypsies, Philip V attempted a new approach, theoretically more rational but more brutal than ever before. He wanted to decrease the numbers of antisocial or delinquent groups, if not integrating them into society then at least making the groups more useful to Spain. He used this end to justify incredibly cruel and repressive measures, including a 1705 edict that allowed ministers of justice to treat Gypsies as public enemies and fire at them at any sign of resistance to punishment. Also in 1705, the council of Madrid published a schedule for the apprehension and punishment of the Gypsies, in which their description of the situation made it sound as though the country was so overrun with Gypsies that there was no peace or safety for any of the Spanish people.[54]

In 1717, Philip V added to his laws of 1705, issuing a pragmatíca that confirmed previous legislation but still contained evidence that Spain was not yet ready to fully devote itself to Gypsy assimilation. Gypsies were excluded from many areas throughout Spain, and indeed, their approved places of residence were limited to forty-one specific towns across the country. On October 1, 1726, another law was passed, saying that Gypsies could not file any complaints against inferior justices being heard in higher tribunals or leave their homes except in urgent cases. Gypsy women were also banished from Madrid, and in fact, all Gypsy women were forbidden to enter any town where there were royal audiences because it was customary for women to flock to royal gatherings to perform, peddle goods, and tell fortunes. Philip V authorized, with the same law, the hunting down of Gypsies with firepower or sword, and even chasing Gypsies from churches to which they had fled for protection.[55] Despite the Bourbon attempt to produce more effective anti-Gypsy laws, this law was no more successful than any before it. Historian George Borrow writes:

> This law was attended with the same success as the others; the Gitános left their places of domicile whenever they thought proper, frequented various fairs, and played off their jockey tricks as usual, or traversed the country in armed gangs, plundering the small villages, and assaulting travelers.[56]

The middle of the eighteenth century brought a major change to anti-Gypsy law. While the galleys since 1530 had been used as a form of punishment, in 1748 naval technological improvements made the galleys obsolete. Thus, Spain had to find a form of punishment to replace the one that had been preferred since Charles I in 1539. This would have been a logical time to make the laws point decisively toward either elimination of the Gypsies or their integration into society, but Ferdinand VI, the next ruler, instead continued to use Gypsies as a labor force—within Spain but outside of society. Now Ferdinand VI demanded that Gypsies be sent into forced labor in numerous areas as chosen by the government, mostly spinning for women, factories for boys, and mines and shipyards for men.[57]

In 1749, a raid occurred reminiscent of Philip II's 1575 Gypsy-hunt. Like Philip II's, Ferdinand's raid was somewhat successful. In just one night an estimated six to twelve thousand Gypsy men were rounded up. The raid was recommended by Reverend Gaspar Vázquez Tablada, Bishop of Oviedo and governor of the Council of Castile, and supported by armed forces. Most of the men ended up in naval arsenals converted to penal establishments where they performed heavy labor. Ferdinand VI did, however, recognize that some Gypsies might be "good" people, and if they could substantiate claims to a family and honest work, they were allowed to return home.[58]

Ferdinand VI also continued his father's 1705 pragmatíca but designated thirty-four more towns as acceptable places of residence for Gypsies. His hope, with this modification, was to disperse Gypsy families. With seventy-five towns that Gypsies could live in, he calculated that there would be approximately one per one hundred people. This demonstrated some interest in assimilating the Gypsies.[59]

The small shifts in Gypsy policy finally culminated under Spain's next ruler, Ferdinand VI's successor and half-brother, Carlos Tercero or Charles III. He was the monarch who would finally create the law that had been eluding rulers for almost three hundred years, and in doing so he would begin to tackle the Gypsy problem. He had a reputation for tolerance, and this attitude seems to have come through in his Gypsy legislation. His first act in regard to the Gypsies marked change: in 1763, he attempted to set free the men held from the 1749 raid. He was strongly opposed by his advisors for two years, but in 1765 he succeeded in releasing the Gypsies.[60]

This was a minor step, however, compared to his law that would be passed in 1783. It was largely the product of a report written in 1772 by Pedro Valiente and Pedro Rodriguez. The report provided the basis for future legislation and pointed out that while the previous laws' trend had been toward assimilation, the national sentiment remained overwhelmingly against Gypsy assimilation. Valiente and Rodriguez suggested that, like under Philip IV, the word "Gitáno" be prohibited and "New Castilian" used instead. They also thought that Gypsies should be able to have any trade and should have access to a good education. Looking at past legislation, the two showed that its penal attempts had been ineffective. Charles III gave a mixed reception to their proposals, but in the end he incorporated many of their ideas into his next law.[61]

This new law, passed on September 19, 1783, was a product of the Enlightenment's thought: Charles III's hope was to make the Gypsies more useful to Spain by integrating them and offering them unprecedented opportunities. The law's framers saw that the previous three hundred years of legislation had been largely futile, and they set out to fix its problems.[62] The statute was addressed to the Gypsies and tried to convince them that it was in their best interest to give up their traditional ways, though there were also many restrictions to help convince them: Gypsies were still barred from their traditional trades of animal trading, sheep shearing, metal working, music, and dance; they were not to keep horses, leave their homes, or take refuge in churches; and the earlier laws against speaking Romany were confirmed.[63]

In addition, these laws were backed up with severe penalties, perhaps even more harsh than ever before. Any Gypsy who was caught living a nomadic lifestyle would have, upon first offense, any children younger than sixteen taken away, and upon second offense, be executed. These punishments, however, were enforced effectively only while Charles III remained on the throne until his death in 1788.[64]

Although it continued many of the prior policies, Charles III's law broke with most past legislation in one very significant way: it did not distinguish between a regular Spaniard and a Gypsy who had given up his traditional ways, reminiscent of Philip IV's first law. Charles III declared that Gypsies were, in fact, not a tainted race,[65] saying: "they are not...nor do they come from, any infected stock whatever."[66]

Despite its strict requirements and penalties, this law provided Gypsies with unprecedented opportunities. They were allowed occupations in any non-Gypsy trade they wished, though they could not work in Madrid or any royal residences. Gradually, this new law led to an increase in the settled Gypsy population and marked the end of a major emphasis on anti-Gypsy legislation.[67] In 1841, George Borrow wrote:

> We should not have said thus much of Carlos Tercero...if a law passed during his reign did not connect him intimately with the history of Gitános, whose condition to a certain extent it has already altered, over whose future destinies there can be no doubt that it will exert considerable influence.[68, 69]

The law's framers were also realistic about the Spanish justice system, realizing that Gypsies had always found ways to avoid the laws' enforcement. Therefore, the writers provided means to avoid reliance on corregidors, chief royal agents in cities who presided over city council meetings and acted as appeals judges, and alguazils, municipal constables or sheriffs, who could hamper the law's enforcement.[70] Thus, Charles III insured that unlike those before him, his law would truly have an effect on the Gypsies in Spain.

Gypsy legislation in Spain is a curious subject; in a span of only three hundred years there were huge variances in what rulers wanted to do with the Gypsies and also how they went about it. Indeed, many of the policy changes did not even represent a slow shifting as time progressed, but were large, often erratic changes in goals and methods as different rulers ascended to the Spanish throne and attempted to make their laws more successful than those of their predecessors. Finally, though, Charles III was able to create a law that began the slow process of minimizing the conflict between Gypsies and the state, its rulers, and its people. Yet, the period in Spain from the fifteenth to the eighteenth centuries is only a minute slice of Gypsy history. Experiences like those in Spain at this time were commonplace across Europe. Gypsy persecution also was far from over by the end of the eighteenth century. Of course the most infamous episode of killing Gypsies in large numbers would not occur until under the Nazis in the twentieth century,[71] but Gypsies found enemies before and after that episode, with stigma and persecution still existing today. It should be noted, however, that Spain and the Gypsies have not always been at odds. Despite the laws against them and their lifestyle, Gypsies have made a significant contribution to Spanish culture, especially in their song and dance, and Spanish Gypsies today are some of Europe's most integrated and free people.[72]

Notes

[1] Bertha Quintana, Qué Gitáno!: Gypsies of Southern Spain (New York: Holt, Rinehart, and Winston, Inc., 1972) p. 13; Teofilo Ruiz, Spanish Society, 1400-1600 (Harrow, England: Pearson Education Limited, 2001) p. 114; Donald Kenrick, The Destiny of Europe's Gypsies (New York: Basic Books, Inc., 1972) p. 42; Ian Hancock, The Pariah Syndrome (Ann Arbor, MI: Karoma Publishers, Inc., 1987) p. 53

[2] Quintana, Gitáno, p. 20

[3] Angus Fraser, The Gypsies (Cambridge, Massachusetts: Basil Blackwell Inc., 1992) p. 160

[4] The study of Spanish anti-Gypsy legislation has been a much overlooked subject, at least in the English language. There are very few historians who address this topic, and I have found none who have presented any extended analysis of the entire period from Ferdinand and Isabella to Charles III.

[5] Kenrick, Destiny, p. 13; Quintana, Gitáno, pp. 14-15; David Vassberg, The Village and the Outside World in Golden Age Castile (Cambridge, United Kingdom: Cambridge University Press, 1996) p. 143

[6] Jean-Paul Clebert, The Gypsies (New York: E.P. Dutton & Co., Inc., 1963) pp. 23-24

[7] Ibid., pp. 28, 82; Allen Josephs, White Wall of Spain (Ames, Iowa: The Iowa State University Press, 1983) p. 28

[8] Quintana, Gitáno, p. 16

[9] Vassberg, Castile, p. 143; Charles Chapman, A History of Spain (New York: The MacMillan Company, 1918) p. 275; Quintana, Gitáno, p. 17; Fraser, Gypsies, p. 205

[10] While 1447 is the date recognized by most historians, Angus Fraser states that a safe-conduct dating from January 12, 1425, was the first document relating to Gypsies in Spain. It was granted to a Gypsy calling himself "Don Johan de Egipte Menor" by Alfonso V of Aragon in Saragossa, valid for three months. Alfonso "the Magnanimous" issued a second safe-conduct that year to another Gypsy, Count Thomas of Little Egypt. The conflicting dates can perhaps be attributed to the distinction between Gypsies living their lives within certain Spanish regions as opposed to simply passing through the areas.

[11] Quintana, Gitáno, p. 14; Fraser, Gypsies, p. 97

[12] Quintana, Gitáno, pp. 15-16, Josephs, White Wall, p. 85; Fraser, Gypsies, p. 98

[13] Quintana, Gitáno, p. 17; Fraser, Gypsies, p. 205; Vassberg, Castile, pp. 143, 245; Antonio Dominguez, The Golden Age of Spain (New York: Basic Books Inc. Publishers, 1971) p. 165; Chapman, Spain, p. 276

[14] Vassberg, Castile, p. 144

[15] Chapman, Spain, p. 276

[16] Vassberg, Castile, p. 144

[17] Henry Kamen, Spain in the Later Seventeenth Century (London: Longman Group Limited, 1980) p. 282; Quintana, Gitáno, pp. 19-20; Vassberg, Castile, p. 144

[18] Quintana, Gitáno, pp. 16, 20; Fraser, Gypsies, p. 97

[19] George Borrow, The Zincali: An Account of the Gypsies of Spain (London: Hazell, Watson & Viney, Ld., 1923) p. 152

[20] Ibid., p. 153

[21] Kamen, Seventeenth Century, p. 282; Quintana, Gitáno, p. 21

[22] Jean Hippolyte Mariejol, The Spain of Ferdinand and Isabella (New Brunswick, New Jersey: Rutgers University Press, 1961) pp. xii, 15; Fraser, Gypsies, p. 98

[23] Fraser, Gypsies, p. 98

[24] Quintana, Gitáno, p. 19; Chapman, Spain, p. 276; Fraser, Gypsies, p. 98; Borrow, Zincali, p. 155

[25] Vassberg, Castile, p. 143; Chapman, Spain, p. 276

[26] Rafael Altamira, A History of Spain, (Princeton, New Jersey: D. Van Nostrand Company, Inc., 1949) p. 340

[27] Hancock, Pariah, p. 54

[28] Ibid., pp. 53-54

[29] The first law to extend galley service to any type of legal offender was issued in 1530.

[30] Vassberg, Castile, p. 144; Ruth Pike, Penal Servitude in Early Modern Spain, (Madison, Wisconsin: The University of Wisconsin Press, 1983) p. 6; Borrow, Zincali, p. 156; Quintana, Gitáno, p. 19; Ruiz, Spanish Society, p. 108; Fraser, Gypsies, p. 99

[31] Fraser, Gypsies, p. 160

[32] Ibid., p. 160; Pike, Penal Servitude, p. 6; Vassberg, Castile, p. 144

[33] Borrow, Zincali, p. 156

[34] Fraser, Gypsies, p. 160; Kenrick, Destiny, p. 50

[35] Fraser, Gypsies, pp. 99, 160

[36] Vassberg, Castile, p. 144

[37] Kamen, Seventeenth Century, p. 282; Quintana, Gitáno, p. 19; Fraser, Gypsies, pp. 156-157, 161

[38] Fraser, Gypsies, p. 157

[39] Ibid, p. 161

[40] Kamen, Seventeenth Century, p. 282; Fraser, Gypsies, pp. 161-162

[41] Borrow, Zincali, p. 158

[42] Fraser, Gypsies, p. 161

[43] Quintana, Gitáno, pp. 19-20; Kamen, Seventeenth Century, p. 282; Kenrick, Destiny, p. 50; Fraser, Gypsies,   pp. 161-162

[44] Quintana, Gitáno, p. 21; Borrow, Zincali, p. 153

[45] Trevor Davies, Spain in Decline: 1621-1700 (London: MacMillan & Co. Ltd., 1965) p. 98

[46] Vassberg, Castile, p. 145; Fraser, Gypsies, p. 161

[47] Vassberg, Castile, p. 144

[48] Ruth Mackay, The Limits of Royal Authority (Cambridge, United Kingdom: Cambridge University Press, 1999) p. 139

[49] Ibid., pp. 139, 179

[50] Borrow, Zincali, p. 160

[51] Ibid., pp. 160-161; Fraser, Gypsies, p. 163

[52] Quintana, Gitáno, p. 21; Fraser, Gypsies, p. 163

[53] Fraser, Gypsies, p. 163; Kamen, Seventeenth Century,   p. 282

[54] Antonio Dominguez Ortiz, The Golden Age of Spain 1516-1659 (New York: Basic Books Inc. Publishers, 1971) p. 166; Borrow, Zincali, p. 162; Fraser, Gypsies, p. 163

[55] Fraser, Gypsies, p. 163; Borrow, Zincali, p. 163

[56] Borrow, Zincali, p. 163

[57] Fraser, Gypsies, pp. 164-165; Pike, Penal Servitude, p. 6

[58] Fraser, Gypsies, pp. 164-165

[59] Ibid., p. 164

[60] Borrow, Zincali, pp. 165-166; Altamira, Spain, p. 462; Fraser, Gypsies, p. 165

[61] Fraser, Gypsies, pp. 165-166

[62] Borrow, Zincali, pp. 168-169; Fraser, Gypsies, p. 166

[63] Vassberg, Castile, p. 143; Quintana, Gitáno, p. 20; Kenrick, Destiny, p. 50

[64] Fraser, Gypsies, pp. 166-167; Borrow, Zincali, p. 166

[65] Chapman, Spain, p. 414

[66] Altamira, Spain, p. 462

[67] Borrow, Zincali, p. 170; Fraser, Gypsies, p. 166; Quintana, Gitáno, p. 22

[68] Borrow, Zincali, p. 168

[69] Borrow is also, however, skeptical of Charles III's active role in this very important legislation. He questions whether Charles had any more to do with the law than its signing, saying: "there is damning evidence to prove that in many respects he was a mere Nimrod, and it is not probable that such a character would occupy his thoughts much with plans for the welfare of his people, especially such a class as the Gitános..."

[70] Mackay, Royal Authority, pp. 178-179; Borrow, Zincali, p. 169

[71] Hancock, Pariah, p. 53; Isabel Fonseca, Bury Me Standing (New York: Vintage Books, 1995) pp. 241-277

[72] Clebert, Gypsies, p. 203

Bibliography

Altamira, Rafael, A History of Spain: From the Beginnings to the Present Day Princeton, New Jersey: D. Van Nostrand Company, Inc., 1949

Borrow, George, The Zincali: An Account of the Gypsies of Spain London: Hazell, Watson & Viney, Ld., 1923

Chapman, Charles E., A History of Spain New York: The MacMillan Company, 1918

Clebert, Jean-Paul, The Gypsies New York: E.P. Dutton & Co., Inc., 1963

Davies, R. Trevor, Spain in Decline: 1621-1700 London: MacMillan & Co. Ltd., 1965

Fonseca, Isabel, Bury Me Standing: The Gypsies and Their Journey New York: Vintage Books, 1995

Fraser, Angus, The Gypsies Cambridge, Massachusetts: Basil Blackwell Inc., 1992

Hancock, Ian, The Pariah Syndrome: An account of Gypsy slavery and persecution Ann Arbor, Michigan: Karoma Publishers, Inc., 1987

Josephs, Allen, White Wall of Spain: The Mysteries of Andalusian Culture Ames, Iowa: The Iowa State University Press, 1983

Kamen, Henry, Spain in the Later Seventeenth Century, 1665-1700 London: Longman Group Limited, 1980

Kenrick, Donald, and Grattan Puxon, The Destiny of Europe's Gypsies New York: Basic Books, Inc., 1972

Mackay, Ruth, The Limits of Royal Authority: Resistance and Obedience in Seventeenth-Century Castile Cambridge, United Kingdom: Cambridge University Press, 1999

Mariéjol, Jean Hippolyte, The Spain of Ferdinand and Isabella New Brunswick, New Jersey: Rutgers University Press, 1961

Ortiz, Antonia Dominguez, The Golden Age of Spain 1516-1659 New York: Basic Books, Inc. Publishers, 1971

Pike, Ruth, Penal Servitude in Early Modern Spain Madison, Wisconsin: The University of Wisconsin Press, 1983

Quintana, Bertha B., and Lois Gray Floyd. Qué Gitáno!: Gypsies of Southern Spain New York: Holt, Rinehart, and Winston, Inc., 1972

Ruiz, Teofilo F., Spanish Society, 1400-1600 Harlow, England: Pearson, Education Limited, 2001

Vassberg, David E., The Village and the Outside World in Golden Age Castile: Mobility and migration in everyday rural life Cambridge, United Kingdom: Cambridge University Press, 1996

Other Sources:

Highfield, Roger, ed., Spain in the Fifteenth Century, 1369-1516: Essays and Extracts by Historians of Spain London: The MacMillan Press Ltd., 1972

Liegeois, Jean-Pierre, "The Cave-Dwellers of Andalusia," 50 Journal of the Gyspy Lore Society (1971) pp. 3-19

Mangen, S.P., Spanish Society after Franco: Regime Transition and the Welfare State New York: Palgrave, 2001

Walker, Virginia, "Gypsies, Grottoes, and Granada: Notes on The Canyon of the 'Black Men,'" 49 Journal of the Gypsy Lore Society (1970) pp. 45-50

Ralph Waldo Emerson Prize 2012

TRANSFORMATION OF THE HUMAN CONSCIOUSNESS:
THE ORIGINS OF SOCIALIST REALISM
IN THE SOVIET UNION

Maya Iyer Krishnan

Abstract

The Soviet Union endorsed Socialist Realism as its official artistic style in 1932. This style used depictions of workers, factories and agriculture to idealize the Soviet State, essentially turning the arts into a form of government propaganda. While the adoption of Socialist Realism as artistic policy is frequently traced to Joseph Stalin's rise to political preeminence after 1928 and his solidification of power from 1932 to 1936, the true origins of Socialist Realism can be found earlier.

This paper seeks to trace the formation of Socialist Realism as an artistic policy and to demonstrate the continuity in official attitudes toward art from 1917 through 1932. It finds the policy's origins in state sponsorship of propaganda during the Russian Civil War (c.a. 1918-1921), the constant ideological commitment of Bolshevik officials to the use of art for social benefit, and the institution of harsh censorship throughout the 1920s. Socialist

The author is at Stanford. She wrote this International Baccalaureate Extended Essay for Robert Thomas at Richard Montgomery High School during the 2009-2010 academic year.

Realism did not emerge from Stalin's dictatorship. Rather, it was the culmination of developments that had occurred in Soviet artistic policy since the Bolsheviks' rise to power.

Introduction

"Comrade Stalin has called our writers 'engineers of the human soul,'" said Soviet culture boss Andrei Zhdanov at the 1934 First All-Union Congress of Soviet Writers. "What does this mean? What obligations does this title impose on us?"[1]

Zhdanov's words illuminate the attitudes and expectations underlying the artistic doctrine known as Socialist Realism. This doctrine became an official part of Soviet cultural policy in 1932, and would remain in place for decades after. Mandating that artists must depict reality 'in its revolutionary development,'[2] it imposed aesthetic and ideological uniformity on art. The doctrine was not a written law or document, but was rather an orthodoxy that formed around the state's belief that art should be realistic in style and propagandistic in intent. A series of speeches and proclamations from prominent figures such as Stalin and Zhdanov form the core of the doctrine. The main directive Zhdanov issued was to "depict reality in its revolutionary development,"[3] focusing content on the transformation of the Soviet state into the ideal Communist society. In 1932, Stalin stated, "[t]he artist ought to show life truthfully. And if he shows it truthfully, he cannot fail to show it moving to socialism. This is and will be socialist realism."[4] The imperative to depict life 'truthfully' was intertwined with the imperative to glorify socialism and the State. The Socialist Realist doctrine rested upon the expectation that artists would align their work with the interests of the government.

A substantial body of historical work portrays this artistic policy as the product of Joseph Stalin's totalitarian state. Sheila Fitzpatrick, one of the most prominent cultural historians of the Soviet Union, argues that the State had a moderate and tolerant attitude toward artists until the rise of Stalin. Fitzpatrick finds that literary policy prior to 1928, "was soft, insofar as it existed at all"[5] and then notes that State tolerance "ended abruptly"[6] under Stalin's auspices. Fitzpatrick identifies an abrupt policy reversal in 1928 and portrays artistic oppression as a byproduct of Stalin's desire to solidify his power. Such an approach to Soviet cultural policy interprets Socialist Realism as the result of a single leader's ambitions.

This paper argues that Socialist Realism was not, fundamentally, a Stalinist doctrine. Rather, it argues that Socialist Realism was the logical continuation of the actions and values of the early Bolshevik state. Prior to Stalin's political hegemony in the 1930s, the core ideas of Socialist Realism were already in place. While Stalin did officially implement the policy, the concept of controlling artists and using them to serve the Soviet people was a part of Bolshevik mindset and practice from the very beginning of the regime. Top officials such as Lenin and Trotsky spoke of art as a tool for both educating the masses and buttressing the State. Several left-wing artists themselves contributed to this vision by calling for more art oriented toward social improvement and more government intervention in art. While the chaos of the Civil War, which lasted from 1918 to 1921, prevented the government from systematically oppressing artists, the government did commission propagandistic art in the hope of uplifting and educating its people. The propaganda projects the state sponsored were an early example of the government's vision of "appropriate" socialist art. Directly after the close of the Civil War, the State began to implement that vision by putting an extensive censorship apparatus into place. From 1922 onward, documents detailing censorship operations demonstrate that the Bolshevik (Communist) State sought to control artists for the protection and benefit of the proletarian masses. Censors evaluated workers' responses to art in order to determine whether certain works should be allowed, providing a precedent for Socialist Realism's prioritization of the impact of art on the proletariat. After 1928, the state controlled artists through a series of artistic organizations and unions. The final result of these actions was that by the time Socialist Realism became policy in 1932, the foundational components of the doctrine had long since been in place: censorship and control, for the sake of the people, was already reality. Socialist Realism possessed a strong sequence of historical precedents, and was not the unique policy of Stalin's totalitarian regime.

Foundations of Socialist Realism in the Early Bolshevik Regime

The ideological foundations of government control over artists existed from the very beginning of the Bolshevik regime. Lenin was suspicious of the notion of artistic freedom, noting in a letter to German Communist Clara Zetkin, "every artist...claims as his proper right the liberty to work freely according to his idea, whether it is any good or not. There you have the ferment, the experiment, the chaos."[7] Lenin presents the concept of artistic freedom as an excuse for mediocrity and closely associates "experiment" with "chaos," implying that the creative process is analogous to social disorder. He believes that the role of the Communist is to "guide this development consciously, clearly, and to shape and determine its results."[8] To Lenin, artistic liberty is fundamentally opposed to social stability, while artistic control can serve the purpose of statecraft. Trotsky shares this view of art as a powerful, but dangerous, tool. In his 1923 essay *Literature and Revolution,* he refers to "the plow of the new art,"[9] comparing art to a productive implement that leads to a quantifiable social gain. This metaphor implies that the artist will be akin to the farm worker, engaging in a task that requires neither creativity nor experimentation. Trotsky also issues judgments regarding style, claiming that "[t]he Revolution cannot live together with mysticism. Nor can the Revolution live together with romanticism..."[10] Although *Literature and Revolution* contains no specific policy recommendations, it demonstrates a presupposition that the government should determine artistic direction; this attitude provides a clear ideological precedent for the 1932 Socialist Realist doctrine.

The State's extensive sponsorship of art during the Civil War was its first practical implementation of the concepts of Socialist Realism, as first articulated by Trotsky and Lenin. The large quantity of propagandistic art that the government commissioned demonstrates its profound faith in the power of art to both educate the population and strengthen the State. The theater was the area in which the Bolsheviks were most involved. The 1919 First National Conference on Extra-Mural Education spoke of theater as an educational and revolutionary force,[11] and by October 1920, the Red Army had organized 1,415 theaters and 250 cinemas to "educate" the population about the revolution.[12] The government instituted a 500 percent tax on private theater profits in 1918, and then officially nationalized the theater in 1919.[13] As private theaters closed in Petrograd, the Commissariat of Enlightenment sent various state-approved theater groups into the old performance spaces.[14] One of the most iconic works the Bolsheviks sponsored was the 1920 reenactment of the storming of the winter palace in Petrograd, in which the director of the spectacle, Nikolay Yevreinov, used 8,000 actors and counted 100,000 in the audience.[15] Members of the Red Army, in addition to professional actors, worked in the play. The dramatized reenactment included "capitalists push[ing] sacks of money with their bellies toward Kerensky's throne," mock combat between Red Army and White Army forces, and a rousing rendition of the national anthem. Yevreinov noted that "the man of the theater possessing social ideals" would see the spectacle as "a revelation, pregnant with suggestion towards that theater of the future which shall fully answer the need of spiritual social service."[16] Yevreinov's concept of the theater as "social service" is an early articulation of the idea that would become fundamental to Socialist Realism.[17] He associates the interests of the government with those of society: the play, which was a celebration of the new State, is now conceptualized as a celebration of the people.

Government sponsorship of art was by no means confined to the theater. In 1918 Lenin approached Anatoly Lunacharsky, head of the culturally and educationally focused Commissariat of Enlightenment, to request a series of statues of revolutionary figures,[18] each of which was intended to inspire a sense of awe in the Communist regime. Lunacharsky ultimately produced a list of 67 socialist heroes for the state to monumentalize.[19] In the field of propagandistic poster design, the state commissioned artists such as Aleksandr Rodchenko to create new styles to support the revolution.[20] Various artistic groups competed for a commission to design decorations for Petrograd's 1919 May Day celebration of the revolution.[21] The government's propagandistic commissions demonstrate a clear vision for the use of art in the new regime. Art was a public utility that could educate the people and thereby support the State.

While the government attempted to use art for social benefit during the Civil War period, it did not actively repress artists. Practical restraints prevented the government from translating the oppressive will of Lenin and Trotsky into reality. From 1917 to 1921, the government was embroiled in a bloody civil war that ultimately resulted in the death of millions.[22] The resources and administrative oversight necessary to suppress dissident artists had to be allocated to the state's primary goal: winning the war. Art was important, but not a priority. Symptomatically, when the government moved from Petrograd to Moscow in 1921, the Commissariat of Enlightenment was one of the last departments to move.[23] When it did at last move, it took several months to do so, and during that time, branches operated semi-autonomously in both cities.[24] Centralizing and coordinating policy would have been nearly impossible, given the severe logistical constraints. Furthermore, the fact that the Commissariat of Enlightenment was one of the last departments to move demonstrates its relative unimportance to the State during the Civil War. Defeating the White Army took precedence over cultural and artistic policy.

The seeds of Socialist Realism were thus present both in 1917 and through the close of the Civil War in 1921. During the earliest years of the Bolshevik regime, the ideological impetus to use art for a social purpose was strong. Although the government was not able to take significant steps toward oppressing artists during this period, its sponsorship of art expressed a clear faith in the power of art to educate the people and legitimize its own existence.

Radicalization of the Artists: 1917-1929

The actions of artists themselves also provided a substantial precedent for Socialist Realism. Many left-wing artists and culturati called for greater government intervention in art, as they believed this intervention would further the goals of the revolution. Revolutionary artists were intolerant of approaches other than their own and accused one another of 'counter-revolutionary' or 'bourgeois' tendencies. The overall result was the repeated validation of government oppression and intervention in art and the strengthening of the core values of Socialist Realism.

Prominent members of the radical cultural intelligentsia believed that the government should become more actively involved in art in order to benefit the masses. Dramaturge Adrian Piotrovsky, in a 1920 article entitled "Dictatorship," contended that the Bolsheviks should have a "repressive policy in the arts." Piotrovsky noted, "either the proletariat will make art, or it will be made by petty shopkeepers." In response to the dangerous influence of the "superficially educated," the government must "show another way by force."[25] Piotrovsky's article provides an early example of support by artists of repressive government interference for the benefit of the proletariat. Proletarian culture movements of the pre-Stalinist regime echoed Piotrovsky's beliefs. The Proletkult group formed in 1917 to promote the art of the working class over 'bourgeois' art. The group asked the government for the authority to independently create proletarian revolution in the cultural sphere, but by 1919 Lenin had grown weary of the group's request for autonomous power and withdrew his support.[26] The concept of totalitarian control over the arts did not, therefore, originate with Stalin, and was not even unique to top Bolsheviks such as Lenin and Trotsky. Although not all artists supported increased government intervention, there was certainly a group of artists in the early Soviet Union who provided a precedent for Socialist Realism. As a result of the influence of artistic radicals, relatively moderate artists continually faced attacks from the far left. Bolshevik supporter and Futurist poet Vladimir Mayakovsky created a journal called *Left Front of Literature* [LEF] in 1923, but militant proletarian groups called the magazine 'bourgeois'. A group of proletariat-supporting writers then created *On Guard*, a competing magazine that claimed revolutionary content was more important than literary form. Facing mounting criticism, LEF later dissolved.[27] The fate of LEF was in many ways emblematic of the pressures artists in the early Bolshevik regime faced. Even a poet as pro-revolution as Mayakovsky, who titled his journal "Left Front," could receive heavy criticism for being 'bourgeois'. According to Proletkult, movements such as Futurism focused on aesthetic form rather than uplifting content, rendering them unsuitable for a new proletariat culture.[28] Proletkult viewed artistic unsuitability as a sign of political deviance, a viewpoint that cast artists such as Mayakovsky as enemies of the State. The actions of left-wing artists themselves thus provided a precedent for the monolithic Socialist Realist doctrine. The concept of artistic control implemented by the State, for the good of the people, was common to both top Bolshevik officials and radical artists.

The foregoing reflects how the core idea of Socialist Realism did not originate in the 1930s and was not fundamentally Stalinist. Rather, it was a part of the Bolshevik revolutionary attitude, and had been present at all levels of discourse since the very beginning of the regime.

Apparatus of Oppression: 1922-1928

The conclusion of the Civil War afforded the government the time and resources with which to develop an extensive censorship apparatus. This apparatus provided the State with the organizational infrastructure it could use to further the goals central to Socialist Realism. From 1922 on, the apparatus worked to centralize its control over artistic production and eliminate private publishing. Using this control, censors attempted to reform artistic expression to maximize social good. This situation provides a strong precedent for Socialist Realism's control over art for the supposed benefit of the people. Ideological commitment combined with government resources to help create the first practical example of Socialist Realism in action. It is significant that this apparatus expanded concurrently with Lenin's decline and the power struggle following his death in 1924. Stalin was not the central authority until several years following Lenin's death,[29] which indicates that censorship and oppression increased under non-Stalinist auspices.

The first step toward control was the development of a centralized bureaucratic structure that extensively censored works. While Gosizdat, the state publishing house, had served as an ad hoc censorship agency during the Civil War,[30] in 1922, a new department became responsible for censorship: *Glavlit*.[31] The fact that censorship received its own department merely one year after the conclusion of the Civil War indicates its importance to the government. In the absence of the practical and logistical constraints of war, the State could implement Trotsky and Lenin's ideological will. Control was centralized and extensive, since works could face two rounds of censorship, as both a regional censor and the central office frequently reviewed the same titles.[32] *Glavlit* exercised substantial power over the literary world. Of the 497 works *Glavlit* reviewed in the 3rd quarter of 1923, 20 percent faced cuts or changes and 6 percent were banned.[33] A 1923 State decree created another department called *Glavrepertkom* to oversee art, cinema, and music. The decree mandated that institutions register lists of their workers and programs with *Glavrepertkom*, and ordered all texts to be submitted for censorship in their final form,[34] reflecting how centralization of the artistic world began before Stalin's rise. *Glavlit* further increased its control in a mid-1920s campaign to consolidate the printing industry under its supervision. The department began to limit presses to certain predefined genres, forbidding presses to publish works outside of their assigned scope.[35] After 1926, the number of private presses dropped sharply,[36] and although private presses printed 23 percent of works in 1925, by 1926 they printed only 10 percent.[37] The establishment of *Glavlit*

was the first step toward making the Bolshevik leaders' dream of
control over artists a practical reality.

The goals and expectations for 1920s censorship provided
a significant precedent for Zhdanov's 1934 exhortation for writers
to lead a "transformation of the human consciousness."[38] Censors
used the new censorship infrastructure to reshape artistic expression for what they believed was in the didactic interest of the masses.
In one report to *Orgburo*, a department that oversaw personnel
issues and policy implementation,[39] *Glavlit* head Lebedev-Polyansky
contended that *Glavlit* censorship had a "pedagogical bias," making its decisions based on the educational value a text might yield
to workers.[40] In the same report, Lebedev-Polyansky asserted that
Glavlit suppressed "the flow of vulgar literature" but allowed certain works "of a light genre which help spread Soviet influence to
the broad philistine masses."[41] While Lebedev-Polyansky clearly
disapproved of the 'light' literature, he felt that the social benefit
it brought overruled all other considerations. His judgment of
'vulgar' literature also demonstrates that censorship was used to
direct public tastes, not just to conceal State secrets. One 1928
Glavlit report counts the pages of 'worthless reading' published in
the past year: 3,607,730.[42] Another *Glavlit* report contended, "[p]
etty-bourgeouis and low-brow tastes, the sentimental, philistine and
erotic novel, adventures, ridiculous science fiction, eroticism and
boulevard tastes—such are the main forms of belles-lettres production by private presses."[43] Defending the masses against their own
poor taste, for their own welfare, emerged as a central goal for
Glavlit. *Glavlit* reported to Politburo, the executive branch of the
Communist Party, which also served as the Soviet Union's most
powerful final censorship authority and displayed an attitude similar
to that of *Glavlit*. The State's vision of an "appropriate" culture for
the proletariat served as an important factor in deciding which
works were to be permitted. In 1929, the Agitation and Propaganda Committee (*Agitprop*) wrote a report to Politburo speaking
against Mikhail Bulgakov's play *Flight*, contending that to permit
the production of the play "would only make it harder to bring
Soviet theater closer to the worker-audience."[44] Once more the
government's vision of proletarian social benefit proved a crucial

consideration. When Zhdanov spoke in 1934 of the "education of the working people in the spirit of Socialism,"[45] he was really articulating the policy that the government had implemented a decade before. *Glavlit* had transformed the Civil War-era intent of artists and Bolsheviks into a system of oppression and control.

One of the most important aspects of Socialist Realism was its concern with mass reaction to art. The consideration of workers' and factory representatives' opinions during the censorship process indicates that the government strongly considered this factor prior to the solidification of Stalin's power in the 1930s. Not only was censorship implemented for the benefit of the proletariat, it was implemented by the proletariat. Agitprop member S. Krylov's correspondence regarding Mikhail Levidov's play *Conspiracy of Equals* refers to "responsible worker Communists—thirty to thirty-five people" invited to a viewing of the play.[46] Though the final decision itself was intended to be secret and made by a central authority, the reactions and impressions of workers would inform that decision. Other documents confirm the importance of worker response to the censorship process. In 1931, out-of-favor writer Eugeny Zamyatin wrote to Stalin protesting the 1928 censorship of his play *Attila* and asking for permission to emigrate. In his own support, Zamyatin noted that the play had already been read at a session of the Bolshoi Theater with "representatives from eighteen Leningrad factories" in attendance.[47] Zamyatin quoted the responses of various factory representatives in the letter, including the Volodarsky Factory representative's impression that the play "treats the theme of class struggle in ancient times...in [a manner] in keeping with modern times."[48] Zamyatin's use of worker response as self-defense indicates a desperate faith in the power of proletariat opinion to redeem him.[49] The workers are the jury to Stalin's judge, a source of limited authority in the process of Soviet censorship. The prioritization of the proletariat was a longstanding theme in the Soviet Union's control over artists.

Politburo's extensive involvement in the censorship process placed artistic expression under the complete control of the government. Documents regarding the operations of Politburo demonstrate the extent of the centralization of censorship and control over printing and the arts in pre-Stalinist Russia. One 1926 Politburo resolution on B. A. Pilnyak's "Tale of the Unextinguished Moon" calls the work a "malicious, slanderous, and counterrevolutionary attack" against the Party.[50] Politburo banned all presses from reprinting the story, recommended the seizure of the issues of the journal in which the story appeared, and instructed the state publishing house to examine the remainder of Pilnyak's stories for "unacceptable" political content. Politburo's ability to command such far-reaching consequences suggests that the censorship apparatus was highly developed and coordinated prior to the rise of Stalin. Politburo served as an absolute authority and refused to enter into negotiation or accept appeals. When Politburo considered banning the play *Conspiracy of Equals*, director Alexander Tairov wrote to Politburo member Mikhail Tomsky to testify to the "moral importance of this matter of survival for our theater."[51] By way of response, Tomsky was outraged by the breach of Politburo confidentiality. In an irate memorandum to Molotov he asked, "Isn't it time to put an end to the shameless chatter about the Politburo and its resolutions? How did Tairov find out about the PB resolutions? Why does he need to know this? Can't you instruct someone to investigate?"[52] The involvement of the top echelons of the Soviet State in artistic matters signaled the demise of any limited power the cultural intelligentsia had once enjoyed. Tairov's letter demonstrates a presumption that he can influence the censorship decisions of the government, a presumption that is clearly no longer valid in 1927.

Artistic policy had escalated in importance, as it could now become a State secret. The final Politburo resolution "found it unnecessary to permit the performance of *Conspiracy of Equals*" and asked the Party's Central Control Commission to "investigate those guilty of disclosing the Politburo's resolution on *Conspiracy of Equals*."[53] The language of the resolution, in which Politburo "found it unnecessary to permit" a work, also demonstrates a belief that artistic expression is a privilege or favor granted by the state. The pre-Stalinist government had already managed to erode the foundations of artistic freedom. *Glavrepertkom*'s original decision to allow the play also convinced Politburo that the censorship apparatus needed to become more stringent. The resolution mandated the replacement of current *Glavrepertkom* members with stricter "individuals who can ensure the proper work of *Glavrepertkom*."[54] As testament to the increase in centralized control, the secret police (OGPU) paid *Glavlit* officials' salaries starting in the late 1920s.[55] One account of the department also reports that the censors wore OGPU uniforms.[56] Politburo's pervasive interference in artistic affairs provided yet another limitation on artistic freedom. Secrecy, centralization, and control increased over the course of the decade. Lenin's dream of restricting "the ferment, the experiment, the chaos" had become practical reality.

The effect of these developments was to make the artist into the tool of the State. Artistic freedom was virtually nonexistent by this time, as works now only existed by virtue of Politburo and *Glavlit*'s permission. In this manner, Socialist Realism's unification of artist with State was in place long before 1932.

Consolidation of Control: 1928-1934

From 1928 to 1934, the state organized artists into a series of groups and unions under its control. These groups provided the means through which the state introduced Socialist Realism in 1932. They represent the culmination of the process of control and oppression that began in 1917.

In 1928, the Soviet Union granted the Russian Association of Proletarian Writers (RAPP) and Russian Association of Proletarian Musicians (RAPM) broad authority over the arts. With State support, RAPP pressured LEF to dissolve, gained power over the All-Russian Union of Peasant Writers, and lead campaigns against artists such as Zamyatin and Bulgakov.[57] Sheila Fitzpatrick notes that Politburo began to appoint RAPP members to the editorial boards of non-RAPP journals and grant greater consideration to the opinions of the RAPP group.[58] She interprets the party's decision to grant RAPP special powers as a part of the radicalization surrounding Stalin's rise to power. She identifies RAPP's new-found authority with Stalin's "class war"[59] that included the 1927 Five-Year Plan for the economy, the 1928 Shakhty Trials against engineers for "wrecking" factory equipment, and the movement toward immediate collectivization.[60] According to Fitzpatrick, these decisions were part of a "cultural revolution" that Stalin initiated in order to outmaneuver his political opponents.[61] While Fitzpatrick is correct in identifying the "class war" toward the end of the decade as an immediate motivation for the empowerment of RAPP, the State's actions were in fact completely aligned with developments throughout the 1920s.[62] Viewed in the context of *Glavlit* and Politburo's escalating intervention, it is clear that there was no radical break or "revolution" in cultural policy following Stalin's rise. There was merely an intensification of the preexisting trend toward control and centralization.

Although RAPP was technically a non-governmental or-ganization, the State continued to heavily supervise the arts. In 1929, Commissar of Enlightenment Anatoly Lunacharsky resigned under rising pressure from radical elements in the Party and was rapidly replaced by the more intolerant Zhdanov.[63] The OGPU also remained highly involved in the arts. A 1931 secret police report celebrated the "rout of counterrevolutionary organizations of the intelligentsia" but noted that individual members of the intelli-gentsia remained "counterrevolutionary."[64] This report illustrates both the government's sense of triumph at successful suppression of the cultural intelligentsia and its desire to further consolidate control. It predates the formation of the Union of Soviet Writers by barely one year. The report also lists the attitudes and "creative moods of right-wing film directors," such as that of a Leningrad director, Beresnev: "I don't understand politics in art, I hate all that. Just think what themes we have in cinema and art—tractor building, diesel building, and muck like that."[65] Beresnev's criti-cism of the predominance of agricultural and industrial themes in art marked him as a subversive, indicating both the prevalence of propagandistic art prior to 1932 and the controlling attitude of the state. Politburo also continued to interfere in the arts. Though

Politburo chose to appoint many RAPP-connected artists to the boards of journals, it retained the power to make these editorial appointments without RAPP input, thereby continuing the control it exercised throughout the 1920s. The State also began awarding its own artistic ranks and titles during this period,[66] further underscoring its authority over RAPP. While RAPP proved a convenient means of organizing the artistic milieu, the State never lessened its grip on the arts. The overall trend of rising government control continued from 1928 through the 1930s.

In 1932 the State created the Union of Soviet Writers, the body that served as the first official Socialist Realist organization. The 1932 Politburo resolution, "On restructuring literary and arts organizations" removed power from RAPP and proposed a new national organization to replace it.[67] A Union of Architects and a Union of Artists were also created alongside the Union of Soviet Writers.[68] Politburo affirmed that, "major quantitative and qualitative growth has been achieved in literature and art," but feared that RAPP alienated some pro-Soviet artists through its aggressive attitude. To this end, Politburo aimed to "unite all writers [and artists] who support the platform of Soviet power,"[69] a decision that promoted increased centralization of control over the arts and ultimately brought Socialist Realism into being. At a 1932 meeting at Soviet cultural leader Maxim Gorky's house, Stalin issued his famous statement about how "the artist ought to show life truthfully."[70] This statement was the founding principle of the Union,[71] of which Gorky was the head. Support of the State and portrayal of Soviet triumph formed the core principles of both the Union and Socialist Realism. P. Iudin, a leader of the 1932 Union of Soviet Writers, proclaimed in a speech, "[i]n their works, with their books and at their first congress, Soviet writers affirm openly before all the world that they are proponents of the communist worldview, that they are firmly behind the positions of Soviet power..."[72] Iudin presents the unification of artist and State as a triumph for both parties and reduces the artist to one more voice in a supportive chorus for the State. This development occurred under the auspices of Stalin but was by no means purely Stalinist. The Union of Soviet Writers was one more step in the escalation of control the government had initiated, and represented the formalization of the propagandistic intent of early Bolshevik art.

In 1934, Politburo replaced the Union of Soviet Writers within the All-Union Congress of Soviet Writers, as the former grew paralyzed by internal division and bickering,[73] but retained the focus on Socialist Realism in the new organization. Since the aesthetic was still inherently political, the artist was still the agent of the government. At the end of his 1934 speech to the Congress, Zhdanov exhorted, "Be as active as you can in organizing the transformation of the human consciousness in the spirit of Socialism!"[74] Zhdanov contended that the job of the artist was to reshape the people to suit the vision of the government, ostensibly for the benefit of the people themselves. The 1934 meeting of the Congress reiterated the basic principles of the 1932 Union and Stalin's declaration on the nature of Socialist Realism. Ideology and policy that had existed from 1917 through 1932 became orthodoxy. Socialist Realism had officially arrived.

Conclusion

From the beginning of Bolshevik rule, top officials had viewed art as the tool of the revolution. The events from 1917 to 1932 are thus best viewed as manifestations of this belief; the logical consequences of a philosophy of artistic control. This thesis is part of a broader historiographical trend of identifying continuity throughout the stages of Soviet rule. In *Lenin, Stalin, and Hitler,* an analysis of early 20th-century dictatorship, historian Robert Gellately argues that the violence of Lenin's regime provided a direct predecessor for the brutality of Stalin's state. Gellately vigorously contests the idea that Stalin "polluted"[75] Lenin's ideals, proposing instead that "Stalin was Lenin's logical successor."[76] Gellately finds the source of Stalin's policy of violence in the ideology and early actions of the Bolshevik state.

Likewise, I reject Sheila Fitzpatrick's notion of a Stalinist "class war" that ended prior respect for freedom in the arts. Socialist Realism was the result of a deeply-held belief in the need to use art to reshape society into a "better" State for the workers. Under Lenin's rule, the government began wide-scale propaganda projects to influence the masses, and an invasive censorship apparatus began to form. The expansion and centralization of power over artists throughout the 1920s served as an elaboration of Lenin and Trotsky's vision of art as a tool of the State. Meanwhile, censors and Politburo members repeatedly spoke of the educational value of art and considered proletarian response of utmost importance to a work's value. By the time Stalin first uttered the words "socialist realism" at Maxim Gorky's house,[77] the infrastructure and ideology of oppression were already in place. Socialist Realism should not, therefore, be primarily identified with Stalin. It is fundamentally linked to the words and actions of government officials and left-wing artists who shared a common goal of creating an appropriate art form for the new State.

The development of Socialist Realism relied upon the participation and contributions of countless individuals in Soviet Russia. To grant Stalin primary responsibility denies the contributions numerous artists, censors and ideologues made to the policy. This episode in Soviet history serves as a reminder of how oppression develops: not by the will of one, but through the actions of many.

[1] Andrei Zhdanov, "From Speech at the First All-Union Congress of Soviet Writers 1934" in Modernism: An Anthology of Sources and Documents ed. Vassiliki Kolocotroni, Jane Goldman, Olga Taxidou (Chicago: The University of Chicago Press, 1998) p. 525

[2] Ibid., p. 525

[3] Ibid., p. 525

[4] David Hoffman, Stalinist Values: The Cultural Norms of Soviet Modernity (1917-1941) (Ithaca: Cornell University Press, 2003) p. 161

[5] Sheila Fitzpatrick, The Cultural Front: Power and Culture in Revolutionary Russia (Ithaca: Cornell University Press, 1992) p. 105

[6] Ibid., p. 112

[7] Donald Treadgold, Twentieth Century Russia: Seventh Edition (Boulder: Westview Press, 1990) p. 222

[8] Ibid., p. 222

[9] Leon Trotsky, "Literature and Revolution" in Modernism: An Anthology of Sources and Documents p. 229

[10] Ibid., p. 230

[11] Katerina Clark, Petersburg: Crucible of Cultural Revolution (Cambridge: Harvard University Press, 1998) p. 108

[12] Ibid., p. 104

[13] Ibid., p. 108

[14] Ibid., p. 118

[15] Nikolay Yevreinov, "A Member of the Audience: Storming the Winter Palace" in Modernism: An Anthology of Sources and Documents, p. 224

[16] Ibid., p. 225

[17] William J. Leatherbarrow and Derek Offord, A Documentary History of Russian Thought: from the Enlightenment to Marxism (New York: Ardis, 1987) pp. 136-148, 199-227

My research suggests that the culture and philosophy of the 19th-century liberal intelligentsia may have also have contributed to the ideology behind Socialist Realism. The concept of the art as an instrument of social improvement appears throughout the writings of key members of this liberal intelligentsia. For example, writer and prominent socialist Alexander Herzen noted that the role of the artist was to utter "what exists in the dim consciousness of the masses," while the author and philosopher Nikolay Cherneshevsky spoke of "the direct duty" authors felt to speak for their country. An examination of the influence of the 19th-century intelligentsia is not within the scope of this paper, and is a topic for later exploration.

   [18] Victoria E. Bonnell, Iconography of Power: Soviet Political Posters under Lenin and Stalin (Berkeley: University of California Press, 1999) pp. 21-22
   [19] Ibid., p. 138
   [20] Stephen J. Eskilson, Graphic Design: A New History (New Haven: Yale University Press, 2007) pp. 204-206
   [21] Clark, p. 103
   [22] Robert Gellately, Lenin, Stalin, and Hitler: The Age of Social Catastrophe (New York: Alfred A. Knopf, 2007) p. 71
   [23] Clark, p. 101
   [24] Ibid., p. 101
   [25] Ibid., p. 119
   [26] Hoffman, pp. 38-39
   [27] Treadgold, p. 227
   [28] Clark, p. 103
   [29] Gellately, p. 159
   [30] Michael S. Fox, "Glavlit, Censorship, and the Problem of Party Policy in Cultural Affairs, 1922-8," Soviet Studies 44, no. 6, (1992) p. 1052, www.jstor.org/stable/152329 (accessed March 2, 2010)
   [31] Ibid., p. 1052
   [32] Ibid., pp. 1054-1055
   [33] Ibid., p. 1054
   [34] Ibid., p. 1056
   [35] Ibid., p. 1059
   [36] Only 78 of the 1,000 presses in the Soviet Union were private, as opposed to 232 in 1923. Ibid., p. 1060
   [37] Ibid., p. 1060
   [38] Zhdanov, p. 526
   [39] Gellately, pp. 146-148

Orgburo and Politburo were the two main committees of the Central Committee of the Communist Party. Politburo served as the executive branch and strategic head of the Party, whereas Orgburo dealt with the logistical and personnel-related issues arising from Politburo directives. The Communist Party dominated the structure of the actual 'state' to such an extent that the Party was the government and vice versa. The main political body of the 'state' was Sovnarkom, or the Council of People's Commissars, of which Lenin was chair. For this reason, references to the "state" and the "government" in this paper also refer to Communist Party apparati.

[40] P.I. Lebedev-Polyansky, "On the activities of Glavlit" in Soviet Culture and Power: A History in Documents, ed. Katerina Clark and Evgeny Dobrenko with Andrei Artizov and Oleg Naumov (New Haven: Yale University Press, 2007) p. 124

[41] Ibid., p. 123

[42] Fox, p. 1061

[43] Ibid., p. 1061

[44] P.M. Kerzhentsev, "Report from P.M. Kerzhentsev, Deputy Head of Agitprop TsK VKP(b), to the Politburo of the TsK VKP(b) on M.A. Bulgakov's Flight," in Soviet Culture and Power pp. 98-103

[45] Yevreinov, p. 225

[46] S.N. Krylov, "Letter from Deputy Chief of Agitpropotdel TsK VKP (b) to V.M. Molotov" in Soviet Culture and Power pp. 94-96

[47] E.I. Zamyatin, "Letter from E.I. Zamyatin to I.V. Stalin," in Soviet Culture and Power pp. 109-110

[48] Ibid., p. 110

[49] Stalin ultimately allowed Zamyatin to leave the Soviet Union. Zamyatin died in Paris in 1937.

[50] Politburo, "Resolution of the Politburo TsK VKP(b) on B.A. Pilnyak's 'Tale of the Unextinguished Moon,'" in Soviet Culture and Power: A History in Documents pp. 90-91

[51] A.Y. Tairov, "Letter from A.Y. Tairov to M.P. Tomsky," in Soviet Culture and Power p. 96

[52] M.P. Tomsky, "Memorandum from M.P. Tomsky to V.M. Molotov," in Soviet Culture and Power p. 97

[53] Politburo, "Resolution of the Politburo TsK VKP(b) on banning M. Yu. Levidov's play Conspiracy of Equals" in Soviet Culture and Power p. 97

[54] Ibid., p. 98

[55] Jeffrey Brooks, Thank You, Comrade Stalin! (Princeton: Princeton University Press, 2000) p. 4

[56] Ibid., p. 4

[57] Katerina Clark and Evgeny Dobrenko, "The Demise of RAPP," in Soviet Culture and Power p. 150

[58] Fitzpatrick, p. 52

[59] Ibid., p. 115

[60] Ibid., p. 119

[61] Ibid., p. 113

[62] Fitzpatrick views the Central Committee's 1925 refusal to endorse far-left proletarian groups as evidence of the Party's initial reluctance to interfere in the arts. But while Fitzpatrick justifiably interprets the refusal as a sign of relative moderation, the Party was still extensively involved in censorship at that time.

[63] Irina Lunacharskaia and Kurt S. Schultz, "Why Did Commissar of Enlightenment A. V. Lunacharskii Resign?" Russian Review 51, no. 3 (1992) p. 335, www.jstor.org/stable/131115 (accessed March 2, 2010)

[64] OGPU Secret Police Department, "On anti-Soviet activity among the intelligentsia in 1931," in Soviet Culture and Power pp. 130-133

[65] Ibid., p. 131

[66] Brooks, p. 126

[67] Politburo, "On Restructuring literary and arts organizations," in Soviet Culture and Power pp. 151-152

[68] Ibid., p. 151

[69] Ibid., p. 152

[70] Simon Sebag Montefiore, Stalin: The Court of the Red Tsar (New York: Alfred A. Knopf, 2004) p. 96

[71] Ibid., p. 95

[72] Brooks, p 111

[73] A.E. Nikitin, "On the situation in the Union of Soviet Writers," in Soviet Culture and Power pp. 202-205

[74] Zhdanov, p. 526

[75] Gellately, p. 7

[76] Ibid., p. 9

[77] Montefiore, p. 96

Bibliography

Primary Sources

Kerzhentsev, P.M., "Report from P.M. Kerzhentsev, Deputy Head of Agitprop TsK VKP(b), to the Politburo of the TsK VKP(b) on M.A. Bulgakov's <u>Flight</u>," from <u>Soviet Culture and Power: A History in Documents, 1917-1953</u> edited by Katerina Clark and Evgeny Dobrenko with Andrei Artizov and Oleg Naumov, New Haven: Yale University Press, 2007

Krylov, S.N., "Letter from Deputy Chief of Agitpropotdel TsK VKP (b) to V.M. Molotov," from <u>Soviet Culture and Power: A History in Documents, 1917-1953</u> edited by Katerina Clark and Evgeny Dobrenko with Andrei Artizov and Oleg Naumov, New Haven: Yale University Press, 2007

Lebedev-Polyansky, P.I., "On the activities of Glavlit," from <u>Soviet Culture and Power: A History in Documents, 1917-1953</u> edited by Katerina Clark and Evgeny Dobrenko with Andrei Artizov and Oleg Naumov, New Haven: Yale University Press, 2007

Nikitin, A.E., "On the situation in the Union of Soviet Writers," from <u>Soviet Culture and Power: A History in Documents, 1917-1953</u> edited by Katerina Clark and Evgeny Dobrenko with Andrei Artizov and Oleg Naumov, New Haven: Yale University Press, 2007

OGPU Secret Police Department, "On anti-Soviet activity among the intelligentsia in 1931," from <u>Soviet Culture and Power: A History in Documents, 1917-1953</u> edited by Katerina Clark and Evgeny Dobrenko with Andrei Artizov and Oleg Naumov, New Haven: Yale University Press, 2007

Politburo, "On Restructuring literary and arts organizations," from <u>Soviet Culture and Power: A History in Documents, 1917-1953</u> edited by Katerina Clark and Evgeny Dobrenko with Andrei Artizov and Oleg Naumov, New Haven: Yale University Press, 2007

Politburo, "Resolution of the Politburo TsK VKP(b) on B.A. Pilnyak's 'Tale of the Unextinguished Moon,'" from <u>Soviet</u>

Culture and Power: A History in Documents, 1917-1953 edited by Katerina Clark and Evgeny Dobrenko with Andrei Artizov and Oleg Naumov, New Haven: Yale University Press, 2007

Politburo, "Resolution of the Politburo TsK VKP(b) on banning M. Yu. Levidov's play Conspiracy of Equals," from Soviet Culture and Power: A History in Documents, 1917-1953 edited by Katerina Clark and Evgeny Dobrenko with Andrei Artizov and Oleg Naumov, New Haven: Yale University Press, 2007

Tairov, A.Y., "Letter from A.Y. Tairov to M.P. Tomsky," from Soviet Culture and Power: A History in Documents, 1917-1953 edited by Katerina Clark and Evgeny Dobrenko with Andrei Artizov and Oleg Naumov, New Haven: Yale University Press, 2007

Tomsky, M.P., "Memorandum from M.P. Tomsky to V.M. Molotov," from Soviet Culture and Power: A History in Documents, 1917-1953 edited by Katerina Clark and Evgeny Dobrenko with Andrei Artizov and Oleg Naumov, New Haven: Yale University Press, 2007

Trotsky, Leon, "Literature and Revolution," from Modernism: An Anthology of Sources and Documents edited by Vassiliki Kolocotroni, Jane Goldman, Olga Taxidou, Chicago: The University of Chicago Press, 1998

Yevreinov, Nikolay, "A Member of the Audience: Storming the Winter Palace," from Modernism: An Anthology of Sources and Documents edited by Vassiliki Kolocotroni, Jane Goldman, Olga Taxidou, Chicago: The University of Chicago Press, 1998

Zamyatin, E.I., "Letter from E.I. Zamyatin to I.V. Stalin," from Soviet Culture and Power: A History in Documents, 1917-1953 edited by Katerina Clark and Evgeny Dobrenko with Andrei Artizov and Oleg Naumov, New Haven: Yale University Press, 2007

Zhdanov, Andrei, "From Speech at the First All-Union Congress of Soviet Writers 1934," from Modernism: An Anthology of Sources and Documents edited by Vassiliki Kolocotroni, Jane Goldman, Olga Taxidou, Chicago: The University of Chicago Press, 1998

Secondary Sources

Bonnell, Victoria, <u>Iconography of Power: Soviet Political Posters under Lenin and Stalin</u> Berkeley: University of California Press, 1999

Brooks, Jeffrey, <u>Thank You, Comrade Stalin!</u> Princeton: Princeton University Press, 2000

Clark, Katerina, <u>Petersburg: Crucible of Cultural Revolution</u> Cambridge: Harvard University Press, 1998

Eskilson, Stephen J., <u>Graphic Design: A New History</u> New Haven: Yale University Press, 2007

Fitzpatrick, Sheila, The <u>Cultural Front: Power and Culture in Revolutionary Russia</u> Ithaca: Cornell University Press, 1992

Fox, Michael S., "Glavlit, Censorship, and the Problem of Party Policy in Cultural Affairs, 1922-8," <u>Soviet Studies</u> 44, no. 6, 1992, pp. 1045-68, www.jstor.org/stable/152329 (accessed March 2, 2010)

Gellately, Robert, <u>Lenin, Stalin, and Hitler: The Age of Social Catastrophe</u> New York: Alfred A. Knopf, 2007

Hoffman, David, <u>Stalinist Values: The Cultural Norms of Soviet Modernity (1917-1941)</u> Ithaca: Cornell University Press, 2003

Leatherbarrow, William J., and Derek Offord, <u>A Documentary History of Russian Thought: from the Enlightenment to Marxism</u> New York: Ardis, 1987

Montefiore, Simon Sebag, <u>Stalin: The Court of the Red Tsar</u> New York: Alfred A. Knopf, 2004

Lunacharskaia, Irina, and Kurt S. Schultz, "Why Did Commissar of Enlightenment A. V. Lunacharskii Resign?" <u>Russian Review</u> 51, no. 3, 1992, pp. 319-342, www.jstor.org/stable/131115 (accessed March 2, 2010)

Treadgold, Donald, <u>Twentieth Century Russia: Seventh Edition</u> Boulder: Westview Press, 1990

Note: The original authors of the documents obtained through the anthologies <u>Modernism: An Anthology of Sources and Documents</u> and <u>Soviet Culture and Power: A History in Documents, 1917-1953</u> are credited in the endnotes in order to clarify the source of the citation. The full bibliographic details of the anthologies are not repeated after their first citation, although information regarding each individual document is provided in subsequent citations.

NOTES ON CONTRIBUTORS

Rachel E. Hines (Chaim Rumkowski) is an MD/MPH candidate at the University of Maryland. She earned the International Baccalaureate Diploma at Richard Montgomery High School in Rockville, Maryland.

Jessica Leight (Anne Hutchinson) is a Ph.D. candidate at MIT. She graduated summa cum laude from Yale and was a Rhodes Scholar. She graduated early from Cambridge Rindge and Latin School in Cambridge, Massachusetts, where she wrote this paper as a Junior for an independent study supervised by Mr. Michael Desimone in 2001.

Jane Abbottsmith (Irish Nationalism) graduated *magna cum laude* from Princetonand is a Gates Scholar at Cambridge University. She is a graduate of Summit Country Day School in Cincinnati, Ohio.

Wei Li (<u>Convivencia</u> in Medieval Spain) is at Williams College this Fall. She is a graduate of Singapore American School, where she was in the Spanish Honor Society and vice-president of SEED, a service club aiding in earthquake recovery in Sichuan, China.

Caitlin Lu (Matteo Ricci in China) is a Freshman at Stanford. She was a Senior at the Chinese International School in Hong Kong, when she wrote this paper for Mr. Christopher Caves' IB Higher Level History course in the 2010/2011 academic year.

Kaya Nagayo (Ainu Trade, 1650-1720) is at Waseda University in Tokyo. As a Senior at St. Maur International School in Yokohama, Japan, she took the London Guildhall School of Music Exam in piano and the Royal Conservatory of Music Exam in violin. In the summer of 2009 she participated in the Sino-Japan Youth Conference at the United World College in Hong Kong, and she plans a history major at the university.

Jonathan Lu (The Needham Question) is a Freshman at Stanford. He is a graduate of Chinese International School in Hong Kong, where he was the founder of *Xiao Hua* and served as the head of student government.

Sarah Bahn Valkenburgh (The Great Awakening) is a graduate of Dartmouth College (*summa cum laude*) and Harvard Medical School. She wrote this paper as a student at Greens Farms Academy in Greens Farms, Connecticut.

Michael Korzinstone (The Kornilov Affair) is a hedge fund manager in London. He is a graduate of Upper Canada College in Toronto, Canada, and The Wharton School.

Amy Rachel Motomura (Gypsies in Spain) is a graduate of Boulder High School in Boulder, Colorado, and of the Pratt School of Engineering at Duke University, where she was one of three students in the class of 2007 to have a perfect 4.0 record.

Maya Iyer Krishnan (Socialist Realism) is at Stanford. She earned the International Baccalaureate Diploma at Richard Montgomery High School in Rockville, Maryland.

All these authors were awarded the Ralph Waldo Emerson Prize.

SUBMISSIONS

===============

We need the best history research papers we can find, and we welcome a chance to consider your best work.

Essay Requirements

You may submit a history paper to *The Concord Review* if you completed it before starting college.

You must be the sole author.

The paper must be in English and may not have been previously published except in a publication of a secondary school that you attended.

Essays should be in the 4,000-6,000 (or more) word range, with Turabian (Chicago) endnotes and bibliography. The longest paper we have published was 21,000 words (on the Mountain Meadows Massacre. She went to Stanford...see it on www.tcr.org).

Essays may be on any historical topic, ancient or modern, domestic or foreign, and must be typed or printed from a word processor.

Essays must be accompanied by a check for $40, made out to *The Concord Review,* and by our 'Form to Accompany Essays.' The author will receive the next four issues of the journal in pdf.

Essays should have the notes and bibliography placed at the end (Chicago/Turabian style).

For more information, and a submission form, go to:

www.tcr.org and click on "**Submit**"

Send questions to the Editor, Will Fitzhugh, at fitzhugh@tcr.org

CONSORTIUM FOR VARSITY ACADEMICS®

Member Schools
and National Partners in
The Consortium for Varsity Academics®

MEMBER SCHOOLS

Menlo School (CA)
Singapore American School (Singapore)

NATIONAL PARTNERS

American Council of Trustees and Alumni
Anonymous (3)
Carnegie Corporation of New York
Earhart Foundation
The History Channel
Lagemann Foundation
Leadership and Learning Center
National Center on Education and the Economy
Douglas B. Reeves

For information on joining the Consortium,
please contact Will Fitzhugh at fitzhugh@tcr.org
Annual Membership is $5,000, payable to The Concord Review

HARVARD COLLEGE

Office of Admissions and Financial Aid

September 15, 2010

Mr. Will Fitzhugh
The Concord Review
730 Boston Post Road, Suite 24
Sudbury, Massachusetts 01776 USA

Dear Will,

We agree with your argument that high school students who have read a complete nonfiction book or two, and written a serious research paper or two, will be better prepared for college academic work than those who have not.

The Concord Review, founded in 1987, remains the only journal in the world for the academic papers of secondary students, and we in the Admissions Office here are always glad to see reprints of papers which students have had published in the *Review* and which they send to us as part of their application materials. Over the years, more than 10% (112) of these authors have come to college at Harvard.

Since 1998, when it started, we have been supporters of your National Writing Board, which is still unique in supplying independent three-page assessments of the research papers of secondary students. The NWB reports also provide a useful addition to the college application materials of high school students who are seeking admission to selective colleges.

For all our undergraduates, even those in the sciences, such competence, both in reading nonfiction books and in the writing of serious research papers, is essential for academic success. Some of our high schools now place too little emphasis on this, but *The Concord Review* and the National Writing Board are doing a national service in encouraging our secondary students, and their teachers, to spend more time and effort on developing these abilities.

Sincerely,

Bill

William R. Fitzsimmons
Dean of Admissions and Financial Aid
WRF:oap

Administrative Office: 86 Brattle Street • Cambridge, Massachusetts 02138

Made in the USA
Charleston, SC
01 September 2016